The Flavorful Air Fryer

Cookbook for Beginners

2000+ Days of Exciting and Mouthwatering Air Fryer Recipes to Spice Up Your Air-Fried Creations, Making Eating a Pleasure

Robert T. Gard

Table of Contents

INTRODUCTION

Are you tired of feeling guilty after indulging in your favorite fried foods? Do you want to enjoy crispy, delicious meals without the added calories and unhealthy oils? Look no further than an air fryer! This revolutionary kitchen appliance allows you to cook your favorite dishes with little to no oil, resulting in a healthier and guilt-free dining experience. And with this cookbook, you'll discover a whole new world of possibilities for your air fryer. This cookbook has something for everyone. So why wait? Start cooking up a storm and enjoy all the flavor and none of the guilt with the help of this air fryer cookbook!

As a busy writer, I always struggled to find the time to cook healthy meals for my family. With long work hours and a hectic schedule, fast food and takeout became our go-to options. But as my children grew older, I began to worry about their health and the impact our eating habits were having on their well-being.

One day, while browsing through a kitchen supply store, I stumbled upon an air fryer. Intrigued by its promise of healthier cooking with less oil, I decided to give it a try. To my surprise, the results were amazing! My family loved the crispy, delicious meals I was able to make using the air fryer, and I loved how easy and mess-free it was to use.

Inspired by my newfound love for air frying, I started experimenting with different recipes and ingredients, discovering new and exciting ways to cook all our favorite foods. And that's when I realized that there must be other families out there struggling with the same issues I had faced. So, I decided to write this cookbook to share my knowledge and experience with others who want to cook healthier, more delicious meals for their families without sacrificing taste or convenience.

My hope is that this cookbook will inspire others to discover the benefits of air frying and help them lead happier, healthier lives.

Air frying is a cooking method that uses hot air to cook food instead of oil, resulting in many benefits:

1. Healthier meals: Air frying reduces the amount of oil used in cooking, which can lead to healthier meals with fewer calories and less fat.

2. Less mess: With air frying, there's no need for messy oil or deep fryers, making clean-up quick and easy.

3. Versatility: Air fryers can cook a wide range of foods, from vegetables and meats to desserts and snacks.

4. Faster cooking time: Air frying can cook food faster than traditional methods, saving you time in the kitchen.

5. Consistent results: Air frying produces consistent results every time, ensuring your food is cooked evenly and thoroughly.

6. Energy efficient: Air fryers use less energy than traditional ovens, making them an eco-friendly option.

7. Safe and convenient: Air fryers are safe to use and come with features like automatic shut-off and temperature control, making them a convenient addition to any kitchen.

Chapter 1 Breakfasts

Spinach and Feta Egg Bake

Prep time: 7 minutes | Cook time: 23 to 25 minutes |
Serves 2

Avocado oil spray

⅓ cup diced red onion

1 cup frozen chopped spinach, thawed and drained

4 large eggs

¼ cup heavy (whipping) cream

Sea salt and freshly ground black pepper, to taste

¼ teaspoon cayenne pepper

½ cup crumbled feta cheese

¼ cup shredded Parmesan cheese

1. Spray a deep pan with oil. Put the onion in the pan, and place the pan in the air fryer basket. Set the air fryer to 350ºF (177ºC) and bake for 7 minutes. 2. Sprinkle the spinach over the onion. 3. In a medium bowl, beat the eggs, heavy cream, salt, black pepper, and cayenne. Pour this mixture over the vegetables. 4. Top with the feta and Parmesan cheese. Bake for 16 to 18 minutes, until the eggs are set and lightly brown.

Bacon, Broccoli and Cheese Bread Pudding

Prep time: 30 minutes | Cook time: 48 minutes |
Serves 2 to 4

½ pound (227 g) thick cut bacon, cut into ¼-inch pieces

3 cups brioche bread or rolls, cut into ½-inch cubes

3 eggs

1 cup milk

½ teaspoon salt

freshly ground black pepper

1 cup frozen broccoli florets, thawed and chopped

1½ cups grated Swiss cheese

1. Preheat the air fryer to 400ºF (204ºC). 2. Air fry the bacon for 6 to 10 minutes until crispy, shaking the basket a few times while it cooks to help it cook evenly. Remove the bacon and set it aside on a paper towel. 3. Air fry the brioche bread cubes for 2 minutes to dry and toast lightly. (If your brioche is a few days old and slightly stale, you can omit this step.) 4. Butter a cake pan. Combine all the ingredients in a large bowl and toss well. Transfer the mixture to the buttered cake pan, cover with aluminum foil and refrigerate the bread pudding overnight, or for at least 8 hours. 5. Remove the casserole from the refrigerator an hour before you plan to cook, and let it sit on the countertop to come to room temperature. 6. Preheat the air fryer to 330ºF (166ºC). Transfer the covered cake pan, to the basket of the air fryer, lowering the dish into the basket using a sling made of aluminum foil (fold a piece of aluminum foil into a strip about 2-inches wide by 24-inches long). Fold the ends of the aluminum foil over the top of the dish before returning the basket to the air fryer. Air fry for 20 minutes. Remove the foil and air fry for an additional 20 minutes. If the top starts to brown a little too much before the custard has set, simply return the foil to the pan. The bread pudding has cooked through when a skewer inserted into the center comes out clean.

Golden Avocado Tempura

Prep time: 5 minutes | Cook time: 10 minutes |
Serves 4

½ cup bread crumbs

½ teaspoons salt

1 Haas avocado, pitted, peeled

and sliced

Liquid from 1 can white beans

1. Preheat the air fryer to 350ºF (177ºC). 2. Mix the bread crumbs and salt in a shallow bowl until well-incorporated. 3. Dip the avocado slices in the bean liquid, then into the bread crumbs. 4. Put the avocados in the air fryer, taking care not to overlap any slices, and air fry for 10 minutes, giving the basket a good shake at the halfway point. 5. Serve immediately.

Bacon Cheese Egg with Avocado

Prep time: 15 minutes | Cook time: 20 minutes |
Serves 4

6 large eggs

¼ cup heavy whipping cream

1½ cups chopped cauliflower

1 cup shredded medium Cheddar cheese

1 medium avocado, peeled and

pitted

8 tablespoons full-fat sour cream

2 scallions, sliced on the bias

12 slices sugar-free bacon, cooked and crumbled

1. In a medium bowl, whisk eggs and cream together. Pour into a round baking dish. 2. Add cauliflower and mix, then top with Cheddar. Place dish into the air fryer basket. 3. Adjust the temperature to 320ºF (160ºC) and set the timer for 20 minutes. 4. When completely cooked, eggs will be firm and cheese will be browned. Slice into four pieces. 5. Slice avocado and divide evenly among pieces. Top each piece with 2 tablespoons sour cream, sliced scallions, and crumbled bacon.

Bacon, Cheese, and Avocado Melt

Prep time: 5 minutes | Cook time: 3 to 5 minutes | Serves 2

1 avocado
4 slices cooked bacon, chopped
2 tablespoons salsa

1 tablespoon heavy cream
¼ cup shredded Cheddar cheese

1. Preheat the air fryer to 400ºF (204ºC). 2. Slice the avocado in half lengthwise and remove the stone. To ensure the avocado halves do not roll in the basket, slice a thin piece of skin off the base. 3. In a small bowl, combine the bacon, salsa, and cream. Divide the mixture between the avocado halves and top with the cheese. 4. Place the avocado halves in the air fryer basket and air fry for 3 to 5 minutes until the cheese has melted and begins to brown. Serve warm.

Egg White Cups

Prep time: 10 minutes | Cook time: 15 minutes | Serves 4

2 cups 100% liquid egg whites
3 tablespoons salted butter, melted
¼ teaspoon salt
¼ teaspoon onion powder

½ medium Roma tomato, cored and diced
½ cup chopped fresh spinach leaves

1. In a large bowl, whisk egg whites with butter, salt, and onion powder. Stir in tomato and spinach, then pour evenly into four ramekins greased with cooking spray. 2. Place ramekins into air fryer basket. Adjust the temperature to 300ºF (149ºC) and bake for 15 minutes. Eggs will be fully cooked and firm in the center when done. Serve warm.

Mexican Breakfast Pepper Rings

Prep time: 5 minutes | Cook time: 10 minutes | Serves 4

Olive oil
1 large red, yellow, or orange bell pepper, cut into four ¾-inch rings

4 eggs
Salt and freshly ground black pepper, to taste
2 teaspoons salsa

1. Preheat the air fryer to 350ºF (177ºC). Lightly spray a baking pan with olive oil. 2. Place 2 bell pepper rings on the pan. Crack one egg into each bell pepper ring. Season with salt and black pepper. 3. Spoon ½ teaspoon of salsa on top of each egg. 4. Place the pan in the air fryer basket. Air fry until the yolk is slightly runny, 5 to 6 minutes or until the yolk is fully cooked, 8 to 10 minutes. 5. Repeat with the remaining 2 pepper rings. Serve hot.

Chocolate Doughnut Holes

Prep time: 10 minutes | Cook time: 8 to 12 minutes per batch | Makes 24 doughnut holes

1 (8-count) can refrigerated biscuits
Cooking oil spray
48 semisweet chocolate chips

3 tablespoons melted unsalted butter
¼ cup confectioners' sugar

1. Separate the biscuits and cut each biscuit into thirds, for 24 pieces. 2. Flatten each biscuit piece slightly and put 2 chocolate chips in the center. Wrap the dough around the chocolate and seal the edges well. 3. Insert the crisper plate into the basket and the basket into the unit. Preheat the unit by selecting AIR FRY, setting the temperature to 330ºF (166ºC), and setting the time to 3 minutes. Select START/STOP to begin. 4. Once the unit is preheated, spray the crisper plate with cooking oil. Brush each doughnut hole with a bit of the butter and place it into the basket. Select AIR FRY, set the temperature to 330ºF (166ºC), and set the time between 8 and 12 minutes. Select START/STOP to begin. 5. The doughnuts are done when they are golden brown. When the cooking is complete, place the doughnut holes on a plate and dust with the confectioners' sugar. Serve warm.

Honey-Apricot Granola with Greek Yogurt

Prep time: 10 minutes | Cook time: 30 minutes | Serves 6

1 cup rolled oats
¼ cup dried apricots, diced
¼ cup almond slivers
¼ cup walnuts, chopped
¼ cup pumpkin seeds
¼ cup hemp hearts
¼ to ⅓ cup raw honey, plus more for drizzling

1 tablespoon olive oil
1 teaspoon ground cinnamon
¼ teaspoon ground nutmeg
¼ teaspoon salt
2 tablespoons sugar-free dark chocolate chips (optional)
3 cups nonfat plain Greek yogurt

1. Preheat the air fryer to 260°F(127ºC). Line the air fryer basket with parchment paper. 2. In a large bowl, combine the oats, apricots, almonds, walnuts, pumpkin seeds, hemp hearts, honey, olive oil, cinnamon, nutmeg, and salt, mixing so that the honey, oil, and spices are well distributed. 3. Pour the mixture onto the parchment paper and spread it into an even layer. 4. Bake for 10 minutes, then shake or stir and spread back out into an even layer. Continue baking for 10 minutes more, then repeat the process of shaking or stirring the mixture. Bake for an additional 10 minutes before removing from the air fryer. 5. Allow the granola to cool completely before stirring in the chocolate chips (if using) and pouring into an airtight container for storage. 6. For each serving, top ½ cup Greek yogurt with ⅓ cup granola and a drizzle of honey, if needed.

Egg and Bacon Muffins

Prep time: 5 minutes | Cook time: 15 minutes |

Serves 1

2 eggs	3 ounces (85 g) shredded
Salt and ground black pepper,	Cheddar cheese
to taste	5 ounces (142 g) cooked bacon
1 tablespoon green pesto	1 scallion, chopped

1. Preheat the air fryer to 350ºF (177ºC). Line a cupcake tin with parchment paper. 2. Beat the eggs with pepper, salt, and pesto in a bowl. Mix in the cheese. 3. Pour the eggs into the cupcake tin and top with the bacon and scallion. 4. Bake in the preheated air fryer for 15 minutes, or until the egg is set. 5. Serve immediately.

Blueberry Cobbler

Prep time: 5 minutes | Cook time: 15 minutes |

Serves 4

⅓ cup whole-wheat pastry flour	½ teaspoon vanilla extract
¾ teaspoon baking powder	Cooking oil spray
Dash sea salt	½ cup fresh blueberries
½ cup 2% milk	¼ cup granola
2 tablespoons pure maple syrup	

1. In a medium bowl, whisk the flour, baking powder, and salt. Add the milk, maple syrup, and vanilla and gently whisk, just until thoroughly combined. 2. Preheat the unit by selecting BAKE, setting the temperature to 350ºF (177ºC), and setting the time to 3 minutes. Select START/STOP to begin. 3. Spray a 6-by-2-inch round baking pan with cooking oil and pour the batter into the pan. Top evenly with the blueberries and granola. 4. Once the unit is preheated, place the pan into the basket. 5. Select BAKE, set the temperature to 350ºF (177ºC), and set the time to 15 minutes. Select START/STOP to begin. 6. When the cooking is complete, the cobbler should be nicely browned and a knife inserted into the middle should come out clean. Enjoy plain or topped with a little vanilla yogurt.

Bourbon Vanilla French Toast

Prep time: 15 minutes | Cook time: 6 minutes |

Serves 4

2 large eggs	1 teaspoon vanilla extract
2 tablespoons water	8 (1-inch-thick) French bread
⅔ cup whole or 2% milk	slices
1 tablespoon butter, melted	Cooking spray
2 tablespoons bourbon	

1. Preheat the air fryer to 320ºF (160ºC). Line the air fryer basket with parchment paper and spray it with cooking spray. 2. Beat the eggs with the water in a shallow bowl until combined. Add the milk, melted butter, bourbon, and vanilla and stir to mix well. 3. Dredge 4 slices of bread in the batter, turning to coat both sides evenly. Transfer the bread slices onto the parchment paper. 4. Bake for 6 minutes until nicely browned. Flip the slices halfway through the cooking time. 5. Remove from the basket to a plate and repeat with the remaining 4 slices of bread. 6. Serve warm.

Bacon, Egg, and Cheese Roll Ups

Prep time: 15 minutes | Cook time: 15 minutes |

Serves 4

2 tablespoons unsalted butter	12 slices sugar-free bacon
¼ cup chopped onion	1 cup shredded sharp Cheddar
½ medium green bell pepper,	cheese
seeded and chopped	½ cup mild salsa, for dipping
6 large eggs	

1. In a medium skillet over medium heat, melt butter. Add onion and pepper to the skillet and sauté until fragrant and onions are translucent, about 3 minutes. 2. Whisk eggs in a small bowl and pour into skillet. Scramble eggs with onions and peppers until fluffy and fully cooked, about 5 minutes. Remove from heat and set aside. 3. On work surface, place three slices of bacon side by side, overlapping about ¼ inch. Place ¼ cup scrambled eggs in a heap on the side closest to you and sprinkle ¼ cup cheese on top of the eggs. 4. Tightly roll the bacon around the eggs and secure the seam with a toothpick if necessary. Place each roll into the air fryer basket. 5. Adjust the temperature to 350ºF (177ºC) and air fry for 15 minutes. Rotate the rolls halfway through the cooking time. 6. Bacon will be brown and crispy when completely cooked. Serve immediately with salsa for dipping.

Johnny Cakes

Prep time: 10 minutes | Cook time: 10 to 12 minutes |

| Serves 4

½ cup all-purpose flour	1 cup milk, whole or 2%
1½ cups yellow cornmeal	1 tablespoon butter, melted
2 tablespoons sugar	1 large egg, lightly beaten
1 teaspoon baking powder	1 to 2 tablespoons oil
1 teaspoon salt	

1. In a large bowl, whisk the flour, cornmeal, sugar, baking powder, and salt until blended. Whisk in the milk, melted butter, and egg until the mixture is sticky but still lumpy. 2. Preheat the air fryer to 350ºF (177ºC). Line the air fryer basket with parchment paper. 3. For each cake, drop 1 heaping tablespoon of batter onto the parchment paper. The fryer should hold 4 cakes. 4. Spritz the cakes with oil and cook for 3 minutes. Turn the cakes, spritz with oil again, and cook for 2 to 3 minutes more. Repeat with a second batch of cakes.

Breakfast Cobbler

Filling:

10 ounces (283 g) bulk pork sausage, crumbled

¼ cup minced onions

2 cloves garlic, minced

½ teaspoon fine sea salt

½ teaspoon ground black pepper

1 (8 ounces / 227 g) package cream cheese (or Kite Hill brand cream cheese style spread

for dairy-free), softened

¾ cup beef or chicken broth

Biscuits:

3 large egg whites

¾ cup blanched almond flour

1 teaspoon baking powder

¼ teaspoon fine sea salt

2½ tablespoons very cold unsalted butter, cut into ¼-inch pieces

Fresh thyme leaves, for garnish

1. Preheat the air fryer to 400ºF (204ºC). 2. Place the sausage, onions, and garlic in a pie pan. Using your hands, break up the sausage into small pieces and spread it evenly throughout the pie pan. Season with the salt and pepper. Place the pan in the air fryer and bake for 5 minutes. 3. While the sausage cooks, place the cream cheese and broth in a food processor or blender and purée until smooth. 4. Remove the pork from the air fryer and use a fork or metal spatula to crumble it more. Pour the cream cheese mixture into the sausage and stir to combine. Set aside. 5. Make the biscuits: Place the egg whites in a medium-sized mixing bowl or the bowl of a stand mixer and whip with a hand mixer or stand mixer until stiff peaks form. 6. In a separate medium-sized bowl, whisk together the almond flour, baking powder, and salt, then cut in the butter. When you are done, the mixture should still have chunks of butter. Gently fold the flour mixture into the egg whites with a rubber spatula. 7. Use a large spoon or ice cream scoop to scoop the dough into 4 equal-sized biscuits, making sure the butter is evenly distributed. Place the biscuits on top of the sausage and cook in the air fryer for 5 minutes, then turn the heat down to 325ºF (163ºC) and bake for another 17 to 20 minutes, until the biscuits are golden brown. Serve garnished with fresh thyme leaves. 8. Store leftovers in an airtight container in the refrigerator for up to 3 days. Reheat in a preheated 350ºF (177ºC) air fryer for 5 minutes, or until warmed through.

Whole Wheat Banana-Walnut Bread

Olive oil cooking spray

2 ripe medium bananas

1 large egg

¼ cup nonfat plain Greek yogurt

¼ cup olive oil

½ teaspoon vanilla extract

2 tablespoons raw honey

1 cup whole wheat flour

¼ teaspoon salt

¼ teaspoon baking soda

½ teaspoon ground cinnamon

¼ cup chopped walnuts

1. Preheat the air fryer to 360°F(182ºC). Lightly coat the inside of a 8-by-4-inch loaf pan with olive oil cooking spray. (Or use two 5 ½-by-3-inch loaf pans.) 2. In a large bowl, mash the bananas with a fork. Add the egg, yogurt, olive oil, vanilla, and honey. Mix until well combined and mostly smooth. 3. Sift the whole wheat flour, salt, baking soda, and cinnamon into the wet mixture, then stir until just combined. Do not overmix. 4. Gently fold in the walnuts. 5. Pour into the prepared loaf pan and spread to distribute evenly. 6. Place the loaf pan in the air fryer basket and bake for 20 to 23 minutes, or until golden brown on top and a toothpick inserted into the center comes out clean. 7. Allow to cool for 5 minutes before serving.

Hole in One

1 slice bread

1 teaspoon soft butter

1 egg

Salt and pepper, to taste

1 tablespoon shredded Cheddar cheese

2 teaspoons diced ham

1. Place a baking dish inside air fryer basket and preheat the air fryer to 330ºF (166ºC). 2. Using a 2½-inch-diameter biscuit cutter, cut a hole in center of bread slice. 3. Spread softened butter on both sides of bread. 4. Lay bread slice in baking dish and crack egg into the hole. Sprinkle egg with salt and pepper to taste. 5. Cook for 5 minutes. 6. Turn toast over and top it with shredded cheese and diced ham. 7. Cook for 1 to 2 more minutes or until yolk is done to your liking.

Whole Wheat Blueberry Muffins

Olive oil cooking spray

½ cup unsweetened applesauce

¼ cup raw honey

½ cup nonfat plain Greek yogurt

1 teaspoon vanilla extract

1 large egg

1½ cups plus 1 tablespoon whole wheat flour, divided

½ teaspoon baking soda

½ teaspoon baking powder

½ teaspoon salt

½ cup blueberries, fresh or frozen

1. Preheat the air fryer to 360°F(182ºC). Lightly coat the inside of six silicone muffin cups or a six-cup muffin tin with olive oil cooking spray. 2. In a large bowl, combine the applesauce, honey, yogurt, vanilla, and egg and mix until smooth. 3. Sift in 1½ cups of the flour, the baking soda, baking powder, and salt into the wet mixture, then stir until just combined. 4. In a small bowl, toss the blueberries with the remaining 1 tablespoon flour, then fold the mixture into the muffin batter. 5. Divide the mixture evenly among the prepared muffin cups and place into the basket of the air fryer. Bake for 12 to 15 minutes, or until golden brown on top and a toothpick inserted into the middle of one of the muffins comes out clean. 6. Allow to cool for 5 minutes before serving.

Breakfast Calzone

Prep time: 15 minutes | Cook time: 15 minutes |

Serves 4

1½ cups shredded Mozzarella cheese	1 large whole egg
½ cup blanched finely ground almond flour	4 large eggs, scrambled
1 ounce (28 g) full-fat cream cheese	½ pound (227 g) cooked breakfast sausage, crumbled
	8 tablespoons shredded mild Cheddar cheese

1. In a large microwave-safe bowl, add Mozzarella, almond flour, and cream cheese. Microwave for 1 minute. Stir until the mixture is smooth and forms a ball. Add the egg and stir until dough forms. 2. Place dough between two sheets of parchment and roll out to ¼-inch thickness. Cut the dough into four rectangles. 3. Mix scrambled eggs and cooked sausage together in a large bowl. Divide the mixture evenly among each piece of dough, placing it on the lower half of the rectangle. Sprinkle each with 2 tablespoons Cheddar. 4. Fold over the rectangle to cover the egg and meat mixture. Pinch, roll, or use a wet fork to close the edges completely. 5. Cut a piece of parchment to fit your air fryer basket and place the calzones onto the parchment. Place parchment into the air fryer basket. 6. Adjust the temperature to 380ºF (193ºC) and air fry for 15 minutes. 7. Flip the calzones halfway through the cooking time. When done, calzones should be golden in color. Serve immediately.

Hearty Cheddar Biscuits

Prep time: 10 minutes | Cook time: 22 minutes |

Makes 8 biscuits

2⅓ cups self-rising flour	plus more to melt on top
2 tablespoons sugar	1⅓ cups buttermilk
½ cup butter (1 stick), frozen for 15 minutes	1 cup all-purpose flour, for shaping
½ cup grated Cheddar cheese,	1 tablespoon butter, melted

1. Line a buttered 7-inch metal cake pan with parchment paper or a silicone liner. 2. Combine the flour and sugar in a large mixing bowl. Grate the butter into the flour. Add the grated cheese and stir to coat the cheese and butter with flour. Then add the buttermilk and stir just until you can no longer see streaks of flour. The dough should be quite wet. 3. Spread the all-purpose (not self-rising) flour out on a small cookie sheet. With a spoon, scoop 8 evenly sized balls of dough into the flour, making sure they don't touch each other. With floured hands, coat each dough ball with flour and toss them gently from hand to hand to shake off any excess flour. Put each floured dough ball into the prepared pan, right up next to the other. This will help the biscuits rise, rather than spreading out. 4. Preheat the air fryer to 380ºF (193ºC). 5. Transfer the cake pan to the basket of the air fryer. Let the ends of the aluminum foil sling hang across the cake pan before returning the basket to the air fryer. 6. Air fry for 20 minutes. Check the biscuits twice to make sure they are not getting too brown on top. If they are, re-arrange the aluminum foil strips to cover any brown parts. After 20 minutes, check the biscuits by inserting a toothpick into the center of the biscuits. It should come out clean. If it needs a little more time, continue to air fry for two extra minutes. Brush the tops of the biscuits with some melted butter and sprinkle a little more grated cheese on top if desired. Pop the basket back into the air fryer for another 2 minutes. 7. Remove the cake pan from the air fryer. Let the biscuits cool for just a minute or two and then turn them out onto a plate and pull apart. Serve immediately.

Red Pepper and Feta Frittata

Prep time: 10 minutes | Cook time: 20 minutes |

Serves 4

Olive oil cooking spray	½ teaspoon black pepper
8 large eggs	1 garlic clove, minced
1 medium red bell pepper, diced	½ cup feta, divided
½ teaspoon salt	

1. Preheat the air fryer to 360ºF(182ºC). Lightly coat the inside of a 6-inch round cake pan with olive oil cooking spray. 2. In a large bowl, beat the eggs for 1 to 2 minutes, or until well combined. 3. Add the bell pepper, salt, black pepper, and garlic to the eggs, and mix together until the bell pepper is distributed throughout. 4. Fold in ¼ cup of the feta cheese. 5. Pour the egg mixture into the prepared cake pan, and sprinkle the remaining ¼ cup of feta over the top. 6. Place into the air fryer and bake for 18 to 20 minutes, or until the eggs are set in the center. 7. Remove from the air fryer and allow to cool for 5 minutes before serving.

Poached Eggs on Whole Grain Avocado Toast

Prep time: 5 minutes | Cook time: 7 minutes | Serves 4

Olive oil cooking spray	4 pieces whole grain bread
4 large eggs	1 avocado
Salt	Red pepper flakes (optional)
Black pepper	

1. Preheat the air fryer to 320ºF(160ºC). Lightly coat the inside of four small oven-safe ramekins with olive oil cooking spray. 2. Crack one egg into each ramekin, and season with salt and black pepper. 3. Place the ramekins into the air fryer basket. Close and set the timer to 7 minutes. 4. While the eggs are cooking, toast the bread in a toaster. 5. Slice the avocado in half lengthwise, remove the pit, and scoop the flesh into a small bowl. Season with salt, black pepper, and red pepper flakes, if desired. Using a fork, smash the avocado lightly. 6. Spread a quarter of the smashed avocado evenly over each slice of toast. 7. Remove the eggs from the air fryer, and gently spoon one onto each slice of avocado toast before serving.

Breakfast Pita

Prep time: 5 minutes | Cook time: 6 minutes | Serves 2

1 whole wheat pita	¼ teaspoon dried oregano
2 teaspoons olive oil	¼ teaspoon dried thyme
½ shallot, diced	⅛ teaspoon salt
¼ teaspoon garlic, minced	2 tablespoons shredded
1 large egg	Parmesan cheese

1. Preheat the air fryer to 380°F(193°C). 2. Brush the top of the pita with olive oil, then spread the diced shallot and minced garlic over the pita. 3. Crack the egg into a small bowl or ramekin, and season it with oregano, thyme, and salt. 4. Place the pita into the air fryer basket, and gently pour the egg onto the top of the pita. Sprinkle with cheese over the top. 5. Bake for 6 minutes. 6. Allow to cool for 5 minutes before cutting into pieces for serving.

Breakfast Sammies

Prep time: 15 minutes | Cook time: 20 minutes | Serves 5

Biscuits:	Eggs:
6 large egg whites	5 large eggs
2 cups blanched almond flour, plus more if needed	½ teaspoon fine sea salt
1½ teaspoons baking powder	¼ teaspoon ground black pepper
½ teaspoon fine sea salt	5 (1 ounce / 28 g) slices
¼ cup (½ stick) very cold unsalted butter (or lard for dairy-free), cut into ¼-inch pieces	Cheddar cheese (omit for dairy-free)
	10 thin slices ham

1. Spray the air fryer basket with avocado oil. Preheat the air fryer to 350°F (177°C). Grease two pie pans or two baking pans that will fit inside your air fryer. 2. Make the biscuits: In a medium-sized bowl, whip the egg whites with a hand mixer until very stiff. Set aside. 3. In a separate medium-sized bowl, stir together the almond flour, baking powder, and salt until well combined. Cut in the butter. Gently fold the flour mixture into the egg whites with a rubber spatula. If the dough is too wet to form into mounds, add a few tablespoons of almond flour until the dough holds together well. 4. Using a large spoon, divide the dough into 5 equal portions and drop them about 1 inch apart on one of the greased pie pans. (If you're using a smaller air fryer, work in batches if necessary.) Place the pan in the air fryer and bake for 11 to 14 minutes, until the biscuits are golden brown. Remove from the air fryer and set aside to cool. 5. Make the eggs: Set the air fryer to 375°F (191°C). Crack the eggs into the remaining greased pie pan and sprinkle with the salt and pepper. Place the eggs in the air fryer to bake for 5 minutes, or until they are cooked to your liking. 6. Open the air fryer and top each egg yolk with a slice of cheese (if using). Bake for another minute, or until the cheese is melted. 7. Once the biscuits are cool, slice them in half lengthwise. Place 1 cooked egg

topped with cheese and 2 slices of ham in each biscuit. 8. Store leftover biscuits, eggs, and ham in separate airtight containers in the fridge for up to 3 days. Reheat the biscuits and eggs on a baking sheet in a preheated 350°F (177°C) air fryer for 5 minutes, or until warmed through.

Oat Bran Muffins

Prep time: 10 minutes | Cook time: 10 to 12 minutes per batch | Makes 8 muffins

⅔ cup oat bran	1 egg
½ cup flour	2 tablespoons canola oil
¼ cup brown sugar	½ cup chopped dates, raisins, or
1 teaspoon baking powder	dried cranberries
½ teaspoon baking soda	24 paper muffin cups
⅛ teaspoon salt	Cooking spray
½ cup buttermilk	

1. Preheat the air fryer to 330°F (166°C). 2. In a large bowl, combine the oat bran, flour, brown sugar, baking powder, baking soda, and salt. 3. In a small bowl, beat together the buttermilk, egg, and oil. 4. Pour buttermilk mixture into bowl with dry ingredients and stir just until moistened. Do not beat. 5. Gently stir in dried fruit. 6. Use triple baking cups to help muffins hold shape during baking. Spray them with cooking spray, place 4 sets of cups in air fryer basket at a time, and fill each one ¾ full of batter. 7. Cook for 10 to 12 minutes, until top springs back when lightly touched and toothpick inserted in center comes out clean. 8. Repeat for remaining muffins.

Quesadillas

Prep time: 10 minutes | Cook time: 15 minutes | Serves 4

4 eggs	4 tablespoons salsa
2 tablespoons skim milk	2 ounces (57 g) Cheddar
Salt and pepper, to taste	cheese, grated
Oil for misting or cooking spray	½ small avocado, peeled and
4 flour tortillas	thinly sliced

1. Preheat the air fryer to 270°F (132°C). 2. Beat together eggs, milk, salt, and pepper. 3. Spray a baking pan lightly with cooking spray and add egg mixture. 4. Bake for 8 to 9 minutes, stirring every 1 to 2 minutes, until eggs are scrambled to your liking. Remove and set aside. 5. Spray one side of each tortilla with oil or cooking spray. Flip over. 6. Divide eggs, salsa, cheese, and avocado among the tortillas, covering only half of each tortilla. 7. Fold each tortilla in half and press down lightly. 8. Place 2 tortillas in air fryer basket and air fry at 390°F (199°C) for 3 minutes or until cheese melts and outside feels slightly crispy. Repeat with remaining two tortillas. 9. Cut each cooked tortilla into halves or thirds.

Sausage and Egg Breakfast Burrito

Prep time: 5 minutes | Cook time: 30 minutes |

Serves 6

6 eggs

Salt and pepper, to taste

Cooking oil

½ cup chopped red bell pepper

½ cup chopped green bell pepper

8 ounces (227 g) ground chicken sausage

½ cup salsa

6 medium (8-inch) flour tortillas

½ cup shredded Cheddar cheese

1. In a medium bowl, whisk the eggs. Add salt and pepper to taste. 2. Place a skillet on medium-high heat. Spray with cooking oil. Add the eggs. Scramble for 2 to 3 minutes, until the eggs are fluffy. Remove the eggs from the skillet and set aside. 3. If needed, spray the skillet with more oil. Add the chopped red and green bell peppers. Cook for 2 to 3 minutes, until the peppers are soft. 4. Add the ground sausage to the skillet. Break the sausage into smaller pieces using a spatula or spoon. Cook for 3 to 4 minutes, until the sausage is brown. 5. Add the salsa and scrambled eggs. Stir to combine. Remove the skillet from heat. 6. Spoon the mixture evenly onto the tortillas. 7. To form the burritos, fold the sides of each tortilla in toward the middle and then roll up from the bottom. You can secure each burrito with a toothpick. Or you can moisten the outside edge of the tortilla with a small amount of water. I prefer to use a cooking brush, but you can also dab with your fingers. 8. Spray the burritos with cooking oil and place them in the air fryer. Do not stack. Cook the burritos in batches if they do not all fit in the basket. Air fry at 400ºF (204ºC) for 8 minutes. 9. Open the air fryer and flip the burritos. Cook for an additional 2 minutes or until crisp. 10. If necessary, repeat steps 8 and 9 for the remaining burritos. 11. Sprinkle the Cheddar cheese over the burritos. Cool before serving.

Easy Buttermilk Biscuits

Prep time: 5 minutes | Cook time: 18 minutes |

Makes 16 biscuits

2½ cups all-purpose flour

1 tablespoon baking powder

1 teaspoon kosher salt

1 teaspoon sugar

½ teaspoon baking soda

8 tablespoons (1 stick) unsalted butter, at room temperature

1 cup buttermilk, chilled

1. Stir together the flour, baking powder, salt, sugar, and baking powder in a large bowl. 2. Add the butter and stir to mix well. Pour in the buttermilk and stir with a rubber spatula just until incorporated. 3. Place the dough onto a lightly floured surface and roll the dough out to a disk, ½ inch thick. Cut out the biscuits with a 2-inch round cutter and re-roll any scraps until you have 16 biscuits. 4. Preheat the air fryer to 325ºF (163ºC). 5. Working in batches, arrange the biscuits in the air fryer basket in a single layer. Bake for about 18 minutes until the biscuits are golden brown. 6. Remove from the basket to a plate and repeat with the remaining biscuits. 7. Serve hot.

Everything Bagels

Prep time: 15 minutes | Cook time: 14 minutes |

Makes 6 bagels

1¾ cups shredded Mozzarella cheese or goat cheese Mozzarella

2 tablespoons unsalted butter or coconut oil

1 large egg, beaten

1 tablespoon apple cider

vinegar

1 cup blanched almond flour

1 tablespoon baking powder

⅛ teaspoon fine sea salt

1½ teaspoons everything bagel seasoning

1. Make the dough: Put the Mozzarella and butter in a large microwave-safe bowl and microwave for 1 to 2 minutes, until the cheese is entirely melted. Stir well. Add the egg and vinegar. Using a hand mixer on medium, combine well. Add the almond flour, baking powder, and salt and, using the mixer, combine well. 2. Lay a piece of parchment paper on the countertop and place the dough on it. Knead it for about 3 minutes. The dough should be a little sticky but pliable. (If the dough is too sticky, chill it in the refrigerator for an hour or overnight.) 3. Preheat the air fryer to 350ºF (177ºC). Spray a baking sheet or pie pan that will fit into your air fryer with avocado oil. 4. Divide the dough into 6 equal portions. Roll 1 portion into a log that is 6 inches long and about ½ inch thick. Form the log into a circle and seal the edges together, making a bagel shape. Repeat with the remaining portions of dough, making 6 bagels. 5. Place the bagels on the greased baking sheet. Spray the bagels with avocado oil and top with everything bagel seasoning, pressing the seasoning into the dough with your hands. 6. Place the bagels in the air fryer and bake for 14 minutes, or until cooked through and golden brown, flipping after 6 minutes. 7. Remove the bagels from the air fryer and allow them to cool slightly before slicing them in half and serving. Store leftovers in an airtight container in the fridge for up to 4 days or in the freezer for up to a month.

Pizza Eggs

Prep time: 5 minutes | Cook time: 10 minutes |

Serves 2

1 cup shredded Mozzarella cheese

7 slices pepperoni, chopped

1 large egg, whisked

¼ teaspoon dried oregano

¼ teaspoon dried parsley

¼ teaspoon garlic powder

¼ teaspoon salt

1. Place Mozzarella in a single layer on the bottom of an ungreased round nonstick baking dish. Scatter pepperoni over cheese, then pour egg evenly around baking dish. 2. Sprinkle with remaining ingredients and place into air fryer basket. Adjust the temperature to 330ºF (166ºC) and bake for 10 minutes. When cheese is brown and egg is set, dish will be done. 3. Let cool in dish 5 minutes before serving.

Cheesy Cauliflower "Hash Browns"

Prep time: 30 minutes | Cook time: 24 minutes | Makes 6 hash browns

2 ounces (57 g) 100% cheese crisps	instructions
1 (12-ounce / 340-g) steamer bag cauliflower, cooked according to package	1 large egg
	½ cup shredded sharp Cheddar cheese
	½ teaspoon salt

1. Let cooked cauliflower cool 10 minutes. 2. Place cheese crisps into food processor and pulse on low 30 seconds until crisps are finely ground. 3. Using a kitchen towel, wring out excess moisture from cauliflower and place into food processor. 4. Add egg to food processor and sprinkle with Cheddar and salt. Pulse five times until mixture is mostly smooth. 5. Cut two pieces of parchment to fit air fryer basket. Separate mixture into six even scoops and place three on each piece of ungreased parchment, keeping at least 2 inch of space between each scoop. Press each into a hash brown shape, about ¼ inch thick. 6. Place one batch on parchment into air fryer basket. Adjust the temperature to 375ºF (191ºC) and air fry for 12 minutes, turning hash browns halfway through cooking. Hash browns will be golden brown when done. Repeat with second batch. 7. Allow 5 minutes to cool. Serve warm.

Strawberry Toast

Prep time: 10 minutes | Cook time: 8 minutes | Makes 4 toasts

4 slices bread, ½-inch thick	1 cup sliced strawberries
Butter-flavored cooking spray	1 teaspoon sugar

1. Spray one side of each bread slice with butter-flavored cooking spray. Lay slices sprayed side down. 2. Divide the strawberries among the bread slices. 3. Sprinkle evenly with the sugar and place in the air fryer basket in a single layer. 4. Air fry at 390ºF (199ºC) for 8 minutes. The bottom should look brown and crisp and the top should look glazed.

Three-Berry Dutch Pancake

Prep time: 10 minutes | Cook time: 12 to 16 minutes | Serves 4

2 egg whites	1 tablespoon unsalted butter, melted
1 egg	
½ cup whole-wheat pastry flour	1 cup sliced fresh strawberries
½ cup 2% milk	½ cup fresh blueberries
1 teaspoon pure vanilla extract	½ cup fresh raspberries

1. In a medium bowl, use an eggbeater or hand mixer to quickly mix the egg whites, egg, pastry flour, milk, and vanilla until well combined. 2. Use a pastry brush to grease the bottom of a baking pan with the melted butter. Immediately pour in the batter and put the basket back in the fryer. Bake at 330ºF (166ºC) for 12 to 16 minutes, or until the pancake is puffed and golden brown. 3. Remove the pan from the air fryer; the pancake will fall. Top with the strawberries, blueberries, and raspberries. Serve immediately.

Apple Rolls

Prep time: 20 minutes | Cook time: 20 to 24 minutes | Makes 12 rolls

Apple Rolls:	1 teaspoon ground cinnamon
2 cups all-purpose flour, plus more for dusting	1 large Granny Smith apple, peeled and diced
2 tablespoons granulated sugar	1 to 2 tablespoons oil
1 teaspoon salt	Icing:
3 tablespoons butter, at room temperature	½ cup confectioners' sugar
	½ teaspoon vanilla extract
¾ cup milk, whole or 2%	2 to 3 tablespoons milk, whole or 2%
½ cup packed light brown sugar	

Make the Apple Rolls 1. In a large bowl, whisk the flour, granulated sugar, and salt until blended. Stir in the butter and milk briefly until a sticky dough forms. 2. In a small bowl, stir together the brown sugar, cinnamon, and apple. 3. Place a piece of parchment paper on a work surface and dust it with flour. Roll the dough on the prepared surface to ¼ inch thickness. 4. Spread the apple mixture over the dough. Roll up the dough jelly roll-style, pinching the ends to seal. Cut the dough into 12 rolls. 5. Preheat the air fryer to 320ºF (160ºC). 6. Line the air fryer basket with parchment paper and spritz it with oil. Place 6 rolls on the prepared parchment. 7. Bake for 5 minutes. Flip the rolls and bake for 5 to 7 minutes more until lightly browned. Repeat with the remaining rolls. Make the Icing 8. In a medium bowl, whisk the confectioners' sugar, vanilla, and milk until blended. 9. Drizzle over the warm rolls.

Pancake Cake

Prep time: 10 minutes | Cook time: 7 minutes | Serves 4

½ cup blanched finely ground almond flour	softened
	1 large egg
¼ cup powdered erythritol	½ teaspoon unflavored gelatin
½ teaspoon baking powder	½ teaspoon vanilla extract
2 tablespoons unsalted butter,	½ teaspoon ground cinnamon

1. In a large bowl, mix almond flour, erythritol, and baking powder. Add butter, egg, gelatin, vanilla, and cinnamon. Pour into a round baking pan. 2. Place pan into the air fryer basket. 3. Adjust the temperature to 300ºF (149ºC) and set the timer for 7 minutes. 4. When the cake is completely cooked, a toothpick will come out clean. Cut cake into four and serve.

Drop Biscuits

Prep time: 10 minutes | Cook time: 9 to 10 minutes | Serves 5

4 cups all-purpose flour

1 tablespoon baking powder

1 tablespoon sugar (optional)

1 teaspoon salt

6 tablespoons butter, plus more

for brushing on the biscuits (optional)

¾ cup buttermilk

1 to 2 tablespoons oil

1. In a large bowl, whisk the flour, baking powder, sugar (if using), and salt until blended. 2. Add the butter. Using a pastry cutter or 2 forks, work the dough until pea-size balls of the butter-flour mixture appear. Stir in the buttermilk until the mixture is sticky. 3. Preheat the air fryer to 330ºF (166ºC). Line the air fryer basket with parchment paper and spritz it with oil. 4. Drop the dough by the tablespoonful onto the prepared basket, leaving 1 inch between each, to form 10 biscuits. 5. Bake for 5 minutes. Flip the biscuits and cook for 4 minutes more for a light brown top, or 5 minutes more for a darker biscuit. Brush the tops with melted butter, if desired.

Parmesan Ranch Risotto

Prep time: 10 minutes | Cook time: 30 minutes | Serves 2

1 tablespoon olive oil

1 clove garlic, minced

1 tablespoon unsalted butter

1 onion, diced

¾ cup Arborio rice

2 cups chicken stock, boiling

½ cup Parmesan cheese, grated

1. Preheat the air fryer to 390ºF (199ºC). 2. Grease a round baking tin with olive oil and stir in the garlic, butter, and onion. 3. Transfer the tin to the air fryer and bake for 4 minutes. Add the rice and bake for 4 more minutes. 4. Turn the air fryer to 320ºF (160ºC) and pour in the chicken stock. Cover and bake for 22 minutes. 5. Scatter with cheese and serve.

Cinnamon Rolls

Prep time: 10 minutes | Cook time: 20 minutes | Makes 12 rolls

2½ cups shredded Mozzarella cheese

2 ounces (57 g) cream cheese, softened

1 cup blanched finely ground

almond flour

½ teaspoon vanilla extract

½ cup confectioners' erythritol

1 tablespoon ground cinnamon

1. In a large microwave-safe bowl, combine Mozzarella cheese, cream cheese, and flour. Microwave the mixture on high 90 seconds until cheese is melted. 2. Add vanilla extract and erythritol, and mix

2 minutes until a dough forms. 3. Once the dough is cool enough to work with your hands, about 2 minutes, spread it out into a 12 × 4-inch rectangle on ungreased parchment paper. Evenly sprinkle dough with cinnamon. 4. Starting at the long side of the dough, roll lengthwise to form a log. Slice the log into twelve even pieces. 5. Divide rolls between two ungreased round nonstick baking dishes. Place one dish into air fryer basket. Adjust the temperature to 375ºF (191ºC) and bake for 10 minutes. 6. Cinnamon rolls will be done when golden around the edges and mostly firm. Repeat with second dish. Allow rolls to cool in dishes 10 minutes before serving.

Cinnamon-Raisin Bagels

Prep time: 30 minutes | Cook time: 10 minutes | Makes 4 bagels

Oil, for spraying

¼ cup raisins

1 cup self-rising flour, plus more for dusting

1 cup plain Greek yogurt

1 teaspoon ground cinnamon

1 large egg

1. Line the air fryer basket with parchment and spray lightly with oil. 2. Place the raisins in a bowl of hot water and let sit for 10 to 15 minutes, until they have plumped. This will make them extra juicy. 3. In a large bowl, mix together the flour, yogurt, and cinnamon with your hands or a large silicone spatula until a ball is formed. It will be quite sticky for a while. 4. Drain the raisins and gently work them into the ball of dough. 5. Place the dough on a lightly floured work surface and divide into 4 equal pieces. Roll each piece into an 8- or 9-inch-long rope and shape it into a circle, pinching the ends together to seal. 6. In a small bowl, whisk the egg. Brush the egg onto the tops of the dough. 7. Place the dough in the prepared basket. 8. Air fry at 350ºF (177ºC) for 10 minutes. Serve immediately.

Two-Cheese Grits

Prep time: 10 minutes | Cook time: 10 to 12 minutes | Serves 4

⅔ cup instant grits

1 teaspoon salt

1 teaspoon freshly ground black pepper

¾ cup milk, whole or 2%

1 large egg, beaten

3 ounces (85 g) cream cheese, at room temperature

1 tablespoon butter, melted

1 cup shredded mild Cheddar cheese

1 to 2 tablespoons oil

1. In a large bowl, combine the grits, salt, and pepper. Stir in the milk, egg, cream cheese, and butter until blended. Stir in the Cheddar cheese. 2. Preheat the air fryer to 400ºF (204ºC). Spritz a baking pan with oil. 3. Pour the grits mixture into the prepared pan and place it in the air fryer basket. 4. Cook for 5 minutes. Stir the mixture and cook for 5 minutes more for soupy grits or 7 minutes more for firmer grits.

Cheddar Eggs

Prep time: 5 minutes | Cook time: 15 minutes |
Serves 2

4 large eggs

2 tablespoons unsalted butter, melted

½ cup shredded sharp Cheddar cheese

1. Crack eggs into a round baking dish and whisk. Place dish into the air fryer basket. 2. Adjust the temperature to 400°F (204°C) and set the timer for 10 minutes. 3. After 5 minutes, stir the eggs and add the butter and cheese. Let cook 3 more minutes and stir again. 4. Allow eggs to finish cooking an additional 2 minutes or remove if they are to your desired liking. 5. Use a fork to fluff. Serve warm.

Savory Sweet Potato Hash

Prep time: 15 minutes | Cook time: 18 minutes |
Serves 6

2 medium sweet potatoes, peeled and cut into 1-inch cubes

½ green bell pepper, diced

½ red onion, diced

4 ounces (113 g) baby bella mushrooms, diced

2 tablespoons olive oil

1 garlic clove, minced

½ teaspoon salt

½ teaspoon black pepper

½ tablespoon chopped fresh rosemary

1. Preheat the air fryer to 380°F(193°C). 2. In a large bowl, toss all ingredients together until the vegetables are well coated and seasonings distributed. 3. Pour the vegetables into the air fryer basket, making sure they are in a single even layer. (If using a smaller air fryer, you may need to do this in two batches.) 4. Roast for 9 minutes, then toss or flip the vegetables. Roast for 9 minutes more. 5. Transfer to a serving bowl or individual plates and enjoy.

Berry Muffins

Prep time: 15 minutes | Cook time: 12 to 17 minutes
| Makes 8 muffins

1⅓ cups plus 1 tablespoon all-purpose flour, divided

¼ cup granulated sugar

2 tablespoons light brown sugar

2 teaspoons baking powder

2 eggs

⅔ cup whole milk

⅓ cup safflower oil

1 cup mixed fresh berries

1. In a medium bowl, stir together 1⅓ cups of flour, the granulated sugar, brown sugar, and baking powder until mixed well. 2. In a small bowl, whisk the eggs, milk, and oil until combined. Stir the egg mixture into the dry ingredients just until combined. 3. In another small bowl, toss the mixed berries with the remaining 1 tablespoon of flour until coated. Gently stir the berries into the batter. 4. Double up 16 foil muffin cups to make 8 cups. 5. Insert

the crisper plate into the basket and the basket into the unit. Preheat the unit by selecting BAKE, setting the temperature to 315°F (157°C), and setting the time to 3 minutes. Select START/STOP to begin. 6. Once the unit is preheated, place 4 cups into the basket and fill each three-quarters full with the batter. 7. Select BAKE, set the temperature to 315°F (157°C), and set the time for 17 minutes. Select START/STOP to begin. 8. After about 12 minutes, check the muffins. If they spring back when lightly touched with your finger, they are done. If not, resume cooking. 9. When the cooking is done, transfer the muffins to a wire rack to cool. 10. Repeat steps 6, 7, and 8 with the remaining muffin cups and batter. 11. Let the muffins cool for 10 minutes before serving.

Cheddar-Ham-Corn Muffins

Prep time: 10 minutes | Cook time: 6 to 8 minutes
per batch | Makes 8 muffins

¾ cup yellow cornmeal

¼ cup flour

1½ teaspoons baking powder

¼ teaspoon salt

1 egg, beaten

2 tablespoons canola oil

½ cup milk

½ cup shredded sharp Cheddar cheese

½ cup diced ham

8 foil muffin cups, liners removed and sprayed with cooking spray

1. Preheat the air fryer to 390°F (199°C). 2. In a medium bowl, stir together the cornmeal, flour, baking powder, and salt. 3. Add egg, oil, and milk to dry ingredients and mix well. 4. Stir in shredded cheese and diced ham. 5. Divide batter among the muffin cups. 6. Place 4 filled muffin cups in air fryer basket and bake for 5 minutes. 7. Reduce temperature to 330°F (166°C) and bake for 1 to 2 minutes or until toothpick inserted in center of muffin comes out clean. 8. Repeat steps 6 and 7 to cook remaining muffins.

Smoky Sausage Patties

Prep time: 30 minutes | Cook time: 9 minutes |
Serves 8

1 pound (454 g) ground pork

1 tablespoon coconut aminos

2 teaspoons liquid smoke

1 teaspoon dried sage

1 teaspoon sea salt

½ teaspoon fennel seeds

½ teaspoon dried thyme

½ teaspoon freshly ground black pepper

¼ teaspoon cayenne pepper

1. In a large bowl, combine the pork, coconut aminos, liquid smoke, sage, salt, fennel seeds, thyme, black pepper, and cayenne pepper. Work the meat with your hands until the seasonings are fully incorporated. 2. Shape the mixture into 8 equal-size patties. Using your thumb, make a dent in the center of each patty. Place the patties on a plate and cover with plastic wrap. Refrigerate the patties for at least 30 minutes. 3. Working in batches if necessary, place the patties in a single layer in the air fryer, being careful not to overcrowd them. 4. Set the air fryer to 400°F (204°C) and air fry for 5 minutes. Flip and cook for about 4 minutes more.

Creamy Cinnamon Rolls

Prep time: 10 minutes | Cook time: 9 minutes |

Serves 8

1 pound (454 g) frozen bread dough, thawed	Cream Cheese Glaze:
¼ cup butter, melted	4 ounces (113 g) cream cheese, softened
¾ cup brown sugar	2 tablespoons butter, softened
1½ tablespoons ground cinnamon	1¼ cups powdered sugar
	½ teaspoon vanilla extract

1. Let the bread dough come to room temperature on the counter. On a lightly floured surface, roll the dough into a 13-inch by 11-inch rectangle. Position the rectangle so the 13-inch side is facing you. Brush the melted butter all over the dough, leaving a 1-inch border uncovered along the edge farthest away from you. 2. Combine the brown sugar and cinnamon in a small bowl. Sprinkle the mixture evenly over the buttered dough, keeping the 1-inch border uncovered. Roll the dough into a log, starting with the edge closest to you. Roll the dough tightly, rolling evenly, and push out any air pockets. When you get to the uncovered edge of the dough, press the dough onto the roll to seal it together. 3. Cut the log into 8 pieces, slicing slowly with a sawing motion so you don't flatten the dough. Turn the slices on their sides and cover with a clean kitchen towel. Let the rolls sit in the warmest part of the kitchen for 1½ to 2 hours to rise. 4. To make the glaze, place the cream cheese and butter in a microwave-safe bowl. Soften the mixture in the microwave for 30 seconds at a time until it is easy to stir. Gradually add the powdered sugar and stir to combine. Add the vanilla extract and whisk until smooth. Set aside. 5. When the rolls have risen, preheat the air fryer to 350ºF (177ºC). 6. Transfer 4 of the rolls to the air fryer basket. Air fry for 5 minutes. Turn the rolls over and air fry for another 4 minutes. Repeat with the remaining 4 rolls. 7. Let the rolls cool for two minutes before glazing. Spread large dollops of cream cheese glaze on top of the warm cinnamon rolls, allowing some glaze to drip down the side of the rolls. Serve warm.

Hearty Blueberry Oatmeal

Prep time: 10 minutes | Cook time: 25 minutes |

Serves 6

1½ cups quick oats	1 teaspoon vanilla extract
1¼ teaspoons ground cinnamon, divided	1 egg, beaten
½ teaspoon baking powder	2 cups blueberries
Pinch salt	Olive oil
1 cup unsweetened vanilla almond milk	1½ teaspoons sugar, divided
¼ cup honey	6 tablespoons low-fat whipped topping (optional)

1. In a large bowl, mix together the oats, 1 teaspoon of cinnamon, baking powder, and salt. 2. In a medium bowl, whisk together the almond milk, honey, vanilla and egg. 3. Pour the liquid ingredients into the oats mixture and stir to combine. Fold in the blueberries. 4. Lightly spray a baking pan with oil. 5. Add half the blueberry mixture to the pan. 6. Sprinkle ⅛ teaspoon of cinnamon and ½ teaspoon sugar over the top. 7. Cover the pan with aluminum foil and place gently in the air fryer basket. 8. Air fry at 360ºF (182ºC) for 20 minutes. Remove the foil and air fry for an additional 5 minutes. Transfer the mixture to a shallow bowl. 9. Repeat with the remaining blueberry mixture, ½ teaspoon of sugar, and ⅛ teaspoon of cinnamon. 10. To serve, spoon into bowls and top with whipped topping.

Pita and Pepperoni Pizza

Prep time: 10 minutes | Cook time: 6 minutes |

Serves 1

1 teaspoon olive oil	¼ cup grated Mozzarella cheese
1 tablespoon pizza sauce	¼ teaspoon garlic powder
1 pita bread	¼ teaspoon dried oregano
6 pepperoni slices	

1. Preheat the air fryer to 350ºF (177ºC). Grease the air fryer basket with olive oil. 2. Spread the pizza sauce on top of the pita bread. Put the pepperoni slices over the sauce, followed by the Mozzarella cheese. 3. Season with garlic powder and oregano. 4. Put the pita pizza inside the air fryer and place a trivet on top. 5. Bake in the preheated air fryer for 6 minutes and serve.

Peppered Maple Bacon Knots

Prep time: 5 minutes | Cook time: 7 to 8 minutes |

Serves 6

1 pound (454 g) maple smoked center-cut bacon	¼ cup brown sugar
¼ cup maple syrup	Coarsely cracked black peppercorns, to taste

1. Preheat the air fryer to 390ºF (199ºC). 2. On a clean work surface, tie each bacon strip in a loose knot. 3. Stir together the maple syrup and brown sugar in a bowl. Generously brush this mixture over the bacon knots. 4. Working in batches, arrange the bacon knots in the air fryer basket. Sprinkle with the coarsely cracked black peppercorns. 5. Air fry for 5 minutes. Flip the bacon knots and continue cooking for 2 to 3 minutes more, or until the bacon is crisp. 6. Remove from the basket to a paper towel-lined plate. Repeat with the remaining bacon knots. 7. Let the bacon knots cool for a few minutes and serve warm.

Turkey Sausage Breakfast Pizza

Prep time: 15 minutes | Cook time: 24 minutes | Serves 2

4 large eggs, divided
1 tablespoon water
½ teaspoon garlic powder
½ teaspoon onion powder
½ teaspoon dried oregano
2 tablespoons coconut flour

3 tablespoons grated Parmesan cheese
½ cup shredded provolone cheese
1 link cooked turkey sausage, chopped (about 2 ounces / 57 g)
2 sun-dried tomatoes, finely chopped
2 scallions, thinly sliced

1. Preheat the air fryer to 400°F (204°C). Line a cake pan with parchment paper and lightly coat the paper with olive oil. 2. In a large bowl, whisk 2 of the eggs with the water, garlic powder, onion powder, and dried oregano. Add the coconut flour, breaking up any lumps with your hands as you add it to the bowl. Stir the coconut flour into the egg mixture, mixing until smooth. Stir in the Parmesan cheese. Allow the mixture to rest for a few minutes until thick and dough-like. 3. Transfer the mixture to the prepared pan. Use a spatula to spread it evenly and slightly up the sides of the pan. Air fry until the crust is set but still light in color, about 10 minutes. Top with the cheeses, sausage, and sun-dried tomatoes. 4. Break the remaining 2 eggs into a small bowl, then slide them onto the pizza. Return the pizza to the air fryer. Air fry 10 to 14 minutes until the egg whites are set and the yolks are the desired doneness. Top with the scallions and allow to rest for 5 minutes before serving.

Chapter 2 Family Favorites

Coconut Chicken Tenders

Prep time: 10 minutes | Cook time: 12 minutes |
Serves 4

Oil, for spraying	¾ cup panko bread crumbs
2 large eggs	1 teaspoon salt
¼ cup milk	½ teaspoon freshly ground
1 tablespoon hot sauce	black pepper
1½ cups sweetened flaked coconut	1 pound (454 g) chicken tenders

1. Line the air fryer basket with parchment and spray lightly with oil. 2. In a small bowl, whisk together the eggs, milk, and hot sauce. 3. In a shallow dish, mix together the coconut, bread crumbs, salt, and black pepper. 4. Coat the chicken in the egg mix, then dredge in the coconut mixture until evenly coated. 5. Place the chicken in the prepared basket and spray liberally with oil. 6. Air fry at 400ºF (204ºC) for 6 minutes, flip, spray with more oil, and cook for another 6 minutes, or until the internal temperature reaches 165ºF (74ºC).

Beignets

Prep time: 30 minutes | Cook time: 6 minutes |
Makes 9 beignets

Oil, for greasing and spraying	1 cup milk
3 cups all-purpose flour, plus more for dusting	2 tablespoons packed light brown sugar
1½ teaspoons salt	1 tablespoon unsalted butter
1 (2¼ teaspoons) envelope active dry yeast	1 large egg
	1 cup confectioners' sugar

1. Oil a large bowl. 2. In a small bowl, mix together the flour, salt, and yeast. Set aside. 3. Pour the milk into a glass measuring cup and microwave in 1-minute intervals until it boils. 4. In a large bowl, mix together the brown sugar and butter. Pour in the hot milk and whisk until the sugar has dissolved. Let cool to room temperature. 5. Whisk the egg into the cooled milk mixture and fold in the flour mixture until a dough forms. 6. On a lightly floured work surface, knead the dough for 3 to 5 minutes. 7. Place the dough in the oiled bowl and cover with a clean kitchen towel. Let rise in a warm place for about 1 hour, or until doubled in size. 8. Roll the dough out on a lightly floured work surface until it's about ¼ inch thick. Cut the dough into 3-inch squares and place them on a lightly floured baking sheet. Cover loosely with a kitchen towel and let rise again until doubled in size, about 30 minutes. 9. Line the air fryer basket with parchment and spray lightly with oil. 10. Place the dough squares in the prepared basket and spray lightly with oil. You may need to work in batches, depending on the size of your air fryer. 11. Air fry at 390ºF (199ºC) for 3 minutes, flip, spray with oil, and cook for another 3 minutes, until crispy. 12. Dust with the confectioners' sugar before serving.

Beef Jerky

Prep time: 30 minutes | Cook time: 2 hours | Serves 8

Oil, for spraying	brown sugar
1 pound (454 g) round steak, cut into thin, short slices	1 tablespoon minced garlic
¼ cup soy sauce	1 teaspoon ground ginger
3 tablespoons packed light	1 tablespoon water

1. Line the air fryer basket with parchment and spray lightly with oil. 2. Place the steak, soy sauce, brown sugar, garlic, ginger, and water in a zip-top plastic bag, seal, and shake well until evenly coated. Refrigerate for 30 minutes. 3. Place the steak in the prepared basket in a single layer. You may need to work in batches, depending on the size of your air fryer. 4. Air fry at 180ºF (82ºC) for at least 2 hours. Add more time if you like your jerky a bit tougher.

Cheesy Roasted Sweet Potatoes

Prep time: 7 minutes | Cook time: 18 to 23 minutes |
Serves 4

2 large sweet potatoes, peeled and sliced	vinegar
1 teaspoon olive oil	1 teaspoon dried thyme
1 tablespoon white balsamic	¼ cup grated Parmesan cheese

1. In a large bowl, drizzle the sweet potato slices with the olive oil and toss. 2. Sprinkle with the balsamic vinegar and thyme and toss again. 3. Sprinkle the potatoes with the Parmesan cheese and toss to coat. 4. Roast the slices, in batches, in the air fryer basket at 400ºF (204ºC) for 18 to 23 minutes, tossing the sweet potato slices in the basket once during cooking, until tender. 5. Repeat with the remaining sweet potato slices. Serve immediately.

Bacon-Wrapped Hot Dogs

Prep time: 5 minutes | Cook time: 10 minutes | Serves 4

Oil, for spraying
4 bacon slices
4 all-beef hot dogs
4 hot dog buns
Toppings of choice

1. Line the air fryer basket with parchment and spray lightly with oil. 2. Wrap a strip of bacon tightly around each hot dog, taking care to cover the tips so they don't get too crispy. Secure with a toothpick at each end to keep the bacon from shrinking. 3. Place the hot dogs in the prepared basket. 4. Air fry at 380ºF (193ºC) for 8 to 9 minutes, depending on how crispy you like the bacon. For extra-crispy, cook the hot dogs at 400ºF (204ºC) for 6 to 8 minutes. 5. Place the hot dogs in the buns, return them to the air fryer, and cook for another 1 to 2 minutes, or until the buns are warm. Add your desired toppings and serve.

Pork Stuffing Meatballs

Prep time: 10 minutes | Cook time: 12 minutes | Makes 35 meatballs

Oil, for spraying
1½ pounds (680 g) ground pork
1 cup bread crumbs
½ cup milk
¼ cup minced onion
1 large egg
1 tablespoon dried rosemary
1 tablespoon dried thyme
1 teaspoon salt
1 teaspoon freshly ground black pepper
1 teaspoon finely chopped fresh parsley

1. Line the air fryer basket with parchment and spray lightly with oil. 2. In a large bowl, mix together the ground pork, bread crumbs, milk, onion, egg, rosemary, thyme, salt, black pepper, and parsley. 3. Roll about 2 tablespoons of the mixture into a ball. Repeat with the rest of the mixture. You should have 30 to 35 meatballs. 4. Place the meatballs in the prepared basket in a single layer, leaving space between each one. You may need to work in batches, depending on the size of your air fryer. 5. Air fry at 390ºF (199ºC) for 10 to 12 minutes, flipping after 5 minutes, or until golden brown and the internal temperature reaches 160ºF (71ºC).

Avocado and Egg Burrito

Prep time: 10 minutes | Cook time: 3 to 5 minutes | Serves 4

2 hard-boiled egg whites, chopped
1 hard-boiled egg, chopped
1 avocado, peeled, pitted, and chopped
1 red bell pepper, chopped
3 tablespoons low-sodium salsa, plus additional for serving (optional)
1 (1.2 ounces / 34 g) slice low-sodium, low-fat American cheese, torn into pieces
4 low-sodium whole-wheat flour tortillas

1. In a medium bowl, thoroughly mix the egg whites, egg, avocado, red bell pepper, salsa, and cheese. 2. Place the tortillas on a work surface and evenly divide the filling among them. Fold in the edges and roll up. Secure the burritos with toothpicks if necessary. 3. Put the burritos in the air fryer basket. Air fry at 390ºF (199ºC) for 3 to 5 minutes, or until the burritos are light golden brown and crisp. Serve with more salsa (if using).

Churro Bites

Prep time: 5 minutes | Cook time: 6 minutes | Makes 36 bites

Oil, for spraying
1 (17¼ ounces / 489 g) package frozen puffed pastry, thawed
1 cup granulated sugar
1 tablespoon ground cinnamon
½ cup confectioners' sugar
1 tablespoon milk

1. Preheat the air fryer to 400ºF (204ºC). Line the air fryer basket with parchment and spray lightly with oil. 2. Unfold the puff pastry onto a clean work surface. Using a sharp knife, cut the dough into 36 bite-size pieces. 3. Place the dough pieces in one layer in the prepared basket, taking care not to let the pieces touch or overlap. 4. Cook for 3 minutes, flip, and cook for another 3 minutes, or until puffed and golden. 5. In a small bowl, mix together the granulated sugar and cinnamon. 6. In another small bowl, whisk together the confectioners' sugar and milk. 7. Dredge the bites in the cinnamon-sugar mixture until evenly coated. 8. Serve with the icing on the side for dipping.

Pork Burgers with Red Cabbage Salad

Prep time: 20 minutes | Cook time: 7 to 9 minutes | Serves 4

½ cup Greek yogurt
2 tablespoons low-sodium mustard, divided
1 tablespoon lemon juice
¼ cup sliced red cabbage
¼ cup grated carrots
1 pound (454 g) lean ground pork
½ teaspoon paprika
1 cup mixed baby lettuce greens
2 small tomatoes, sliced
8 small low-sodium whole-wheat sandwich buns, cut in half

1. In a small bowl, combine the yogurt, 1 tablespoon mustard, lemon juice, cabbage, and carrots; mix and refrigerate. 2. In a medium bowl, combine the pork, remaining 1 tablespoon mustard, and paprika. Form into 8 small patties. 3. Put the sliders into the air fryer basket. Air fry at 400ºF (204ºC) for 7 to 9 minutes, or until the sliders register 165ºF (74ºC) as tested with a meat thermometer. 4. Assemble the burgers by placing some of the lettuce greens on a bun bottom. Top with a tomato slice, the burgers, and the cabbage mixture. Add the bun top and serve immediately.

Veggie Tuna Melts

Prep time: 15 minutes | Cook time: 7 to 11 minutes |
Serves 4

2 low-sodium whole-wheat
English muffins, split
1 (6 ounces / 170 g) can chunk
light low-sodium tuna, drained
1 cup shredded carrot
⅓ cup chopped mushrooms
2 scallions, white and green

parts, sliced
⅓ cup nonfat Greek yogurt
2 tablespoons low-sodium stone
ground mustard
2 slices low-sodium low-fat
Swiss cheese, halved

1. Place the English muffin halves in the air fryer basket. Air fry at 340ºF (171ºC) for 3 to 4 minutes, or until crisp. Remove from the basket and set aside. 2. In a medium bowl, thoroughly mix the tuna, carrot, mushrooms, scallions, yogurt, and mustard. Top each half of the muffins with one-fourth of the tuna mixture and a half slice of Swiss cheese. 3. Air fry for 4 to 7 minutes, or until the tuna mixture is hot and the cheese melts and starts to brown. Serve immediately.

Steak Tips and Potatoes

Prep time: 10 minutes | Cook time: 20 minutes |
Serves 4

Oil, for spraying
8 ounces (227 g) baby gold
potatoes, cut in half
½ teaspoon salt
1 pound (454 g) steak, cut into
½-inch pieces

1 teaspoon Worcestershire
sauce
1 teaspoon granulated garlic
½ teaspoon salt
½ teaspoon freshly ground
black pepper

1. Line the air fryer basket with parchment and spray lightly with oil. 2. In a microwave-safe bowl, combine the potatoes and salt, then pour in about ½ inch of water. Microwave for 7 minutes, or until the potatoes are nearly tender. Drain. 3. In a large bowl, gently mix together the steak, potatoes, Worcestershire sauce, garlic, salt, and black pepper. Spread the mixture in an even layer in the prepared basket. 4. Air fry at 400ºF (204ºC) for 12 to 17 minutes, stirring after 5 to 6 minutes. The cooking time will depend on the thickness of the meat and preferred doneness.

Puffed Egg Tarts

Prep time: 10 minutes | Cook time: 42 minutes |
Makes 4 tarts

Oil, for spraying
All-purpose flour, for dusting
1 (12 ounces / 340 g) sheet
frozen puff pastry, thawed
¾ cup shredded Cheddar

cheese, divided
4 large eggs
2 teaspoons chopped fresh
parsley
Salt and freshly ground black

pepper, to taste

1. Preheat the air fryer to 390ºF (199ºC). Line the air fryer basket with parchment and spray lightly with oil. 2. Lightly dust your work surface with flour. Unfold the puff pastry and cut it into 4 equal squares. Place 2 squares in the prepared basket. 3. Cook for 10 minutes. 4. Remove the basket. Press the center of each tart shell with a spoon to make an indentation. 5. Sprinkle 3 tablespoons of cheese into each indentation and crack 1 egg into the center of each tart shell. 6. Cook for another 7 to 11 minutes, or until the eggs are cooked to your desired doneness. 7. Repeat with the remaining puff pastry squares, cheese, and eggs. 8. Sprinkle evenly with the parsley, and season with salt and black pepper. Serve immediately.

Fish and Vegetable Tacos

Prep time: 15 minutes | Cook time: 9 to 12 minutes |
Serves 4

1 pound (454 g) white fish
fillets, such as sole or cod
2 teaspoons olive oil
3 tablespoons freshly squeezed
lemon juice, divided
1½ cups chopped red cabbage

1 large carrot, grated
½ cup low-sodium salsa
⅓ cup low-fat Greek yogurt
4 soft low-sodium whole-wheat
tortillas

1. Brush the fish with the olive oil and sprinkle with 1 tablespoon of lemon juice. Air fry in the air fryer basket at 390ºF (199ºC) for 9 to 12 minutes, or until the fish just flakes when tested with a fork. 2. Meanwhile, in a medium bowl, stir together the remaining 2 tablespoons of lemon juice, the red cabbage, carrot, salsa, and yogurt. 3. When the fish is cooked, remove it from the air fryer basket and break it up into large pieces. 4. Offer the fish, tortillas, and the cabbage mixture, and let each person assemble a taco.

Fried Green Tomatoes

Prep time: 15 minutes | Cook time: 6 to 8 minutes |
Serves 4

4 medium green tomatoes
⅓ cup all-purpose flour
2 egg whites
¼ cup almond milk
1 cup ground almonds

½ cup panko bread crumbs
2 teaspoons olive oil
1 teaspoon paprika
1 clove garlic, minced

1. Rinse the tomatoes and pat dry. Cut the tomatoes into ½-inch slices, discarding the thinner ends. 2. Put the flour on a plate. In a shallow bowl, beat the egg whites with the almond milk until frothy. And on another plate, combine the almonds, bread crumbs, olive oil, paprika, and garlic and mix well. 3. Dip the tomato slices into the flour, then into the egg white mixture, then into the almond mixture to coat. 4. Place four of the coated tomato slices in the air fryer basket. Air fry at 400ºF (204ºC) for 6 to 8 minutes or until the tomato coating is crisp and golden brown. Repeat with remaining tomato slices and serve immediately.

Chinese-Inspired Spareribs

Prep time: 30 minutes | Cook time: 8 minutes | Serves 4

Oil, for spraying
12 ounces (340 g) boneless pork spareribs, cut into 3-inch-long pieces
1 cup soy sauce
¾ cup sugar

½ cup beef or chicken stock
¼ cup honey
2 tablespoons minced garlic
1 teaspoon ground ginger
2 drops red food coloring (optional)

1. Line the air fryer basket with parchment and spray lightly with oil. 2. Combine the ribs, soy sauce, sugar, beef stock, honey, garlic, ginger, and food coloring (if using) in a large zip-top plastic bag, seal, and shake well until completely coated. Refrigerate for at least 30 minutes. 3. Place the ribs in the prepared basket. 4. Air fry at 375°F (191°C) for 8 minutes, or until the internal temperature reaches 165°F (74°C).

Berry Cheesecake

Prep time: 5 minutes | Cook time: 10 minutes | Serves 4

Oil, for spraying
8 ounces (227 g) cream cheese
6 tablespoons sugar
1 tablespoon sour cream

1 large egg
½ teaspoon vanilla extract
¼ teaspoon lemon juice
½ cup fresh mixed berries

1. Preheat the air fryer to 350°F (177°C). Line the air fryer basket with parchment and spray lightly with oil. 2. In a blender, combine the cream cheese, sugar, sour cream, egg, vanilla, and lemon juice and blend until smooth. Pour the mixture into a 4-inch springform pan. 3. Place the pan in the prepared basket. 4. Cook for 8 to 10 minutes, or until only the very center jiggles slightly when the pan is moved. 5. Refrigerate the cheesecake in the pan for at least 2 hours. 6. Release the sides from the springform pan, top the cheesecake with the mixed berries, and serve.

Apple Pie Egg Rolls

Prep time: 10 minutes | Cook time: 8 minutes | Makes 6 rolls

Oil, for spraying
1 (21 ounces / 595 g) can apple pie filling
1 tablespoon all-purpose flour

½ teaspoon lemon juice
¼ teaspoon ground nutmeg
¼ teaspoon ground cinnamon
6 egg roll wrappers

1. Preheat the air fryer to 400°F (204°C). Line the air fryer basket with parchment and spray lightly with oil. 2. In a medium bowl, mix together the pie filling, flour, lemon juice, nutmeg, and cinnamon. 3. Lay out the egg roll wrappers on a work surface and spoon a dollop of pie filling in the center of each. 4. Fill a small bowl with water. Dip your finger in the water and, working one at a time, moisten the edges of the wrappers. Fold the wrapper like an envelope: First fold one corner into the center. Fold each side corner in, and then fold over the remaining corner, making sure each corner overlaps a bit and the moistened edges stay closed. Use additional water and your fingers to seal any open edges. 5. Place the rolls in the prepared basket and spray liberally with oil. You may need to work in batches, depending on the size of your air fryer. 6. Cook for 4 minutes, flip, spray with oil, and cook for another 4 minutes, or until crispy and golden brown. Serve immediately.

Meatball Subs

Prep time: 15 minutes | Cook time: 19 minutes | Serves 6

Oil, for spraying
1 pound (454 g) 85% lean ground beef
½ cup Italian bread crumbs
1 tablespoon dried minced onion
1 tablespoon minced garlic
1 large egg

1 teaspoon salt
1 teaspoon freshly ground black pepper
6 hoagie rolls
1 (18 ounces / 510 g) jar marinara sauce
1½ cups shredded Mozzarella cheese

1. Line the air fryer basket with parchment and spray lightly with oil. 2. In a large bowl, mix together the ground beef, bread crumbs, onion, garlic, egg, salt, and black pepper. Roll the mixture into 18 meatballs. 3. Place the meatballs in the prepared basket. 4. Air fry at 390°F (199°C) for 15 minutes. 5. Place 3 meatballs in each hoagie roll. Top with marinara and Mozzarella cheese. 6. Place the loaded rolls in the air fryer and cook for 3 to 4 minutes, or until the cheese is melted. You may need to work in batches, depending on the size of your air fryer. Serve immediately.

Elephant Ears

Prep time: 5 minutes | Cook time: 5 minutes | Serves 8

Oil, for spraying
1 (8 ounces / 227 g) can buttermilk biscuits
3 tablespoons sugar
1 tablespoon ground cinnamon

3 tablespoons unsalted butter, melted
8 scoops vanilla ice cream (optional)

1. Line the air fryer basket with parchment and spray lightly with oil. 2. Separate the dough. Using a rolling pin, roll out the biscuits into 6- to 8-inch circles. 3. Place the dough circles in the prepared basket and spray liberally with oil. You may need to work in batches, depending on the size of your air fryer. 4. Air fry at 350°F (177°C) for 5 minutes, or until lightly browned. 5. In a small bowl, mix together the sugar and cinnamon. 6. Brush the elephant ears with the melted butter and sprinkle with the cinnamon-sugar mixture. 7. Top each serving with a scoop of ice cream (if using).

Phyllo Vegetable Triangles

Prep time: 15 minutes | Cook time: 6 to 11 minutes | Serves 6

3 tablespoons minced onion

2 garlic cloves, minced

2 tablespoons grated carrot

1 teaspoon olive oil

3 tablespoons frozen baby peas, thawed

2 tablespoons nonfat cream cheese, at room temperature

6 sheets frozen phyllo dough, thawed

Olive oil spray, for coating the dough

1. In a baking pan, combine the onion, garlic, carrot, and olive oil. Air fry at 390°F (199°C) for 2 to 4 minutes, or until the vegetables are crisp-tender. Transfer to a bowl. 2. Stir in the peas and cream cheese to the vegetable mixture. Let cool while you prepare the dough. 3. Lay one sheet of phyllo on a work surface and lightly spray with olive oil spray. Top with another sheet of phyllo. Repeat with the remaining 4 phyllo sheets; you'll have 3 stacks with 2 layers each. Cut each stack lengthwise into 4 strips (12 strips total). 4. Place a scant 2 teaspoons of the filling near the bottom of each strip. Bring one corner up over the filling to make a triangle; continue folding the triangles over, as you would fold a flag. Seal the edge with a bit of water. Repeat with the remaining strips and filling. 5. Air fry the triangles, in 2 batches, for 4 to 7 minutes, or until golden brown. Serve.

Chapter 3 Fast and Easy Everyday Favorites

Classic Poutine

Prep time: 15 minutes | Cook time: 25 minutes |

Serves 2

2 russet potatoes, scrubbed and cut into ½-inch sticks	1 teaspoon tomato paste
2 teaspoons vegetable oil	1½ cups beef stock
2 tablespoons butter	2 teaspoons Worcestershire sauce
¼ onion, minced	Salt and freshly ground black pepper, to taste
¼ teaspoon dried thyme	
1 clove garlic, smashed	⅔ cup chopped string cheese
3 tablespoons all-purpose flour	

1. Bring a pot of water to a boil, then put in the potato sticks and blanch for 4 minutes. 2. Preheat the air fryer to 400ºF (204ºC). 3. Drain the potato sticks and rinse under running cold water, then pat dry with paper towels. 4. Transfer the sticks in a large bowl and drizzle with vegetable oil. Toss to coat well. 5. Place the potato sticks in the preheated air fryer. Air fry for 25 minutes or until the sticks are golden brown. Shake the basket at least three times during the frying. 6. Meanwhile, make the gravy: Heat the butter in a saucepan over medium heat until melted. 7. Add the onion, thyme, and garlic and sauté for 5 minutes or until the onion is translucent. 8. Add the flour and sauté for an additional 2 minutes. Pour in the tomato paste and beef stock and cook for 1 more minute or until lightly thickened. 9. Drizzle the gravy with Worcestershire sauce and sprinkle with salt and ground black pepper. Reduce the heat to low to keep the gravy warm until ready to serve. 10. Transfer the fried potato sticks onto a plate, then sprinkle with salt and ground black pepper. Scatter with string cheese and pour the gravy over. Serve warm.

Spicy Air Fried Old Bay Shrimp

Prep time: 7 minutes | Cook time: 10 minutes |

Makes 2 cups

½ teaspoon Old Bay Seasoning	⅛ teaspoon salt
1 teaspoon ground cayenne pepper	½ pound (227 g) shrimps, peeled and deveined
½ teaspoon paprika	Juice of half a lemon
1 tablespoon olive oil	

1. Preheat the air fryer to 390ºF (199ºC). 2. Combine the Old Bay Seasoning, cayenne pepper, paprika, olive oil, and salt in a large bowl, then add the shrimps and toss to coat well. 3. Put the shrimps in the preheated air fryer. Air fry for 10 minutes or until opaque. Flip the shrimps halfway through. 4. Serve the shrimps with lemon juice on top.

Beef Bratwursts

Prep time: 5 minutes | Cook time: 15 minutes |

Serves 4

4 (3-ounce / 85-g) beef bratwursts

1. Preheat the air fryer to 375ºF (191ºC). 2. Place the beef bratwursts in the air fryer basket and air fry for 15 minutes, turning once halfway through. 3. Serve hot.

Bacon Pinwheels

Prep time: 10 minutes | Cook time: 10 minutes | Makes 8 pinwheels

1 sheet puff pastry	8 slices bacon
2 tablespoons maple syrup	Ground black pepper, to taste
¼ cup brown sugar	Cooking spray

1. Preheat the air fryer to 360ºF (182ºC). Spritz the air fryer basket with cooking spray. 2. Roll the puff pastry into a 10-inch square with a rolling pin on a clean work surface, then cut the pastry into 8 strips. 3. Brush the strips with maple syrup and sprinkle with sugar, leaving a 1-inch far end uncovered. 4. Arrange each slice of bacon on each strip, leaving a ⅛-inch length of bacon hang over the end close to you. Sprinkle with black pepper. 5. From the end close to you, roll the strips into pinwheels, then dab the uncovered end with water and seal the rolls. 6. Arrange the pinwheels in the preheated air fryer and spritz with cooking spray. 7. Air fry for 10 minutes or until golden brown. Flip the pinwheels halfway through. 8. Serve immediately.

Simple and Easy Croutons

Prep time: 5 minutes | Cook time: 8 minutes | Serves 4

2 slices friendly bread	Hot soup, for serving
1 tablespoon olive oil	

1. Preheat the air fryer to 390ºF (199ºC). 2. Cut the slices of bread into medium-size chunks. 3. Brush the air fryer basket with the oil. 4. Place the chunks inside and air fry for at least 8 minutes. 5. Serve with hot soup.

Garlicky Baked Cherry Tomatoes

Prep time: 5 minutes | Cook time: 4 to 6 minutes | Serves 2

2 cups cherry tomatoes
1 clove garlic, thinly sliced
1 teaspoon olive oil
⅛ teaspoon kosher salt

1 tablespoon freshly chopped basil, for topping
Cooking spray

1. Preheat the air fryer to 360ºF (182ºC). Spritz the air fryer baking pan with cooking spray and set aside. 2. In a large bowl, toss together the cherry tomatoes, sliced garlic, olive oil, and kosher salt. Spread the mixture in an even layer in the prepared pan. 3. Bake in the preheated air fryer for 4 to 6 minutes, or until the tomatoes become soft and wilted. 4. Transfer to a bowl and rest for 5 minutes. Top with the chopped basil and serve warm.

Indian-Style Sweet Potato Fries

Prep time: 5 minutes | Cook time: 8 minutes | Makes 20 fries

Seasoning Mixture:
¾ teaspoon ground coriander
½ teaspoon garam masala
½ teaspoon garlic powder
½ teaspoon ground cumin

¼ teaspoon ground cayenne pepper
Fries:
2 large sweet potatoes, peeled
2 teaspoons olive oil

1. Preheat the air fryer to 400ºF (204ºC). 2. In a small bowl, combine the coriander, garam masala, garlic powder, cumin, and cayenne pepper. 3. Slice the sweet potatoes into ¼-inch-thick fries. 4. In a large bowl, toss the sliced sweet potatoes with the olive oil and the seasoning mixture. 5. Transfer the seasoned sweet potatoes to the air fryer basket and fry for 8 minutes, until crispy. 6. Serve warm.

Air Fried Shishito Peppers

Prep time: 5 minutes | Cook time: 5 minutes | Serves 4

½ pound (227 g) shishito peppers (about 24)
1 tablespoon olive oil

Coarse sea salt, to taste
Lemon wedges, for serving
Cooking spray

1. Preheat the air fryer to 400ºF (204ºC). Spritz the air fryer basket with cooking spray. 2. Toss the peppers with olive oil in a large bowl to coat well. 3. Arrange the peppers in the preheated air fryer. 4. Air fryer for 5 minutes or until blistered and lightly charred. Shake the basket and sprinkle the peppers with salt halfway through the cooking time. 5. Transfer the peppers onto a plate and squeeze the lemon wedges on top before serving.

Corn Fritters

Prep time: 15 minutes | Cook time: 8 minutes | Serves 6

1 cup self-rising flour
1 tablespoon sugar
1 teaspoon salt
1 large egg, lightly beaten

¼ cup buttermilk
¾ cup corn kernels
¼ cup minced onion
Cooking spray

1. Preheat the air fryer to 350ºF (177ºC). Line the air fryer basket with parchment paper. 2. In a medium bowl, whisk the flour, sugar, and salt until blended. Stir in the egg and buttermilk. Add the corn and minced onion. Mix well. Shape the corn fritter batter into 12 balls. 3. Place the fritters on the parchment and spritz with oil. Bake for 4 minutes. Flip the fritters, spritz them with oil, and bake for 4 minutes more until firm and lightly browned. 4. Serve immediately.

Frico

Prep time: 5 minutes | Cook time: 5 minutes | Serves 2

1 cup shredded aged Manchego cheese
1 teaspoon all-purpose flour

½ teaspoon cumin seeds
¼ teaspoon cracked black pepper

1. Preheat the air fryer to 375ºF (191ºC). Line the air fryer basket with parchment paper. 2. Combine the cheese and flour in a bowl. Stir to mix well. Spread the mixture in the basket into a 4-inch round. 3. Combine the cumin and black pepper in a small bowl. Stir to mix well. Sprinkle the cumin mixture over the cheese round. 4. Air fry 5 minutes or until the cheese is lightly browned and frothy. 5. Use tongs to transfer the cheese wafer onto a plate and slice to serve.

Cheesy Baked Grits

Prep time: 10 minutes | Cook time: 12 minutes | Serves 6

¾ cup hot water
2 (1 ounce / 28 g) packages instant grits
1 large egg, beaten
1 tablespoon butter, melted

2 cloves garlic, minced
½ to 1 teaspoon red pepper flakes
1 cup shredded Cheddar cheese or jalapeño Jack cheese

1. Preheat the air fryer to 400ºF (204ºC). 2. In a baking pan, combine the water, grits, egg, butter, garlic, and red pepper flakes. Stir until well combined. Stir in the shredded cheese. 3. Place the pan in the air fryer basket and air fry for 12 minutes, or until the grits have cooked through and a knife inserted near the center comes out clean. 4. Let stand for 5 minutes before serving.

Spinach and Carrot Balls

Prep time: 10 minutes | Cook time: 10 minutes | Serves 4

2 slices toasted bread
1 carrot, peeled and grated
1 package fresh spinach,
blanched and chopped
½ onion, chopped
1 egg, beaten

½ teaspoon garlic powder
1 teaspoon minced garlic
1 teaspoon salt
½ teaspoon black pepper
1 tablespoon nutritional yeast
1 tablespoon flour

1. Preheat the air fryer to 390ºF (199ºC). 2. In a food processor, pulse the toasted bread to form bread crumbs. Transfer into a shallow dish or bowl. 3. In a bowl, mix together all the other ingredients. 4. Use your hands to shape the mixture into small-sized balls. Roll the balls in the bread crumbs, ensuring to cover them well. 5. Put in the air fryer basket and air fry for 10 minutes. 6. Serve immediately.

Easy Roasted Asparagus

Prep time: 5 minutes | Cook time: 6 minutes | Serves 4

1 pound (454 g) asparagus,
trimmed and halved crosswise
1 teaspoon extra-virgin olive oil

Salt and pepper, to taste
Lemon wedges, for serving

1. Preheat the air fryer to 400ºF (204ºC). 2. Toss the asparagus with the oil, ⅛ teaspoon salt, and ⅛ teaspoon pepper in bowl. Transfer to air fryer basket. 3. Place the basket in air fryer and roast for 6 to 8 minutes, or until tender and bright green, tossing halfway through cooking. 4. Season with salt and pepper and serve with lemon wedges.

Easy Cinnamon Toast

Prep time: 5 minutes | Cook time: 20 minutes | Serves 6

1½ teaspoons cinnamon
1½ teaspoons vanilla extract
½ cup sugar
2 teaspoons ground black

pepper
2 tablespoons melted coconut
oil
12 slices whole wheat bread

1. Preheat the air fryer to 400ºF (204ºC). 2. Combine all the ingredients, except for the bread, in a large bowl. Stir to mix well. 3. Dunk the bread in the bowl of mixture gently to coat and infuse well. Shake the excess off. 4. Arrange the bread slices in the preheated air fryer. Air fry for 5 minutes or until golden brown. Flip the bread halfway through. You may need to cook in batches to avoid overcrowding. 5. Remove the bread slices from the air fryer and slice to serve.

Cheesy Potato Patties

Prep time: 5 minutes | Cook time: 10 minutes | Serves 8

2 pounds (907 g) white potatoes
½ cup finely chopped scallions
½ teaspoon freshly ground
black pepper, or more to taste
1 tablespoon fine sea salt

½ teaspoon hot paprika
2 cups shredded Colby cheese
¼ cup canola oil
1 cup crushed crackers

1. Preheat the air fryer to 360ºF (182ºC). 2. Boil the potatoes until soft. Dry them off and peel them before mashing thoroughly, leaving no lumps. 3. Combine the mashed potatoes with scallions, pepper, salt, paprika, and cheese. 4. Mold the mixture into balls with your hands and press with your palm to flatten them into patties. 5. In a shallow dish, combine the canola oil and crushed crackers. Coat the patties in the crumb mixture. 6. Bake the patties for about 10 minutes, in multiple batches if necessary. 7. Serve hot.

Air Fried Zucchini Sticks

Prep time: 5 minutes | Cook time: 20 minutes | Serves 4

1 medium zucchini, cut into 48
sticks
¼ cup seasoned breadcrumbs

1 tablespoon melted buttery
spread
Cooking spray

1. Preheat the air fryer to 360ºF (182ºC). Spritz the air fryer basket with cooking spray and set aside. 2. In 2 different shallow bowls, add the seasoned breadcrumbs and the buttery spread. 3. One by one, dredge the zucchini sticks into the buttery spread, then roll in the breadcrumbs to coat evenly. Arrange the crusted sticks on a plate. 4. Place the zucchini sticks in the prepared air fryer basket. Work in two batches to avoid overcrowding. 5. Air fry for 10 minutes, or until golden brown and crispy. Shake the basket halfway through to cook evenly. 6. When the cooking time is over, transfer the fries to a wire rack. Rest for 5 minutes and serve warm.

Air Fried Broccoli

Prep time: 5 minutes | Cook time: 6 minutes | Serves 1

4 egg yolks
¼ cup butter, melted
2 cups coconut flower

Salt and pepper, to taste
2 cups broccoli florets

1. Preheat the air fryer to 400ºF (204ºC). 2. In a bowl, whisk the egg yolks and melted butter together. Throw in the coconut flour, salt and pepper, then stir again to combine well. 3. Dip each broccoli floret into the mixture and place in the air fryer basket. Air fry for 6 minutes in batches if necessary. Take care when removing them from the air fryer and serve immediately.

Golden Salmon and Carrot Croquettes

Prep time: 15 minutes | Cook time: 10 minutes |

Serves 6

2 egg whites	2 tablespoons minced garlic
1 cup almond flour	cloves
1 cup panko breadcrumbs	½ cup chopped onion
1 pound (454 g) chopped	2 tablespoons chopped chives
salmon fillet	Cooking spray
⅔ cup grated carrots	

1. Preheat the air fryer to 350ºF (177ºC). Spritz the air fryer basket with cooking spray. 2. Whisk the egg whites in a bowl. Put the flour in a second bowl. Pour the breadcrumbs in a third bowl. Set aside. 3. Combine the salmon, carrots, garlic, onion, and chives in a large bowl. Stir to mix well. 4. Form the mixture into balls with your hands. Dredge the balls into the flour, then egg, and then breadcrumbs to coat well. 5. Arrange the salmon balls in the preheated air fryer and spritz with cooking spray. 6. Air fry for 10 minutes or until crispy and browned. Shake the basket halfway through. 7. Serve immediately.

Air Fried Tortilla Chips

Prep time: 5 minutes | Cook time: 10 minutes |

Serves 4

4 six-inch corn tortillas, cut in	¼ teaspoon kosher salt
half and slice into thirds	Cooking spray
1 tablespoon canola oil	

1. Preheat the air fryer to 360ºF (182ºC). Spritz the air fryer basket with cooking spray. 2. On a clean work surface, brush the tortilla chips with canola oil, then transfer the chips in the preheated air fryer. 3. Air fry for 10 minutes or until crunchy and lightly browned. Shake the basket and sprinkle with salt halfway through the cooking time. 4. Transfer the chips onto a plate lined with paper towels. Serve immediately.

Southwest Corn and Bell Pepper Roast

Prep time: 10 minutes | Cook time: 10 minutes |

Serves 4

For the Corn:	1 teaspoon ground cumin
1½ cups thawed frozen corn	½ teaspoon kosher salt
kernels	Cooking spray
1 cup mixed diced bell peppers	For Serving:
1 jalapeño, diced	¼ cup feta cheese
1 cup diced yellow onion	¼ cup chopped fresh cilantro
½ teaspoon ancho chile powder	1 tablespoon fresh lemon juice
1 tablespoon fresh lemon juice	

1. Preheat the air fryer to 375ºF (191ºC). Spritz the air fryer with cooking spray. 2. Combine the ingredients for the corn in a large bowl. Stir to mix well. 3. Pout the mixture into the air fryer. Air fry for 10 minutes or until the corn and bell peppers are soft. Shake the basket halfway through the cooking time. 4. Transfer them onto a large plate, then spread with feta cheese and cilantro. Drizzle with lemon juice and serve.

Crispy Green Tomatoes Slices

Prep time: 10 minutes | Cook time: 8 minutes |

Makes 12 slices

½ cup all-purpose flour	¼-inch-thick slices, patted dry
1 egg	½ teaspoon salt
½ cup buttermilk	½ teaspoon ground black
1 cup cornmeal	pepper
1 cup panko	Cooking spray
2 green tomatoes, cut into	

1. Preheat the air fryer to 400ºF (204ºC). Line the air fryer basket with parchment paper. 2. Pour the flour in a bowl. Whisk the egg and buttermilk in a second bowl. Combine the cornmeal and panko in a third bowl. 3. Dredge the tomato slices in the bowl of flour first, then into the egg mixture, and then dunk the slices into the cornmeal mixture. Shake the excess off. 4. Transfer the well-coated tomato slices in the preheated air fryer and sprinkle with salt and ground black pepper. 5. Spritz the tomato slices with cooking spray. Air fry for 8 minutes or until crispy and lightly browned. Flip the slices halfway through the cooking time. 6. Serve immediately.

Honey Bartlett Pears with Lemony Ricotta

Prep time: 10 minutes | Cook time: 8 minutes |

Serves 4

2 large Bartlett pears, peeled,	½ cup whole-milk ricotta
cut in half, cored	cheese
3 tablespoons melted butter	1 teaspoon pure lemon extract
½ teaspoon ground ginger	1 teaspoon pure almond extract
¼ teaspoon ground cardamom	1 tablespoon honey, plus
3 tablespoons brown sugar	additional for drizzling

1. Preheat the air fryer to 375ºF (191ºC). 2. Toss the pears with butter, ginger, cardamom, and sugar in a large bowl. Toss to coat well. 3. Arrange the pears in the preheated air fryer, cut side down. Air fry for 5 minutes, then flip the pears and air fry for 3 more minutes or until the pears are soft and browned. 4. In the meantime, combine the remaining ingredients in a separate bowl. Whip for 1 minute with a hand mixer until the mixture is puffed. 5. Divide the mixture into four bowls, then put the pears over the mixture and drizzle with more honey to serve.

Sweet Corn and Carrot Fritters

Prep time: 10 minutes | Cook time: 8 to 11 minutes |
Serves 4

1 medium-sized carrot, grated
1 yellow onion, finely chopped
4 ounces (113 g) canned sweet
corn kernels, drained
1 teaspoon sea salt flakes
1 tablespoon chopped fresh
cilantro

1 medium-sized egg, whisked
2 tablespoons plain milk
1 cup grated Parmesan cheese
¼ cup flour
⅓ teaspoon baking powder
⅓ teaspoon sugar
Cooking spray

1. Preheat the air fryer to 350ºF (177ºC). 2. Place the grated carrot in a colander and press down to squeeze out any excess moisture. Dry it with a paper towel. 3. Combine the carrots with the remaining ingredients. 4. Mold 1 tablespoon of the mixture into a ball and press it down with your hand or a spoon to flatten it. Repeat until the rest of the mixture is used up. 5. Spritz the balls with cooking spray. 6. Arrange in the air fryer basket, taking care not to overlap any balls. Bake for 8 to 11 minutes, or until they're firm. 7. Serve warm.

Easy Air Fried Edamame

Prep time: 5 minutes | Cook time: 7 minutes | Serves 6

1½ pounds (680 g) unshelled
edamame

2 tablespoons olive oil
1 teaspoon sea salt

1. Preheat the air fryer to 400ºF (204ºC). 2. Place the edamame in a large bowl, then drizzle with olive oil. Toss to coat well. 3. Transfer the edamame to the preheated air fryer. Cook for 7 minutes or until tender and warmed through. Shake the basket at least three times during the cooking. 4. Transfer the cooked edamame onto a plate and sprinkle with salt. Toss to combine well and set aside for 3 minutes to infuse before serving.

Peppery Brown Rice Fritters

Prep time: 10 minutes | Cook time: 8 to 10 minutes |
Serves 4

1 (10 ounces / 284 g) bag frozen
cooked brown rice, thawed
1 egg
3 tablespoons brown rice flour
⅓ cup finely grated carrots
⅓ cup minced red bell pepper

2 tablespoons minced fresh
basil
3 tablespoons grated Parmesan
cheese
2 teaspoons olive oil

1. Preheat the air fryer to 380ºF (193ºC). 2. In a small bowl, combine the thawed rice, egg, and flour and mix to blend. 3. Stir

in the carrots, bell pepper, basil, and Parmesan cheese. 4. Form the mixture into 8 fritters and drizzle with the olive oil. 5. Put the fritters carefully into the air fryer basket. Air fry for 8 to 10 minutes, or until the fritters are golden brown and cooked through. 6. Serve immediately.

Baked Chorizo Scotch Eggs

Prep time: 5 minutes | Cook time: 15 to 20 minutes |
Makes 4 eggs

1 pound (454 g) Mexican
chorizo or other seasoned
sausage meat
4 soft-boiled eggs plus 1 raw
egg

1 tablespoon water
½ cup all-purpose flour
1 cup panko bread crumbs
Cooking spray

1. Divide the chorizo into 4 equal portions. Flatten each portion into a disc. Place a soft-boiled egg in the center of each disc. Wrap the chorizo around the egg, encasing it completely. Place the encased eggs on a plate and chill for at least 30 minutes. 2. Preheat the air fryer to 360ºF (182ºC). 3. Beat the raw egg with 1 tablespoon of water. Place the flour on a small plate and the panko on a second plate. Working with 1 egg at a time, roll the encased egg in the flour, then dip it in the egg mixture. Dredge the egg in the panko and place on a plate. Repeat with the remaining eggs. 4. Spray the eggs with oil and place in the air fryer basket. Bake for 10 minutes. Turn and bake for an additional 5 to 10 minutes, or until browned and crisp on all sides. 5. Serve immediately.

Garlicky Zoodles

Prep time: 10 minutes | Cook time: 10 minutes |
Serves 4

2 large zucchini, peeled and
spiralized
2 large yellow summer squash,
peeled and spiralized
1 tablespoon olive oil, divided

½ teaspoon kosher salt
1 garlic clove, whole
2 tablespoons fresh basil,
chopped
Cooking spray

1. Preheat the air fryer to 360ºF (182ºC). Spritz the air fryer basket with cooking spray. 2. Combine the zucchini and summer squash with 1 teaspoon olive oil and salt in a large bowl. Toss to coat well. 3. Transfer the zucchini and summer squash in the preheated air fryer and add the garlic. 4. Air fry for 10 minutes or until tender and fragrant. Toss the spiralized zucchini and summer squash halfway through the cooking time. 5. Transfer the cooked zucchini and summer squash onto a plate and set aside. 6. Remove the garlic from the air fryer and allow to cool for a few minutes. Mince the garlic and combine with remaining olive oil in a small bowl. Stir to mix well. 7. Drizzle the spiralized zucchini and summer squash with garlic oil and sprinkle with basil. Toss to serve.

Classic Latkes

Prep time: 15 minutes | Cook time: 10 minutes | Makes 4 latkes

1 egg

2 tablespoons all-purpose flour

2 medium potatoes, peeled and shredded, rinsed and drained

¼ teaspoon granulated garlic

½ teaspoon salt

Cooking spray

1. Preheat the air fryer to 380°F (193°C). Spritz the air fryer basket with cooking spray. 2. Whisk together the egg, flour, potatoes, garlic, and salt in a large bowl. Stir to mix well. 3. Divide the mixture into four parts, then flatten them into four circles. Arrange the circles into the preheated air fryer. 4. Spritz the circles with cooking spray, then air fry for 10 minutes or until golden brown and crispy. Flip the latkes halfway through. 5. Serve immediately.

Scalloped Veggie Mix

Prep time: 10 minutes | Cook time: 15 minutes | Serves 4

1 Yukon Gold potato, thinly sliced

1 small sweet potato, peeled and thinly sliced

1 medium carrot, thinly sliced

¼ cup minced onion

3 garlic cloves, minced

¾ cup 2 percent milk

2 tablespoons cornstarch

½ teaspoon dried thyme

1. Preheat the air fryer to 380°F (193°C). 2. In a baking pan, layer the potato, sweet potato, carrot, onion, and garlic. 3. In a small bowl, whisk the milk, cornstarch, and thyme until blended. Pour the milk mixture evenly over the vegetables in the pan. 4. Bake for 15 minutes. Check the casserole—it should be golden brown on top, and the vegetables should be tender. 5. Serve immediately.

Crunchy Fried Okra

Prep time: 5 minutes | Cook time: 8 to 10 minutes | Serves 4

1 cup self-rising yellow cornmeal

1 teaspoon Italian-style seasoning

1 teaspoon paprika

1 teaspoon salt

½ teaspoon freshly ground black pepper

2 large eggs, beaten

2 cups okra slices

Cooking spray

1. Preheat the air fryer to 400°F (204°C). Line the air fryer basket with parchment paper. 2. In a shallow bowl, whisk the cornmeal, Italian-style seasoning, paprika, salt, and pepper until blended. Place the beaten eggs in a second shallow bowl. 3. Add the okra to the beaten egg and stir to coat. Add the egg and okra mixture to the cornmeal mixture and stir until coated. 4. Place the okra on the parchment and spritz it with oil. 5. Air fry for 4 minutes. Shake the basket, spritz the okra with oil, and air fry for 4 to 6 minutes more until lightly browned and crispy. 6. Serve immediately.

Chapter 4 Poultry

Chicken Croquettes with Creole Sauce

Prep time: 30 minutes | Cook time: 10 minutes |
Serves 4

2 cups shredded cooked chicken	Creole Sauce:
½ cup shredded Cheddar cheese	¼ cup mayonnaise
2 eggs	¼ cup sour cream
¼ cup finely chopped onion	1½ teaspoons Dijon mustard
¼ cup almond meal	1½ teaspoons fresh lemon juice
1 tablespoon poultry seasoning	½ teaspoon garlic powder
Olive oil	½ teaspoon Creole seasoning

1. In a large bowl, combine the chicken, Cheddar, eggs, onion, almond meal, and poultry seasoning. Stir gently until thoroughly combined. Cover and refrigerate for 30 minutes. 2. Meanwhile, to make the Creole sauce: In a small bowl, whisk together the mayonnaise, sour cream, Dijon mustard, lemon juice, garlic powder, and Creole seasoning until thoroughly combined. Cover and refrigerate until ready to serve. 3. Preheat the air fryer to 400°F (204°C). Divide the chicken mixture into 8 portions and shape into patties. 4. Working in batches if necessary, arrange the patties in a single layer in the air fryer basket and coat both sides lightly with olive oil. Pausing halfway through the cooking time to flip the patties, air fry for 10 minutes, or until lightly browned and the cheese is melted. Serve with the Creole sauce.

Chicken Parmesan

Prep time: 15 minutes | Cook time: 10 minutes |
Serves 4

Oil, for spraying	plus ½ cup shredded
2 (8 ounces / 227 g) boneless, skinless chicken breasts	4 tablespoons unsalted butter, melted
1 cup Italian-style bread crumbs	½ cup marinara sauce
¼ cup grated Parmesan cheese,	

1. Preheat the air fryer to 360°F (182°C). Line the air fryer basket with parchment and spray lightly with oil. 2. Cut each chicken breast in half through its thickness to make 4 thin cutlets. Using a meat tenderizer, pound each cutlet until it is about ¾ inch thick. 3. On a plate, mix together the bread crumbs and grated Parmesan cheese. 4. Lightly brush the chicken with the melted butter, then dip into the bread crumb mixture. 5. Place the chicken in the prepared basket and spray lightly with oil. You may need to work in batches,

depending on the size of your air fryer. 6. Cook for 6 minutes. Top the chicken with the marinara and shredded Parmesan cheese, dividing evenly. Cook for another 3 to 4 minutes, or until golden brown, crispy, and the internal temperature reaches 165°F (74°C).

Classic Whole Chicken

Prep time: 5 minutes | Cook time: 50 minutes |
Serves 4

Oil, for spraying	½ teaspoon salt
1 (4 pounds / 1.8 kg) whole chicken, giblets removed	½ teaspoon freshly ground black pepper
1 tablespoon olive oil	¼ teaspoon finely chopped
1 teaspoon paprika	fresh parsley, for garnish
½ teaspoon granulated garlic	

1. Line the air fryer basket with parchment and spray lightly with oil. 2. Pat the chicken dry with paper towels. Rub it with the olive oil until evenly coated. 3. In a small bowl, mix together the paprika, garlic, salt, and black pepper and sprinkle it evenly over the chicken. 4. Place the chicken in the prepared basket, breast-side down. 5. Air fry at 360°F (182°C) for 30 minutes, flip, and cook for another 20 minutes, or until the internal temperature reaches 165°F (74°C) and the juices run clear. 6. Sprinkle with the parsley before serving.

Ginger Turmeric Chicken Thighs

Prep time: 5 minutes | Cook time: 25 minutes |
Serves 4

4 (4 ounces / 113 g) boneless, skin-on chicken thighs	½ teaspoon salt
2 tablespoons coconut oil, melted	½ teaspoon garlic powder
	½ teaspoon ground ginger
½ teaspoon ground turmeric	¼ teaspoon ground black pepper

1. Place chicken thighs in a large bowl and drizzle with coconut oil. Sprinkle with remaining ingredients and toss to coat both sides of thighs. 2. Place thighs skin side up into ungreased air fryer basket. Adjust the temperature to 400°F (204°C) and air fry for 25 minutes. After 10 minutes, turn thighs. When 5 minutes remain, flip thighs once more. Chicken will be done when skin is golden brown and the internal temperature is at least 165°F (74°C). Serve warm.

Bacon-Wrapped Chicken Breasts Rolls

Prep time: 10 minutes | Cook time: 15 minutes |

Serves 4

¼ cup chopped fresh chives	½ teaspoon red pepper flakes
2 tablespoons lemon juice	4 (4 ounces / 113 g) boneless,
1 teaspoon dried sage	skinless chicken breasts,
1 teaspoon fresh rosemary	pounded to ¼ inch thick
leaves	8 slices bacon
½ cup fresh parsley leaves	Sprigs of fresh rosemary, for
4 cloves garlic, peeled	garnish
1 teaspoon ground fennel	Cooking spray
3 teaspoons sea salt	

1. Preheat the air fryer to 340ºF (171ºC). Spritz the air fryer basket with cooking spray. 2. Put the chives, lemon juice, sage, rosemary, parsley, garlic, fennel, salt, and red pepper flakes in a food processor, then pulse to purée until smooth. 3. Unfold the chicken breasts on a clean work surface, then brush the top side of the chicken breasts with the sauce. 4. Roll the chicken breasts up from the shorter side, then wrap each chicken rolls with 2 bacon slices to cover. Secure with toothpicks. 5. Arrange the rolls in the preheated air fryer, then cook for 10 minutes. Flip the rolls halfway through. 6. Increase the heat to 390ºF (199ºC) and air fry for 5 more minutes or until the bacon is browned and crispy. 7. Transfer the rolls to a large plate. Discard the toothpicks and spread with rosemary sprigs before serving.

Pomegranate-Glazed Chicken with Couscous Salad

Prep time: 25 minutes | Cook time: 20 minutes |

Serves 4

3 tablespoons plus 2 teaspoons	1 tablespoon minced fresh
pomegranate molasses	parsley
½ teaspoon ground cinnamon	2 ounces (57 g) cherry
1 teaspoon minced fresh thyme	tomatoes, quartered
Salt and ground black pepper,	1 scallion, white part minced,
to taste	green part sliced thin on bias
2 (12-ounce / 340-g) bone-in	1 tablespoon extra-virgin olive
split chicken breasts, trimmed	oil
¼ cup chicken broth	1 ounce (28 g) feta cheese,
¼ cup water	crumbled
½ cup couscous	Cooking spray

1. Preheat the air fryer to 350ºF (177ºC). Spritz the air fryer basket with cooking spray. 2. Combine 3 tablespoons of pomegranate molasses, cinnamon, thyme, and ⅛ teaspoon of salt in a small bowl. Stir to mix well. Set aside. 3. Place the chicken breasts in the preheated air fryer, skin side down, and spritz with cooking spray. Sprinkle with salt and ground black pepper. 4. Air fry the chicken for 10 minutes, then brush the chicken with half of pomegranate molasses mixture and flip. Air fry for 5 more minutes. 5. Brush the chicken with remaining pomegranate molasses mixture and flip. Air fry for another 5 minutes or until the internal temperature of the chicken breasts reaches at least 165ºF (74ºC). 6. Meanwhile, pour the broth and water in a pot and bring to a boil over medium-high heat. Add the couscous and sprinkle with salt. Cover and simmer for 7 minutes or until the liquid is almost absorbed. 7. Combine the remaining ingredients, except for the cheese, with cooked couscous in a large bowl. Toss to mix well. Scatter with the feta cheese. 8. When the air frying is complete, remove the chicken from the air fryer and allow to cool for 10 minutes. Serve with vegetable and couscous salad.

Cilantro Lime Chicken Thighs

Prep time: 15 minutes | Cook time: 22 minutes |

Serves 4

4 bone-in, skin-on chicken	2 teaspoons chili powder
thighs	1 teaspoon cumin
1 teaspoon baking powder	2 medium limes
½ teaspoon garlic powder	¼ cup chopped fresh cilantro

1. Pat chicken thighs dry and sprinkle with baking powder. 2. In a small bowl, mix garlic powder, chili powder, and cumin and sprinkle evenly over thighs, gently rubbing on and under chicken skin. 3. Cut one lime in half and squeeze juice over thighs. Place chicken into the air fryer basket. 4. Adjust the temperature to 380ºF (193ºC) and roast for 22 minutes. 5. Cut other lime into four wedges for serving and garnish cooked chicken with wedges and cilantro.

Quick Chicken Fajitas

Prep time: 10 minutes | Cook time: 15 minutes |

Serves 2

10 ounces (283 g) boneless,	½ teaspoon garlic powder
skinless chicken breast, sliced	¼ medium onion, peeled and
into ¼-inch strips	sliced
2 tablespoons coconut oil,	½ medium green bell pepper,
melted	seeded and sliced
1 tablespoon chili powder	½ medium red bell pepper,
½ teaspoon cumin	seeded and sliced
½ teaspoon paprika	

1. Place chicken and coconut oil into a large bowl and sprinkle with chili powder, cumin, paprika, and garlic powder. Toss chicken until well coated with seasoning. Place chicken into the air fryer basket. 2. Adjust the temperature to 350ºF (177ºC) and air fry for 15 minutes. 3. Add onion and peppers into the basket when the cooking time has 7 minutes remaining. 4. Toss the chicken two or three times during cooking. Vegetables should be tender and chicken fully cooked to at least 165ºF (74ºC) internal temperature when finished. Serve warm.

Chicken Pesto Parmigiana

Prep time: 10 minutes | Cook time: 23 minutes | Serves 4

2 large eggs
1 tablespoon water
Fine sea salt and ground black pepper, to taste
1 cup powdered Parmesan cheese (about 3 ounces / 85 g)
2 teaspoons Italian seasoning
4 (5-ounce / 142-g) boneless, skinless chicken breasts or

thighs, pounded to ¼ inch thick
1 cup pesto
1 cup shredded Mozzarella cheese (about 4 ounces / 113 g)
Finely chopped fresh basil, for garnish (optional)
Grape tomatoes, halved, for serving (optional)

1. Spray the air fryer basket with avocado oil. Preheat the air fryer to 400°F (204°C). 2. Crack the eggs into a shallow baking dish, add the water and a pinch each of salt and pepper, and whisk to combine. In another shallow baking dish, stir together the Parmesan and Italian seasoning until well combined. 3. Season the chicken breasts well on both sides with salt and pepper. Dip one chicken breast in the eggs and let any excess drip off, then dredge both sides of the breast in the Parmesan mixture. Spray the breast with avocado oil and place it in the air fryer basket. Repeat with the remaining 3 chicken breasts. 4. Air fry the chicken in the air fryer for 20 minutes, or until the internal temperature reaches 165°F (74°C) and the breading is golden brown, flipping halfway through. 5. Dollop each chicken breast with ¼ cup of the pesto and top with the Mozzarella. Return the breasts to the air fryer and cook for 3 minutes, or until the cheese is melted. Garnish with basil and serve with halved grape tomatoes on the side, if desired. 6. Store leftovers in an airtight container in the refrigerator for up to 4 days. Reheat in a preheated 400°F (204°C) air fryer for 5 minutes, or until warmed through.

Fajita Chicken Strips

Prep time: 10 minutes | Cook time: 15 minutes | Serves 4

1 pound (454 g) boneless, skinless chicken tenderloins, cut into strips
3 bell peppers, any color, cut into chunks

1 onion, cut into chunks
1 tablespoon olive oil
1 tablespoon fajita seasoning mix
Cooking spray

1. Preheat the air fryer to 370°F (188°C). 2. In a large bowl, mix together the chicken, bell peppers, onion, olive oil, and fajita seasoning mix until completely coated. 3. Spray the air fryer basket lightly with cooking spray. 4. Place the chicken and vegetables in the air fryer basket and lightly spray with cooking spray. 5. Air fry for 7 minutes. Shake the basket and air fry for an additional 5 to 8 minutes, until the chicken is cooked through and the veggies are starting to char. 6. Serve warm.

Italian Chicken Thighs

Prep time: 5 minutes | Cook time: 20 minutes | Serves 2

4 bone-in, skin-on chicken thighs
2 tablespoons unsalted butter, melted
1 teaspoon dried parsley

1 teaspoon dried basil
½ teaspoon garlic powder
¼ teaspoon onion powder
¼ teaspoon dried oregano

1. Brush chicken thighs with butter and sprinkle remaining ingredients over thighs. Place thighs into the air fryer basket. 2. Adjust the temperature to 380°F (193°C) and roast for 20 minutes. 3. Halfway through the cooking time, flip the thighs. 4. When fully cooked, internal temperature will be at least 165°F (74°C) and skin will be crispy. Serve warm.

Classic Chicken Kebab

Prep time: 35 minutes | Cook time: 25 minutes | Serves 4

¼ cup olive oil
1 teaspoon garlic powder
1 teaspoon onion powder
1 teaspoon ground cumin
½ teaspoon dried oregano
½ teaspoon dried basil
¼ cup lemon juice
1 tablespoon apple cider vinegar
Olive oil cooking spray

1 pound (454 g) boneless skinless chicken thighs, cut into 1-inch pieces
1 red bell pepper, cut into 1-inch pieces
1 red onion, cut into 1-inch pieces
1 zucchini, cut into 1-inch pieces
12 cherry tomatoes

1. In a large bowl, mix together the olive oil, garlic powder, onion powder, cumin, oregano, basil, lemon juice, and apple cider vinegar. 2. Spray six skewers with olive oil cooking spray. 3. On each skewer, slide on a piece of chicken, then a piece of bell pepper, onion, zucchini, and finally a tomato and then repeat. Each skewer should have at least two pieces of each item. 4. Once all of the skewers are prepared, place them in a 9-by-13-inch baking dish and pour the olive oil marinade over the top of the skewers. Turn each skewer so that all sides of the chicken and vegetables are coated. 5. Cover the dish with plastic wrap and place it in the refrigerator for 30 minutes. 6. After 30 minutes, preheat the air fryer to 380°F(193°C). (If using a grill attachment, make sure it is inside the air fryer during preheating.) 7. Remove the skewers from the marinade and lay them in a single layer in the air fryer basket. If the air fryer has a grill attachment, you can also lay them on this instead. 8. Cook for 10 minutes. Rotate the kebabs, then cook them for 15 minutes more. 9. Remove the skewers from the air fryer and let them rest for 5 minutes before serving.

Ranch Chicken Wings

Prep time: 10 minutes | Cook time: 40 minutes |

Serves 4

2 tablespoons water

2 tablespoons hot pepper sauce

2 tablespoons unsalted butter, melted

2 tablespoons apple cider vinegar

1 (1 ounce / 28 g) envelope ranch salad dressing mix

1 teaspoon paprika

4 pounds (1.8 kg) chicken wings, tips removed

Cooking oil spray

1. In a large bowl, whisk the water, hot pepper sauce, melted butter, vinegar, salad dressing mix, and paprika until combined. 2. Add the wings and toss to coat. At this point, you can cover the bowl and marinate the wings in the refrigerator for 4 to 24 hours for best results. However, you can just let the wings stand for 30 minutes in the refrigerator. 3. Insert the crisper plate into the basket and the basket into the unit. Preheat the unit by selecting AIR FRY, setting the temperature to 400°F (204°C), and setting the time to 3 minutes. Select START/STOP to begin. 4. Once the unit is preheated, spray the crisper plate with cooking oil. Working in batches, put half the wings into the basket; it is okay to stack them. Refrigerate the remaining wings. 5. Select AIR FRY, set the temperature to 400°F (204°C), and set the time to 20 minutes. Select START/STOP to begin. 6. After 5 minutes, remove the basket and shake it. Reinsert the basket to resume cooking. Remove and shake the basket every 5 minutes, three more times, until the chicken is browned and glazed and a food thermometer inserted into the wings registers 165°F (74°C). 7. Repeat steps 4, 5, and 6 with the remaining wings. 8. When the cooking is complete, serve warm.

Chicken Pesto Pizzas

Prep time: 10 minutes | Cook time: 12 minutes |

Serves 4

1 pound (454 g) ground chicken thighs

¼ teaspoon salt

⅛ teaspoon ground black pepper

¼ cup basil pesto

1 cup shredded Mozzarella cheese

4 grape tomatoes, sliced

1. Cut four squares of parchment paper to fit into your air fryer basket. 2. Place ground chicken in a large bowl and mix with salt and pepper. Divide mixture into four equal sections. 3. Wet your hands with water to prevent sticking, then press each section into a 6-inch circle onto a piece of ungreased parchment. Place each chicken crust into air fryer basket, working in batches if needed. 4. Adjust the temperature to 350°F (177°C) and air fry for 10 minutes, turning crusts halfway through cooking. 5. Spread 1 tablespoon pesto across the top of each crust, then sprinkle with ¼ cup Mozzarella and top with 1 sliced tomato. Continue cooking at 350°F (177°C) for 2 minutes. Cheese will be melted and brown when done. Serve warm.

Chicken Jalfrezi

Prep time: 15 minutes | Cook time: 15 minutes |

Serves 4

Chicken:

1 pound (454 g) boneless, skinless chicken thighs, cut into 2 or 3 pieces each

1 medium onion, chopped

1 large green bell pepper, stemmed, seeded, and chopped

2 tablespoons olive oil

1 teaspoon ground turmeric

1 teaspoon garam masala

1 teaspoon kosher salt

½ to 1 teaspoon cayenne pepper

Sauce:

¼ cup tomato sauce

1 tablespoon water

1 teaspoon garam masala

½ teaspoon kosher salt

½ teaspoon cayenne pepper

Side salad, rice, or naan bread, for serving

1. For the chicken: In a large bowl, combine the chicken, onion, bell pepper, oil, turmeric, garam masala, salt, and cayenne. Stir and toss until well combined. 2. Place the chicken and vegetables in the air fryer basket. Set the air fryer to 350°F (177°C) for 15 minutes, stirring and tossing halfway through the cooking time. Use a meat thermometer to ensure the chicken has reached an internal temperature of 165°F (74°C). 3. Meanwhile, for the sauce: In a small microwave-safe bowl, combine the tomato sauce, water, garam masala, salt, and cayenne. Microwave on high for 1 minute. Remove and stir. Microwave for another minute; set aside. 4. When the chicken is cooked, remove and place chicken and vegetables in a large bowl. Pour the sauce over all. Stir and toss to coat the chicken and vegetables evenly. 5. Serve with rice, naan, or a side salad.

Jerk Chicken Kebabs

Prep time: 10 minutes | Cook time: 14 minutes |

Serves 4

8 ounces (227 g) boneless, skinless chicken thighs, cut into 1-inch cubes

2 tablespoons jerk seasoning

2 tablespoons coconut oil

½ medium red bell pepper,

seeded and cut into 1-inch pieces

¼ medium red onion, peeled and cut into 1-inch pieces

½ teaspoon salt

1. Place chicken in a medium bowl and sprinkle with jerk seasoning and coconut oil. Toss to coat on all sides. 2. Using eight (6-inch) skewers, build skewers by alternating chicken, pepper, and onion pieces, about three repetitions per skewer. 3. Sprinkle salt over skewers and place into ungreased air fryer basket. Adjust the temperature to 370°F (188°C) and air fry for 14 minutes, turning skewers halfway through cooking. Chicken will be golden and have an internal temperature of at least 165°F (74°C) when done. Serve warm.

Cheesy Pepperoni and Chicken Pizza

Prep time: 15 minutes | Cook time: 15 minutes |

Serves 6

2 cups cooked chicken, cubed
1 cup pizza sauce
20 slices pepperoni
¼ cup grated Parmesan cheese

1 cup shredded Mozzarella cheese
Cooking spray

1. Preheat the air fryer to 375ºF (191ºC). Spritz a baking pan with cooking spray. 2. Arrange the chicken cubes in the prepared baking pan, then top the cubes with pizza sauce and pepperoni. Stir to coat the cubes and pepperoni with sauce. 3. Scatter the cheeses on top, then place the baking pan in the preheated air fryer. Air fryer for 15 minutes or until frothy and the cheeses melt. 4. Serve immediately.

Cranberry Curry Chicken

Prep time: 12 minutes | Cook time: 18 minutes |

Serves 4

3 (5-ounce / 142-g) low-sodium boneless, skinless chicken breasts, cut into 1½-inch cubes
2 teaspoons olive oil
2 tablespoons cornstarch
1 tablespoon curry powder
1 tart apple, chopped

½ cup low-sodium chicken broth
⅓ cup dried cranberries
2 tablespoons freshly squeezed orange juice
Brown rice, cooked (optional)

1. Preheat the air fryer to 380ºF (193ºC). 2. In a medium bowl, mix the chicken and olive oil. Sprinkle with the cornstarch and curry powder. Toss to coat. Stir in the apple and transfer to a metal pan. Bake in the air fryer for 8 minutes, stirring once during cooking. 3. Add the chicken broth, cranberries, and orange juice. Bake for about 10 minutes more, or until the sauce is slightly thickened and the chicken reaches an internal temperature of 165ºF (74ºC) on a meat thermometer. Serve over hot cooked brown rice, if desired.

Chicken and Ham Meatballs with Dijon Sauce

Prep time: 10 minutes | Cook time: 15 minutes |

Serves 4

Meatballs:
½ pound (227 g) ham, diced
½ pound (227 g) ground chicken
½ cup grated Swiss cheese
1 large egg, beaten
3 cloves garlic, minced

¼ cup chopped onions
1½ teaspoons sea salt
1 teaspoon ground black pepper
Cooking spray
Dijon Sauce:
3 tablespoons Dijon mustard
2 tablespoons lemon juice

¼ cup chicken broth, warmed
¾ teaspoon sea salt
¼ teaspoon ground black

pepper
Chopped fresh thyme leaves, for garnish

1. Preheat the air fryer to 390ºF (199ºC). Spritz the air fryer basket with cooking spray. 2. Combine the ingredients for the meatballs in a large bowl. Stir to mix well, then shape the mixture in twelve 1½-inch meatballs. 3. Arrange the meatballs in a single layer in the air fryer basket. Air fry for 15 minutes or until lightly browned. Flip the balls halfway through. You may need to work in batches to avoid overcrowding. 4. Meanwhile, combine the ingredients, except for the thyme leaves, for the sauce in a small bowl. Stir to mix well. 5. Transfer the cooked meatballs on a large plate, then baste the sauce over. Garnish with thyme leaves and serve.

Buffalo Chicken Cheese Sticks

Prep time: 5 minutes | Cook time: 8 minutes | Serves 2

1 cup shredded cooked chicken
¼ cup buffalo sauce
1 cup shredded Mozzarella

cheese
1 large egg
¼ cup crumbled feta

1. In a large bowl, mix all ingredients except the feta. Cut a piece of parchment to fit your air fryer basket and press the mixture into a ½-inch-thick circle. 2. Sprinkle the mixture with feta and place into the air fryer basket. 3. Adjust the temperature to 400ºF (204ºC) and air fry for 8 minutes. 4. After 5 minutes, flip over the cheese mixture. 5. Allow to cool 5 minutes before cutting into sticks. Serve warm.

Hawaiian Chicken Bites

Prep time: 1 hour 15 minutes | Cook time: 15

minutes | Serves 4

½ cup pineapple juice
2 tablespoons apple cider vinegar
½ tablespoon minced ginger
½ cup ketchup
2 garlic cloves, minced

½ cup brown sugar
2 tablespoons sherry
½ cup soy sauce
4 chicken breasts, cubed
Cooking spray

1. Combine the pineapple juice, cider vinegar, ginger, ketchup, garlic, and sugar in a saucepan. Stir to mix well. Heat over low heat for 5 minutes or until thickened. Fold in the sherry and soy sauce. 2. Dunk the chicken cubes in the mixture. Press to submerge. Wrap the bowl in plastic and refrigerate to marinate for at least an hour. 3. Preheat the air fryer to 360ºF (182ºC). Spritz the air fryer basket with cooking spray. 4. Remove the chicken cubes from the marinade. Shake the excess off and put in the preheated air fryer. Spritz with cooking spray. 5. Air fry for 15 minutes or until the chicken cubes are glazed and well browned. Shake the basket at least three times during the frying. 6. Serve immediately.

Chicken and Broccoli Casserole

Prep time: 5 minutes | Cook time: 20 to 25 minutes |

Serves 4

½ pound (227 g) broccoli, chopped into florets	½ teaspoon garlic powder
2 cups shredded cooked chicken	Salt and freshly ground black pepper, to taste
4 ounces (113 g) cream cheese	2 tablespoons chopped fresh basil
⅓ cup heavy cream	1 cup shredded Cheddar cheese
1½ teaspoons Dijon mustard	

1. Preheat the air fryer to 390ºF (199ºC). Lightly coat a casserole dish that will fit in air fryer, with olive oil and set aside. 2. Place the broccoli in a large glass bowl with 1 tablespoon of water and cover with a microwavable plate. Microwave on high for 2 to 3 minutes until the broccoli is bright green but not mushy. Drain if necessary and add to another large bowl along with the shredded chicken. 3. In the same glass bowl used to microwave the broccoli, combine the cream cheese and cream. Microwave for 30 seconds to 1 minute on high and stir until smooth. Add the mustard and garlic powder and season to taste with salt and freshly ground black pepper. Whisk until the sauce is smooth. 4. Pour the warm sauce over the broccoli and chicken mixture and then add the basil. Using a silicone spatula, gently fold the mixture until thoroughly combined. 5. Transfer the chicken mixture to the prepared casserole dish and top with the cheese. Air fry for 20 to 25 minutes until warmed through and the cheese has browned.

Herbed Turkey Breast with Simple Dijon Sauce

Prep time: 5 minutes | Cook time: 30 minutes |

Serves 4

1 teaspoon chopped fresh sage	1½ teaspoons sea salt
1 teaspoon chopped fresh tarragon	1 teaspoon ground black pepper
1 teaspoon chopped fresh thyme leaves	1 (2 pounds / 907 g) turkey breast
1 teaspoon chopped fresh rosemary leaves	3 tablespoons Dijon mustard
	3 tablespoons butter, melted
	Cooking spray

1. Preheat the air fryer to 390ºF (199ºC). Spritz the air fryer basket with cooking spray. 2. Combine the herbs, salt, and black pepper in a small bowl. Stir to mix well. Set aside. 3. Combine the Dijon mustard and butter in a separate bowl. Stir to mix well. 4. Rub the turkey with the herb mixture on a clean work surface, then brush the turkey with Dijon mixture. 5. Arrange the turkey in the preheated air fryer basket. Air fry for 30 minutes or until an instant-read thermometer inserted in the thickest part of the turkey breast reaches at least 165ºF (74ºC). 6. Transfer the cooked turkey breast on a large plate and slice to serve.

Juicy Paprika Chicken Breast

Prep time: 5 minutes | Cook time: 30 minutes |

Serves 4

Oil, for spraying	1 tablespoon packed light brown sugar
4 (6 ounces / 170 g) boneless, skinless chicken breasts	½ teaspoon cayenne pepper
1 tablespoon olive oil	½ teaspoon onion powder
1 tablespoon paprika	½ teaspoon granulated garlic

1. Line the air fryer basket with parchment and spray lightly with oil. 2. Brush the chicken with the olive oil. 3. In a small bowl, mix together the paprika, brown sugar, cayenne pepper, onion powder, and garlic and sprinkle it over the chicken. 4. Place the chicken in the prepared basket. You may need to work in batches, depending on the size of your air fryer. 5. Air fry at 360ºF (182ºC) for 15 minutes, flip, and cook for another 15 minutes, or until the internal temperature reaches 165ºF (74ºC). Serve immediately.

Porchetta-Style Chicken Breasts

Prep time: 10 minutes | Cook time: 15 minutes |

Serves 4

½ cup fresh parsley leaves	1 teaspoon ground fennel
¼ cup roughly chopped fresh chives	½ teaspoon red pepper flakes
4 cloves garlic, peeled	4 (4 ounces / 113 g) boneless, skinless chicken breasts, pounded to ¼ inch thick
2 tablespoons lemon juice	
3 teaspoons fine sea salt	8 slices bacon
1 teaspoon dried rubbed sage	Sprigs of fresh rosemary, for garnish (optional)
1 teaspoon fresh rosemary leaves	

1. Spray the air fryer basket with avocado oil. Preheat the air fryer to 340ºF (171ºC). 2. Place the parsley, chives, garlic, lemon juice, salt, sage, rosemary, fennel, and red pepper flakes in a food processor and purée until a smooth paste forms. 3. Place the chicken breasts on a cutting board and rub the paste all over the tops. With a short end facing you, roll each breast up like a jelly roll to make a log and secure it with toothpicks. 4. Wrap 2 slices of bacon around each chicken breast log to cover the entire breast. Secure the bacon with toothpicks. 5. Place the chicken breast logs in the air fryer basket and air fry for 5 minutes, flip the logs over, and cook for another 5 minutes. Increase the heat to 390ºF (199ºC) and cook until the bacon is crisp, about 5 minutes more. 6. Remove the toothpicks and garnish with fresh rosemary sprigs, if desired, before serving. Store leftovers in an airtight container in the refrigerator for up to 4 days or in the freezer for up to a month. Reheat in a preheated 350ºF (177ºC) air fryer for 5 minutes, then increase the heat to 390ºF (199ºC) and cook for 2 minutes to crisp the bacon.

Gold Livers

Prep time: 10 minutes | Cook time: 20 minutes | Serves 4

2 eggs	½ teaspoon ground black
2 tablespoons water	pepper
¾ cup flour	20 ounces (567 g) chicken
2 cups panko breadcrumbs	livers
1 teaspoon salt	Cooking spray

1. Preheat the air fryer to 390ºF (199ºC). Spritz the air fryer basket with cooking spray. 2. Whisk the eggs with water in a large bowl. Pour the flour in a separate bowl. Pour the panko on a shallow dish and sprinkle with salt and pepper. 3. Dredge the chicken livers in the flour. Shake the excess off, then dunk the livers in the whisked eggs, and then roll the livers over the panko to coat well. 4. Arrange the livers in the preheated air fryer and spritz with cooking spray. Work in batches to avoid overcrowding. 5. Air fry for 10 minutes or until the livers are golden and crispy. Flip the livers halfway through. Repeat with remaining livers. 6. Serve immediately.

Personal Cauliflower Pizzas

Prep time: 10 minutes | Cook time: 25 minutes | Serves 2

1 (12-ounce / 340-g) bag frozen riced cauliflower	4 tablespoons no-sugar-added marinara sauce, divided
⅓ cup shredded Mozzarella cheese	4 ounces (113 g) fresh Mozzarella, chopped, divided
¼ cup almond flour	1 cup cooked chicken breast, chopped, divided
¼ grated Parmesan cheese	
1 large egg	½ cup chopped cherry tomatoes, divided
½ teaspoon salt	
1 teaspoon garlic powder	¼ cup fresh baby arugula,
1 teaspoon dried oregano	divided

1. Preheat the air fryer to 400ºF (204ºC). Cut 4 sheets of parchment paper to fit the basket of the air fryer. Brush with olive oil and set aside. 2. In a large glass bowl, microwave the cauliflower according to package directions. Place the cauliflower on a clean towel, draw up the sides, and squeeze tightly over a sink to remove the excess moisture. Return the cauliflower to the bowl and add the shredded Mozzarella along with the almond flour, Parmesan, egg, salt, garlic powder, and oregano. Stir until thoroughly combined. 3. Divide the dough into two equal portions. Place one piece of dough on the prepared parchment paper and pat gently into a thin, flat disk 7 to 8 inches in diameter. Air fry for 15 minutes until the crust begins to brown. Let cool for 5 minutes. 4. Transfer the parchment paper with the crust on top to a baking sheet. Place a second sheet of parchment paper over the crust. While holding the edges of both sheets together, carefully lift the crust off the baking sheet, flip it, and place it back in the air fryer basket. The new sheet of parchment paper is now on the bottom. Remove the top piece of paper and air fry the crust for another 15 minutes until the top begins to brown.

Remove the basket from the air fryer. 5. Spread 2 tablespoons of the marinara sauce on top of the crust, followed by half the fresh Mozzarella, chicken, cherry tomatoes, and arugula. Air fry for 5 to 10 minutes longer, until the cheese is melted and beginning to brown. Remove the pizza from the oven and let it sit for 10 minutes before serving. Repeat with the remaining ingredients to make a second pizza.

Herb-Buttermilk Chicken Breast

Prep time: 5 minutes | Cook time: 40 minutes | Serves 2

1 large bone-in, skin-on chicken breast	½ teaspoon dried dill
	½ teaspoon onion powder
1 cup buttermilk	¼ teaspoon garlic powder
1½ teaspoons dried parsley	¼ teaspoon dried tarragon
1½ teaspoons dried chives	Cooking spray
¾ teaspoon kosher salt	

1. Place the chicken breast in a bowl and pour over the buttermilk, turning the chicken in it to make sure it's completely covered. Let the chicken stand at room temperature for at least 20 minutes or in the refrigerator for up to 4 hours. 2. Meanwhile, in a bowl, stir together the parsley, chives, salt, dill, onion powder, garlic powder, and tarragon. 3. Preheat the air fryer to 300ºF (149ºC). 4. Remove the chicken from the buttermilk, letting the excess drip off, then place the chicken skin-side up directly in the air fryer. Sprinkle the seasoning mix all over the top of the chicken breast, then let stand until the herb mix soaks into the buttermilk, at least 5 minutes. 5. Spray the top of the chicken with cooking spray. Bake for 10 minutes, then increase the temperature to 350ºF (177ºC) and bake until an instant-read thermometer inserted into the thickest part of the breast reads 160ºF (71ºC) and the chicken is deep golden brown, 30 to 35 minutes. 6. Transfer the chicken breast to a cutting board, let rest for 10 minutes, then cut the meat off the bone and cut into thick slices for serving.

Chipotle Drumsticks

Prep time: 5 minutes | Cook time: 25 minutes | Serves 4

1 tablespoon tomato paste	8 chicken drumsticks
½ teaspoon chipotle powder	½ teaspoon salt
¼ teaspoon apple cider vinegar	⅛ teaspoon ground black
¼ teaspoon garlic powder	pepper

1. In a small bowl, combine tomato paste, chipotle powder, vinegar, and garlic powder. 2. Sprinkle drumsticks with salt and pepper, then place into a large bowl and pour in tomato paste mixture. Toss or stir to evenly coat all drumsticks in mixture. 3. Place drumsticks into ungreased air fryer basket. Adjust the temperature to 400ºF (204ºC) and air fry for 25 minutes, turning drumsticks halfway through cooking. Drumsticks will be dark red with an internal temperature of at least 165ºF (74ºC) when done. Serve warm.

Celery Chicken

Prep time: 10 minutes | Cook time: 15 minutes | Serves 4

½ cup soy sauce	8 boneless, skinless chicken
2 tablespoons hoisin sauce	tenderloins
4 teaspoons minced garlic	1 cup chopped celery
1 teaspoon freshly ground black	1 medium red bell pepper, diced
pepper	Olive oil spray

1. Preheat the air fryer to 375°F (191°C). Spray the air fryer basket lightly with olive oil spray. 2. In a large bowl, mix together the soy sauce, hoisin sauce, garlic, and black pepper to make a marinade. Add the chicken, celery, and bell pepper and toss to coat. 3. Shake the excess marinade off the chicken, place it and the vegetables in the air fryer basket, and lightly spray with olive oil spray. You may need to cook them in batches. Reserve the remaining marinade. 4. Air fry for 8 minutes. Turn the chicken over and brush with some of the remaining marinade. Air fry for an additional 5 to 7 minutes, or until the chicken reaches an internal temperature of at least 165°F (74°C). Serve.

Easy Turkey Tenderloin

Prep time: 20 minutes | Cook time: 30 minutes | Serves 4

Olive oil	black pepper
½ teaspoon paprika	Pinch cayenne pepper
½ teaspoon garlic powder	1½ pounds (680 g) turkey
½ teaspoon salt	breast tenderloin
½ teaspoon freshly ground	

1. Spray the air fryer basket lightly with olive oil. 2. In a small bowl, combine the paprika, garlic powder, salt, black pepper, and cayenne pepper. Rub the mixture all over the turkey. 3. Place the turkey in the air fryer basket and lightly spray with olive oil. 4. Air fry at 370°F (188°C) for 15 minutes. Flip the turkey over and lightly spray with olive oil. Air fry until the internal temperature reaches at least 170°F (77°C) for an additional 10 to 15 minutes. 5. Let the turkey rest for 10 minutes before slicing and serving.

Jalapeño Popper Hasselback Chicken

Prep time: 10 minutes | Cook time: 19 minutes | Serves 2

Oil, for spraying	¼ cup bacon bits
2 (8 ounces / 227 g) boneless,	¼ cup chopped pickled
skinless chicken breasts	jalapeños
2 ounces (57 g) cream cheese,	½ cup shredded Cheddar
softened	cheese, divided

1. Line the air fryer basket with parchment and spray lightly with oil. 2. Make multiple cuts across the top of each chicken breast, cutting only halfway through. 3. In a medium bowl, mix together the cream cheese, bacon bits, jalapeños, and ¼ cup of Cheddar cheese. Spoon some of the mixture into each cut. 4. Place the chicken in the prepared basket. 5. Air fry at 350°F (177°C) for 14 minutes. Scatter the remaining ¼ cup of cheese on top of the chicken and cook for another 2 to 5 minutes, or until the cheese is melted and the internal temperature reaches 165°F (74°C).

Cajun-Breaded Chicken Bites

Prep time: 10 minutes | Cook time: 12 minutes | Serves 4

1 pound (454 g) boneless,	pepper
skinless chicken breasts, cut	1 ounce (28 g) plain pork rinds,
into 1-inch cubes	finely crushed
½ cup heavy whipping cream	¼ cup unflavored whey protein
½ teaspoon salt	powder
¼ teaspoon ground black	½ teaspoon Cajun seasoning

1. Place chicken in a medium bowl and pour in cream. Stir to coat. Sprinkle with salt and pepper. 2. In a separate large bowl, combine pork rinds, protein powder, and Cajun seasoning. Remove chicken from cream, shaking off any excess, and toss in dry mix until fully coated. 3. Place bites into ungreased air fryer basket. Adjust the temperature to 400°F (204°C) and air fry for 12 minutes, shaking the basket twice during cooking. Bites will be done when golden brown and have an internal temperature of at least 165°F (74°C). Serve warm.

Ham Chicken with Cheese

Prep time: 15 minutes | Cook time: 25 minutes | Serves 4

¼ cup unsalted butter, softened	¼ cup water
4 ounces (113 g) cream cheese,	2 cups shredded cooked chicken
softened	¼ pound (113 g) ham, chopped
1½ teaspoons Dijon mustard	4 ounces (113 g) sliced Swiss
2 tablespoons white wine	or Provolone cheese
vinegar	

1. Preheat the air fryer to 380°F (193°C). Lightly coat a casserole dish that will fit in the air fryer, such as an 8-inch round pan, with olive oil and set aside. 2. In a large bowl and using an electric mixer, combine the butter, cream cheese, Dijon mustard, and vinegar. With the motor running at low speed, slowly add the water and beat until smooth. Set aside. 3. Arrange an even layer of chicken in the bottom of the prepared pan, followed by the ham. Spread the butter and cream cheese mixture on top of the ham, followed by the cheese slices on the top layer. Air fry for 20 to 25 minutes until warmed through and the cheese has browned.

Chipotle Aioli Wings

Prep time: 5 minutes | Cook time: 25 minutes |
Serves 6

2 pounds (907 g) bone-in chicken wings	pepper
½ teaspoon salt	2 tablespoons mayonnaise
¼ teaspoon ground black	2 teaspoons chipotle powder
	2 tablespoons lemon juice

1. In a large bowl, toss wings in salt and pepper, then place into ungreased air fryer basket. Adjust the temperature to 400ºF (204ºC) and air fry for 25 minutes, shaking the basket twice while cooking. Wings will be done when golden and have an internal temperature of at least 165ºF (74ºC). 2. In a small bowl, whisk together mayonnaise, chipotle powder, and lemon juice. Place cooked wings into a large serving bowl and drizzle with aioli. Toss to coat. Serve warm.

Yakitori

Prep time: 10 minutes | Cook time: 15 minutes |
Serves 4

½ cup mirin	4 medium scallions, trimmed, cut into 1½-inch pieces
¼ cup dry white wine	Cooking spray
½ cup soy sauce	Special Equipment:
1 tablespoon light brown sugar	4 (4-inch) bamboo skewers, soaked in water for at least 30 minutes
1½ pounds (680 g) boneless, skinless chicken thighs, cut into 1½-inch pieces, fat trimmed	

1. Combine the mirin, dry white wine, soy sauce, and brown sugar in a saucepan. Bring to a boil over medium heat. Keep stirring. 2. Boil for another 2 minutes or until it has a thick consistency. Turn off the heat. 3. Preheat the air fryer to 400ºF (204ºC). Spritz the air fryer basket with cooking spray. 4. Run the bamboo skewers through the chicken pieces and scallions alternatively. 5. Arrange the skewers in the preheated air fryer, then brush with mirin mixture on both sides. Spritz with cooking spray. 6. Air fry for 10 minutes or until the chicken and scallions are glossy. Flip the skewers halfway through. 7. Serve immediately.

Sriracha-Honey Chicken Nuggets

Prep time: 15 minutes | Cook time: 19 minutes |
Serves 6

Oil, for spraying	sugar
1 large egg	½ teaspoon paprika
¾ cup milk	½ teaspoon salt
1 cup all-purpose flour	½ teaspoon freshly ground black pepper
2 tablespoons confectioners'	

2 boneless, skinless chicken breasts, cut into bite-size pieces	2 tablespoons honey
½ cup barbecue sauce	1 tablespoon Sriracha

1. Line the air fryer basket with parchment and spray lightly with oil. 2. In a small bowl, whisk together the egg and milk. 3. In a medium bowl, combine the flour, confectioners' sugar, paprika, salt, and black pepper and stir. 4. Coat the chicken in the egg mixture, then dredge in the flour mixture until evenly coated. 5. Place the chicken in the prepared basket and spray liberally with oil. 6. Air fry at 390ºF (199ºC) for 8 minutes, flip, spray with more oil, and cook for another 6 to 8 minutes, or until the internal temperature reaches 165ºF (74ºC) and the juices run clear. 7. In a large bowl, mix together the barbecue sauce, honey, and Sriracha. 8. Transfer the chicken to the bowl and toss until well coated with the barbecue sauce mixture. 9. Line the air fryer basket with fresh parchment, return the chicken to the basket, and cook for another 2 to 3 minutes, until browned and crispy.

Chicken Rochambeau

Prep time: 15 minutes | Cook time: 20 minutes |
Serves 4

1 tablespoon butter	Sauce:
4 chicken tenders, cut in half crosswise	2 tablespoons butter
Salt and pepper, to taste	½ cup chopped green onions
¼ cup flour	½ cup chopped mushrooms
Oil for misting	2 tablespoons flour
4 slices ham, ¼ to ⅜-inches thick and large enough to cover an English muffin	1 cup chicken broth
	¼ teaspoon garlic powder
2 English muffins, split	1½ teaspoons Worcestershire sauce

1. Place 1 tablespoon of butter in a baking pan and air fry at 390ºF (199ºC) for 2 minutes to melt. 2. Sprinkle chicken tenders with salt and pepper to taste, then roll in the ¼ cup of flour. 3. Place chicken in baking pan, turning pieces to coat with melted butter. 4. Air fry at 390ºF (199ºC) for 5 minutes. Turn chicken pieces over, and spray tops lightly with olive oil. Cook 5 minutes longer or until juices run clear. The chicken will not brown. 5. While chicken is cooking, make the sauce: In a medium saucepan, melt the 2 tablespoons of butter. 6. Add onions and mushrooms and sauté until tender, about 3 minutes. 7. Stir in the flour. Gradually add broth, stirring constantly until you have a smooth gravy. 8. Add garlic powder and Worcestershire sauce and simmer on low heat until sauce thickens, about 5 minutes. 9. When chicken is cooked, remove baking pan from air fryer and set aside. 10. Place ham slices directly into air fryer basket and air fry at 390ºF (199ºC) for 5 minutes or until hot and beginning to sizzle a little. Remove and set aside on top of the chicken for now. 11. Place the English muffin halves in air fryer basket and air fry at 390ºF (199ºC) for 1 minute. 12. Open air fryer and place a ham slice on top of each English muffin half. Stack 2 pieces of chicken on top of each ham slice. Air fry for 1 to 2 minutes to heat through. 13. Place each English muffin stack on a serving plate and top with plenty of sauce.

Chicken and Avocado Fajitas

Prep time: 10 minutes | Cook time: 10 to 14 minutes | Serves 4

Cooking oil spray
4 boneless, skinless chicken breasts, sliced crosswise
1 small red onion, sliced
2 red bell peppers, seeded and sliced
½ cup spicy ranch salad

dressing, divided
½ teaspoon dried oregano
8 corn tortillas
2 cups torn butter lettuce leaves
2 avocados, peeled, pitted, and chopped

1. Insert the crisper plate into the basket and the basket into the unit. Preheat the unit by selecting BAKE, setting the temperature to 375ºF (191ºC), and setting the time to 3 minutes. Select START/STOP to begin. 2. Once the unit is preheated, spray the crisper plate with cooking oil. Place the chicken, red onion, and red bell pepper into the basket. Drizzle with 1 tablespoon of the salad dressing and season with the oregano. Toss to combine. 3. Select BAKE, set the temperature to 375ºF (191ºC), and set the time to 14 minutes. Select START/STOP to begin. 4. After 10 minutes, check the chicken. If a food thermometer inserted into the chicken registers at least 165ºF (74ºC), it is done. If not, resume cooking. 5. When the cooking is complete, transfer the chicken and vegetables to a bowl and toss with the remaining salad dressing. 6. Serve the chicken mixture family-style with the tortillas, lettuce, and avocados, and let everyone make their own plates.

Bacon-Wrapped Stuffed Chicken Breasts

Prep time: 15 minutes | Cook time: 30 minutes | Serves 4

½ cup chopped frozen spinach, thawed and squeezed dry
¼ cup cream cheese, softened
¼ cup grated Parmesan cheese
1 jalapeño, seeded and chopped
½ teaspoon kosher salt
1 teaspoon black pepper

2 large boneless, skinless chicken breasts, butterflied and pounded to ½-inch thickness
4 teaspoons salt-free Cajun seasoning
6 slices bacon

1. In a small bowl, combine the spinach, cream cheese, Parmesan cheese, jalapeño, salt, and pepper. Stir until well combined. 2. Place the butterflied chicken breasts on a flat surface. Spread the cream cheese mixture evenly across each piece of chicken. Starting with the narrow end, roll up each chicken breast, ensuring the filling stays inside. Season chicken with the Cajun seasoning, patting it in to ensure it sticks to the meat. 3. Wrap each breast in 3 slices of bacon. Place in the air fryer basket. Set the air fryer to 350ºF (177ºC) for 30 minutes. Use a meat thermometer to ensure the chicken has reached an internal temperature of 165ºF (74ºC). 4. Let the chicken stand 5 minutes before slicing each rolled-up breast in half to serve.

Broccoli Cheese Chicken

Prep time: 10 minutes | Cook time: 19 to 24 minutes | Serves 6

1 tablespoon avocado oil
¼ cup chopped onion
½ cup finely chopped broccoli
4 ounces (113 g) cream cheese, at room temperature
2 ounces (57 g) Cheddar cheese, shredded
1 teaspoon garlic powder
½ teaspoon sea salt, plus

additional for seasoning, divided
¼ freshly ground black pepper, plus additional for seasoning, divided
2 pounds (907 g) boneless, skinless chicken breasts
1 teaspoon smoked paprika

1. Heat a medium skillet over medium-high heat and pour in the avocado oil. Add the onion and broccoli and cook, stirring occasionally, for 5 to 8 minutes, until the onion is tender. 2. Transfer to a large bowl and stir in the cream cheese, Cheddar cheese, and garlic powder, and season to taste with salt and pepper. 3. Hold a sharp knife parallel to the chicken breast and cut a long pocket into one side. Stuff the chicken pockets with the broccoli mixture, using toothpicks to secure the pockets around the filling. 4. In a small dish, combine the paprika, ½ teaspoon salt, and ¼ teaspoon pepper. Sprinkle this over the outside of the chicken. 5. Set the air fryer to 400ºF (204ºC). Place the chicken in a single layer in the air fryer basket, cooking in batches if necessary, and cook for 14 to 16 minutes, until an instant-read thermometer reads 160ºF (71ºC). Place the chicken on a plate and tent a piece of aluminum foil over the chicken. Allow to rest for 5 to 10 minutes before serving.

Apricot-Glazed Chicken Drumsticks

Prep time: 15 minutes | Cook time: 30 minutes | Makes 6 drumsticks

For the Glaze:
½ cup apricot preserves
½ teaspoon tamari
¼ teaspoon chili powder
2 teaspoons Dijon mustard
For the Chicken:

6 chicken drumsticks
½ teaspoon seasoning salt
1 teaspoon salt
½ teaspoon ground black pepper
Cooking spray

Make the glaze: 1. Combine the ingredients for the glaze in a saucepan, then heat over low heat for 10 minutes or until thickened. 2. Turn off the heat and sit until ready to use. Make the Chicken: 1. Preheat the air fryer to 370ºF (188ºC). Spritz the air fryer basket with cooking spray. 2. Combine the seasoning salt, salt, and pepper in a small bowl. Stir to mix well. 3. Place the chicken drumsticks in the preheated air fryer. Spritz with cooking spray and sprinkle with the salt mixture on both sides. 4. Air fry for 20 minutes or until well browned. Flip the chicken halfway through. 5. Baste the chicken with the glaze and air fryer for 2 more minutes or until the chicken tenderloin is glossy. 6. Serve immediately.

Barbecue Chicken

Prep time: 10 minutes | Cook time: 18 to 20 minutes | Serves 4

⅓ cup no-salt-added tomato sauce

2 tablespoons low-sodium grainy mustard

2 tablespoons apple cider vinegar

1 tablespoon honey

2 garlic cloves, minced

1 jalapeño pepper, minced

3 tablespoons minced onion

4 (5 ounces / 142 g) low-sodium boneless, skinless chicken breasts

1. Preheat the air fryer to 370ºF (188ºC). 2. In a small bowl, stir together the tomato sauce, mustard, cider vinegar, honey, garlic, jalapeño, and onion. 3. Brush the chicken breasts with some sauce and air fry for 10 minutes. 4. Remove the air fryer basket and turn the chicken; brush with more sauce. Air fry for 5 minutes more. 5. Remove the air fryer basket and turn the chicken again; brush with more sauce. Air fry for 3 to 5 minutes more, or until the chicken reaches an internal temperature of 165ºF (74ºC) on a meat thermometer. Discard any remaining sauce. Serve immediately.

Pickle Brined Fried Chicken

Prep time: 30 minutes | Cook time: 47 minutes | Serves 4

4 bone-in, skin-on chicken legs, cut into drumsticks and thighs (about 3½ pounds / 1.6 kg)

Pickle juice from 1 (24 ounces / 680 g) jar kosher dill pickles

½ cup flour

Salt and freshly ground black pepper, to taste

2 eggs

1 cup fine bread crumbs

1 teaspoon salt

1 teaspoon freshly ground black pepper

½ teaspoon ground paprika

⅛ teaspoon ground cayenne pepper

Vegetable or canola oil

1. Place the chicken in a shallow dish and pour the pickle juice over the top. Cover and transfer the chicken to the refrigerator to brine in the pickle juice for 3 to 8 hours. 2. When you are ready to cook, remove the chicken from the refrigerator to let it come to room temperature while you set up a dredging station. Place the flour in a shallow dish and season well with salt and freshly ground black pepper. Whisk the eggs in a second shallow dish. In a third shallow dish, combine the bread crumbs, salt, pepper, paprika and cayenne pepper. 3. Preheat the air fryer to 370ºF (188ºC). 4. Remove the chicken from the pickle brine and gently dry it with a clean kitchen towel. Dredge each piece of chicken in the flour, then dip it into the egg mixture, and finally press it into the bread crumb mixture to coat all sides of the chicken. Place the breaded chicken on a plate or baking sheet and spray each piece all over with vegetable oil. 5.

Air fry the chicken in two batches. Place two chicken thighs and two drumsticks into the air fryer basket. Air fry for 10 minutes. Then, gently turn the chicken pieces over and air fry for another 10 minutes. Remove the chicken pieces and let them rest on plate, do not cover. Repeat with the second batch of chicken, air frying for 20 minutes, turning the chicken over halfway through. 6. Lower the temperature of the air fryer to 340ºF (171ºC). Place the first batch of chicken on top of the second batch already in the basket and air fry for an additional 7 minutes. Serve warm and enjoy.

Almond-Crusted Chicken

Prep time: 15 minutes | Cook time: 25 minutes | Serves 4

¼ cup slivered almonds

2 (6 ounces / 170 g) boneless, skinless chicken breasts

2 tablespoons full-fat mayonnaise

1 tablespoon Dijon mustard

1. Pulse the almonds in a food processor or chop until finely chopped. Place almonds evenly on a plate and set aside. 2. Completely slice each chicken breast in half lengthwise. 3. Mix the mayonnaise and mustard in a small bowl and then coat chicken with the mixture. 4. Lay each piece of chicken in the chopped almonds to fully coat. Carefully move the pieces into the air fryer basket. 5. Adjust the temperature to 350ºF (177ºC) and air fry for 25 minutes. 6. Chicken will be done when it has reached an internal temperature of 165ºF (74ºC) or more. Serve warm.

Ethiopian Chicken with Cauliflower

Prep time: 15 minutes | Cook time: 28 minutes | Serves 6

2 handful fresh Italian parsley, roughly chopped

½ cup fresh chopped chives

2 sprigs thyme

6 chicken drumsticks

1½ small-sized head cauliflower, broken into large-sized florets

2 teaspoons mustard powder

⅓ teaspoon porcini powder

1½ teaspoons berbere spice

⅓ teaspoon sweet paprika

½ teaspoon shallot powder

1 teaspoon granulated garlic

1 teaspoon freshly cracked pink peppercorns

½ teaspoon sea salt

1. Simply combine all items for the berbere spice rub mix. After that, coat the chicken drumsticks with this rub mix on all sides. Transfer them to the baking dish. 2. Now, lower the cauliflower onto the chicken drumsticks. Add thyme, chives and Italian parsley and spritz everything with a pan spray. Transfer the baking dish to the preheated air fryer. 3. Next step, set the timer for 28 minutes; roast at 355ºF (179ºC), turning occasionally. Bon appétit!

Chicken Patties

Prep time: 15 minutes | Cook time: 12 minutes |

Serves 4

1 pound (454 g) ground chicken thigh meat	½ teaspoon garlic powder
½ cup shredded Mozzarella cheese	¼ teaspoon onion powder
1 teaspoon dried parsley	1 large egg
	2 ounces (57 g) pork rinds, finely ground

1. In a large bowl, mix ground chicken, Mozzarella, parsley, garlic powder, and onion powder. Form into four patties. 2. Place patties in the freezer for 15 to 20 minutes until they begin to firm up. 3. Whisk egg in a medium bowl. Place the ground pork rinds into a large bowl. 4. Dip each chicken patty into the egg and then press into pork rinds to fully coat. Place patties into the air fryer basket. 5. Adjust the temperature to 360°F (182°C) and air fry for 12 minutes. 6. Patties will be firm and cooked to an internal temperature of 165°F (74°C) when done. Serve immediately.

Chicken and Vegetable Fajitas

Prep time: 15 minutes | Cook time: 23 minutes |

Serves 6

Chicken:	lengthwise
1 pound (454 g) boneless, skinless chicken thighs, cut crosswise into thirds	1 tablespoon vegetable oil
	½ teaspoon kosher salt
1 tablespoon vegetable oil	½ teaspoon ground cumin
4½ teaspoons taco seasoning	For Serving:
Vegetables:	Tortillas
1 cup sliced onion	Sour cream
1 cup sliced bell pepper	Shredded cheese
1 or 2 jalapeños, quartered	Guacamole
	Salsa

1. For the chicken: In a medium bowl, toss together the chicken, vegetable oil, and taco seasoning to coat. 2. For the vegetables: In a separate bowl, toss together the onion, bell pepper, jalapeño(s), vegetable oil, salt, and cumin to coat. 3. Place the chicken in the air fryer basket. Set the air fryer to 375°F (191°C) for 10 minutes. Add the vegetables to the basket, toss everything together to blend the seasonings, and set the air fryer for 13 minutes more. Use a meat thermometer to ensure the chicken has reached an internal temperature of 165°F (74°C). 4. Transfer the chicken and vegetables to a serving platter. Serve with tortillas and the desired fajita fixings.

Smoky Chicken Leg Quarters

Prep time: 30 minutes | Cook time: 23 to 27 minutes | Serves 6

½ cup avocado oil	½ teaspoon dried thyme
2 teaspoons smoked paprika	½ teaspoon freshly ground black pepper
1 teaspoon sea salt	
1 teaspoon garlic powder	2 pounds (907 g) bone-in, skin-on chicken leg quarters
½ teaspoon dried rosemary	

1. In a blender or small bowl, combine the avocado oil, smoked paprika, salt, garlic powder, rosemary, thyme, and black pepper. 2. Place the chicken in a shallow dish or large zip-top bag. Pour the marinade over the chicken, making sure all the legs are coated. Cover and marinate for at least 2 hours or overnight. 3. Place the chicken in a single layer in the air fryer basket, working in batches if necessary. Set the air fryer to 400°F (204°C) and air fry for 15 minutes. Flip the chicken legs, then reduce the temperature to 350°F (177°C). Cook for 8 to 12 minutes more, until an instant-read thermometer reads 160°F (71°C) when inserted into the thickest piece of chicken. 4. Allow to rest for 5 to 10 minutes before serving.

Curried Orange Honey Chicken

Prep time: 10 minutes | Cook time: 16 to 19 minutes | Serves 4

¾ pound (340 g) boneless, skinless chicken thighs, cut into 1-inch pieces	Olive oil for misting
	¼ cup chicken stock
1 yellow bell pepper, cut into 1½-inch pieces	2 tablespoons honey
	¼ cup orange juice
1 small red onion, sliced	1 tablespoon cornstarch
	2 to 3 teaspoons curry powder

1. Preheat the air fryer to 370°F (188°C). 2. Put the chicken thighs, pepper, and red onion in the air fryer basket and mist with olive oil. 3. Roast for 12 to 14 minutes or until the chicken is cooked to 165°F (74°C), shaking the basket halfway through cooking time. 4. Remove the chicken and vegetables from the air fryer basket and set aside. 5. In a metal bowl, combine the stock, honey, orange juice, cornstarch, and curry powder, and mix well. Add the chicken and vegetables, stir, and put the bowl in the basket. 6. Return the basket to the air fryer and roast for 2 minutes. Remove and stir, then roast for 2 to 3 minutes or until the sauce is thickened and bubbly. 7. Serve warm.

Chapter 5 Beef, Pork, and Lamb

Tuscan Air Fried Veal Loin

Prep time: 1 hour 10 minutes | Cook time: 12 minutes | Makes 3 veal chops

1½ teaspoons crushed fennel seeds
1 tablespoon minced fresh rosemary leaves
1 tablespoon minced garlic
1½ teaspoons lemon zest
1½ teaspoons salt
½ teaspoon red pepper flakes
2 tablespoons olive oil
3 (10-ounce / 284-g) bone-in veal loin, about ½ inch thick

1. Combine all the ingredients, except for the veal loin, in a large bowl. Stir to mix well. 2. Dunk the loin in the mixture and press to submerge. Wrap the bowl in plastic and refrigerate for at least an hour to marinate. 3. Preheat the air fryer to 400ºF (204ºC). 4. Arrange the veal loin in the preheated air fryer and air fry for 12 minutes for medium-rare, or until it reaches your desired doneness. 5. Serve immediately.

Short Ribs with Chimichurri

Prep time: 30 minutes | Cook time: 13 minutes | Serves 4

1 pound (454 g) boneless short ribs
1½ teaspoons sea salt, divided
½ teaspoon freshly ground black pepper, divided
½ cup fresh parsley leaves
½ cup fresh cilantro leaves
1 teaspoon minced garlic
1 tablespoon freshly squeezed lemon juice
½ teaspoon ground cumin
¼ teaspoon red pepper flakes
2 tablespoons extra-virgin olive oil
Avocado oil spray

1. Pat the short ribs dry with paper towels. Sprinkle the ribs all over with 1 teaspoon salt and ¼ teaspoon black pepper. Let sit at room temperature for 45 minutes. 2. Meanwhile, place the parsley, cilantro, garlic, lemon juice, cumin, red pepper flakes, the remaining ½ teaspoon salt, and the remaining ¼ teaspoon black pepper in a blender or food processor. With the blender running, slowly drizzle in the olive oil. Blend for about 1 minute, until the mixture is smooth and well combined. 3. Set the air fryer to 400ºF (204ºC). Spray both sides of the ribs with oil. Place in the basket and air fry for 8 minutes. Flip and cook for another 5 minutes, until an instant-read thermometer reads 125ºF (52ºC) for medium-rare (or to your desired doneness). 4. Allow the meat to rest for 5 to 10 minutes, then slice. Serve warm with the chimichurri sauce.

Cube Steak Roll-Ups

Prep time: 30 minutes | Cook time: 8 to 10 minutes | Serves 4

4 cube steaks (6 ounces / 170 g each)
1 (16 ounces / 454 g) bottle Italian dressing
1 teaspoon salt
½ teaspoon freshly ground black pepper
½ cup finely chopped yellow onion
½ cup finely chopped green bell pepper
½ cup finely chopped mushrooms
1 to 2 tablespoons oil

1. In a large resealable bag or airtight storage container, combine the steaks and Italian dressing. Seal the bag and refrigerate to marinate for 2 hours. 2. Remove the steaks from the marinade and place them on a cutting board. Discard the marinade. Evenly season the steaks with salt and pepper. 3. In a small bowl, stir together the onion, bell pepper, and mushrooms. Sprinkle the onion mixture evenly over the steaks. Roll up the steaks, jelly roll-style, and secure with toothpicks. 4. Preheat the air fryer to 400ºF (204ºC). 5. Place the steaks in the air fryer basket. 6. Cook for 4 minutes. Flip the steaks and spritz them with oil. Cook for 4 to 6 minutes more until the internal temperature reaches 145ºF (63ºC). Let rest for 5 minutes before serving.

Bacon and Cheese Stuffed Pork Chops

Prep time: 10 minutes | Cook time: 12 minutes | Serves 4

½ ounce (14 g) plain pork rinds, finely crushed
½ cup shredded sharp Cheddar cheese
4 slices cooked sugar-free bacon, crumbled
4 (4 ounces / 113 g) boneless pork chops
½ teaspoon salt
¼ teaspoon ground black pepper

1. In a small bowl, mix pork rinds, Cheddar, and bacon. 2. Make a 3-inch slit in the side of each pork chop and stuff with ¼ pork rind mixture. Sprinkle each side of pork chops with salt and pepper. 3. Place pork chops into ungreased air fryer basket, stuffed side up. Adjust the temperature to 400ºF (204ºC) and air fry for 12 minutes. Pork chops will be browned and have an internal temperature of at least 145ºF (63ºC) when done. Serve warm.

Sichuan Cumin Lamb

Prep time: 30 minutes | Cook time: 10 minutes |

Serves 4

Lamb:	1 tablespoon light soy sauce
2 tablespoons cumin seeds	1 tablespoon minced garlic
1 teaspoon Sichuan	2 fresh red chiles, chopped
peppercorns, or ½ teaspoon	1 teaspoon kosher salt
cayenne pepper	¼ teaspoon sugar
1 pound (454 g) lamb	For Serving:
(preferably shoulder), cut into	2 scallions, chopped
½ by 2-inch pieces	Large handful of chopped fresh
2 tablespoons vegetable oil	cilantro

1. For the lamb: In a dry skillet, toast the cumin seeds and Sichuan peppercorns (if using) over medium heat, stirring frequently, until fragrant, 1 to 2 minutes. Remove from the heat and let cool. Use a mortar and pestle to coarsely grind the toasted spices. 2. Use a fork to pierce the lamb pieces to allow the marinade to penetrate better. In a large bowl or resealable plastic bag, combine the toasted spices, vegetable oil, soy sauce, garlic, chiles, salt, and sugar. Add the lamb to the bag. Seal and massage to coat. Marinate at room temperature for 30 minutes. 3. Place the lamb in a single layer in the air fryer basket. Set the air fryer to 350ºF (177ºC) for 10 minutes. Use a meat thermometer to ensure the lamb has reached an internal temperature of 145ºF (63ºC) (medium-rare). 4. Transfer the lamb to a serving bowl. Stir in the scallions and cilantro and serve.

Ground Beef Taco Rolls

Prep time: 20 minutes | Cook time: 10 minutes |

Serves 4

½ pound (227 g) ground beef	2 tablespoons chopped cilantro
⅓ cup water	1½ cups shredded Mozzarella
1 tablespoon chili powder	cheese
2 teaspoons cumin	½ cup blanched finely ground
½ teaspoon garlic powder	almond flour
¼ teaspoon dried oregano	2 ounces (57 g) full-fat cream
¼ cup canned diced tomatoes	cheese
and chiles, drained	1 large egg

1. In a medium skillet over medium heat, brown the ground beef about 7 to 10 minutes. When meat is fully cooked, drain. 2. Add water to skillet and stir in chili powder, cumin, garlic powder, oregano, and tomatoes with chiles. Add cilantro. Bring to a boil, then reduce heat to simmer for 3 minutes. 3. In a large microwave-safe bowl, place Mozzarella, almond flour, cream cheese, and egg. Microwave for 1 minute. Stir the mixture quickly until smooth ball of dough forms. 4. Cut a piece of parchment for your work surface. Press the dough into a large rectangle on the parchment, wetting your hands to prevent the dough from sticking as necessary. Cut the dough into eight rectangles. 5. On each rectangle place a few spoons of the meat mixture. Fold the short ends of each roll toward the center and roll the length as you would a burrito. 6. Cut

a piece of parchment to fit your air fryer basket. Place taco rolls onto the parchment and place into the air fryer basket. 7. Adjust the temperature to 360ºF (182ºC) and air fry for 10 minutes. 8. Flip halfway through the cooking time. 9. Allow to cool 10 minutes before serving.

Apple Cornbread Stuffed Pork Loin

Prep time: 15 minutes | Cook time: 1 hour | Serves 4

to 6

4 strips of bacon, chopped	Apple Gravy:
1 Granny Smith apple, peeled,	2 tablespoons butter
cored and finely chopped	1 shallot, minced
2 teaspoons fresh thyme leaves	1 Granny Smith apple, peeled,
¼ cup chopped fresh parsley	cored and finely chopped
2 cups cubed cornbread	3 sprigs fresh thyme
½ cup chicken stock	2 tablespoons flour
Salt and freshly ground black	1 cup chicken stock
pepper, to taste	½ cup apple cider
1 (2 pounds / 907 g) boneless	Salt and freshly ground black
pork loin	pepper, to taste

1. Preheat the air fryer to 400ºF (204ºC). 2. Add the bacon to the air fryer and air fry for 6 to 8 minutes until crispy. While the bacon is cooking, combine the apple, fresh thyme, parsley and cornbread in a bowl and toss well. Moisten the mixture with the chicken stock and season to taste with salt and freshly ground black pepper. Add the cooked bacon to the mixture. 3. Butterfly the pork loin by holding it flat on the cutting board with one hand, while slicing into the pork loin parallel to the cutting board with the other. Slice into the longest side of the pork loin, but stop before you cut all the way through. You should then be able to open the pork loin up like a book, making it twice as wide as it was when you started. Season the inside of the pork with salt and freshly ground black pepper. 4. Spread the cornbread mixture onto the butterflied pork loin, leaving a one-inch border around the edge of the pork. Roll the pork loin up around the stuffing to enclose the stuffing, and tie the rolled pork in several places with kitchen twine or secure with toothpicks. Try to replace any stuffing that falls out of the roast as you roll it, by stuffing it into the ends of the rolled pork. Season the outside of the pork with salt and freshly ground black pepper. 5. Preheat the air fryer to 360ºF (182ºC). 6. Place the stuffed pork loin into the air fryer, seam side down. Air fry the pork loin for 15 minutes at 360ºF (182ºC). Turn the pork loin over and air fry for an additional 15 minutes. Turn the pork loin a quarter turn and air fry for an additional 15 minutes. Turn the pork loin over again to expose the fourth side, and air fry for an additional 10 minutes. The pork loin should register 155ºF (68ºC) on an instant read thermometer when it is finished. 7. While the pork is cooking, make the apple gravy. Preheat a saucepan over medium heat on the stovetop and melt the butter. Add the shallot, apple and thyme sprigs and sauté until the apple starts to soften and brown a little. Add the flour and stir for a minute or two. Whisk in the stock and apple cider vigorously to prevent the flour from forming lumps. Bring the mixture to a boil to thicken and season to taste with salt and pepper. 8. Transfer the pork loin to a resting plate and loosely tent with foil, letting the pork rest for at least 5 minutes before slicing and serving with the apple gravy poured over the top.

Rosemary Ribeye Steaks

Prep time: 10 minutes | Cook time: 15 minutes | Serves 2

¼ cup butter

1 clove garlic, minced

Salt and ground black pepper, to taste

1½ tablespoons balsamic vinegar

¼ cup rosemary, chopped

2 ribeye steaks

1. Melt the butter in a skillet over medium heat. Add the garlic and fry until fragrant. 2. Remove the skillet from the heat and add the salt, pepper, and vinegar. Allow it to cool. 3. Add the rosemary, then pour the mixture into a Ziploc bag. 4. Put the ribeye steaks in the bag and shake well, coating the meat well. Refrigerate for an hour, then allow to sit for a further twenty minutes. 5. Preheat the air fryer to 400ºF (204ºC). 6. Air fry the ribeye steaks for 15 minutes. 7. Take care when removing the steaks from the air fryer and plate up. 8. Serve immediately.

Five-Spice Pork Belly

Prep time: 10 minutes | Cook time: 17 minutes | Serves 4

1 pound (454 g) unsalted pork belly

2 teaspoons Chinese five-spice powder

Sauce:

1 tablespoon coconut oil

1 (1-inch) piece fresh ginger, peeled and grated

2 cloves garlic, minced

½ cup beef or chicken broth

¼ to ½ cup Swerve confectioners'-style sweetener or equivalent amount of liquid or powdered sweetener

3 tablespoons wheat-free tamari, or ½ cup coconut aminos

1 green onion, sliced, plus more for garnish

1. Spray the air fryer basket with avocado oil. Preheat the air fryer to 400ºF (204ºC). 2. Cut the pork belly into ½-inch-thick slices and season well on all sides with the five-spice powder. Place the slices in a single layer in the air fryer basket (if you're using a smaller air fryer, work in batches if necessary) and cook for 8 minutes, or until cooked to your liking, flipping halfway through. 3. While the pork belly cooks, make the sauce: Heat the coconut oil in a small saucepan over medium heat. Add the ginger and garlic and sauté for 1 minute, or until fragrant. Add the broth, sweetener, and tamari and simmer for 10 to 15 minutes, until thickened. Add the green onion and cook for another minute, until the green onion is softened. Taste and adjust the seasoning to your liking. 4. Transfer the pork belly to a large bowl. Pour the sauce over the pork belly and coat well. Place the pork belly slices on a serving platter and garnish with sliced green onions. 5. Best served fresh. Store leftovers in an airtight container in the fridge for up to 4 days. Reheat in a preheated 400ºF (204ºC) air fryer for 3 minutes, or until heated through.

Chicken-Fried Steak

Prep time: 20 minutes | Cook time: 14 minutes | Serves 2

Steak:

Oil, for spraying

¾ cup all-purpose flour

1 teaspoon salt

1 teaspoon freshly ground black pepper

½ teaspoon paprika

½ teaspoon onion powder

1 teaspoon granulated garlic

¾ cup buttermilk

½ teaspoon hot sauce

2 (5-ounce / 142-g) cube steaks

Gravy:

2 tablespoons unsalted butter

2 tablespoons all-purpose flour

1 cup milk

½ teaspoon salt

½ teaspoon freshly ground black pepper

Make the Steak 1. Line the air fryer basket with parchment and spray lightly with oil. 2. In a medium bowl, mix together the flour, salt, black pepper, paprika, onion powder, and garlic. 3. In another bowl, whisk together the buttermilk and hot sauce. 4. Dredge the steaks in the flour mixture, dip in the buttermilk mixture, and dredge again in the flour until completely coated. Shake off any excess flour. 5. Place the steaks in the prepared basket and spray liberally with oil. 6. Air fry at 400ºF (204ºC) for 7 minutes, flip, spray with oil, and cook for another 6 to 7 minutes, or until crispy and browned. Make the Gravy 7. In a small saucepan, whisk together the butter and flour over medium heat until the butter is melted. Slowly add the milk, salt, and black pepper, increase the heat to medium-high, and continue to cook, stirring constantly, until the mixture thickens. Remove from the heat. 8. Transfer the steaks to plates and pour the gravy over the top. Serve immediately.

Vietnamese Grilled Pork

Prep time: 30 minutes | Cook time: 20 minutes | Serves 6

¼ cup minced yellow onion

2 tablespoons sugar

2 tablespoons vegetable oil

1 tablespoon minced garlic

1 tablespoon fish sauce

1 tablespoon minced fresh lemongrass

2 teaspoons dark soy sauce

½ teaspoon black pepper

1½ pounds (680 g) boneless pork shoulder, cut into ½-inch-thick slices

¼ cup chopped salted roasted peanuts

2 tablespoons chopped fresh cilantro or parsley

1. In a large bowl, combine the onion, sugar, vegetable oil, garlic, fish sauce, lemongrass, soy sauce, and pepper. Add the pork and toss to coat. Marinate at room temperature for 30 minutes, or cover and refrigerate for up to 24 hours. 2. Arrange the pork slices in the air fryer basket; discard the marinade. Set the air fryer to 400ºF (204ºC) for 20 minutes, turning the pork halfway through the cooking time. 3. Transfer the pork to a serving platter. Sprinkle with the peanuts and cilantro and serve.

Sausage and Peppers

Prep time: 7 minutes | Cook time: 35 minutes | Serves 4

Oil, for spraying
2 pounds (907 g) hot or sweet Italian sausage links, cut into thick slices
4 large bell peppers of any color, seeded and cut into slices
1 onion, thinly sliced
1 tablespoon olive oil
1 tablespoon chopped fresh parsley
1 teaspoon dried oregano
1 teaspoon dried basil
1 teaspoon balsamic vinegar

1. Line the air fryer basket with parchment and spray lightly with oil. 2. In a large bowl, combine the sausage, bell peppers, and onion. 3. In a small bowl, whisk together the olive oil, parsley, oregano, basil, and balsamic vinegar. Pour the mixture over the sausage and peppers and toss until evenly coated. 4. Using a slotted spoon, transfer the mixture to the prepared basket, taking care to drain out as much excess liquid as possible. 5. Air fry at 350°F (177°C) for 20 minutes, stir, and cook for another 15 minutes, or until the sausage is browned and the juices run clear.

Buttery Pork Chops

Prep time: 5 minutes | Cook time: 12 minutes | Serves 4

4 (4 ounces / 113 g) boneless pork chops
½ teaspoon salt
¼ teaspoon ground black
pepper
2 tablespoons salted butter, softened

1. Sprinkle pork chops on all sides with salt and pepper. Place chops into ungreased air fryer basket in a single layer. Adjust the temperature to 400°F (204°C) and air fry for 12 minutes. Pork chops will be golden and have an internal temperature of at least 145°F (63°C) when done. 2. Use tongs to remove cooked pork chops from air fryer and place onto a large plate. Top each chop with ½ tablespoon butter and let sit 2 minutes to melt. Serve warm.

Lemon Pork with Marjoram

Prep time: 5 minutes | Cook time: 10 minutes | Serves 4

1 (1 pound / 454 g) pork tenderloin, cut into ½-inch-thick slices
1 tablespoon extra-virgin olive oil
1 tablespoon freshly squeezed lemon juice
1 tablespoon honey
½ teaspoon grated lemon zest
½ teaspoon dried marjoram leaves
Pinch salt
Freshly ground black pepper, to taste

Cooking oil spray

1. Put the pork slices in a medium bowl. 2. In a small bowl, whisk the olive oil, lemon juice, honey, lemon zest, marjoram, salt, and pepper until combined. Pour this marinade over the tenderloin slices and gently massage with your hands to work it into the pork. 3. Insert the crisper plate into the basket and the basket into the unit. Preheat the unit by selecting AIR ROAST, setting the temperature to 400°F (204°C), and setting the time to 3 minutes. Select START/STOP to begin. 4. Once the unit is preheated, spray the crisper plate with cooking oil. Place the pork into the basket. 5. Select AIR ROAST, set the temperature to 400°F (204°C), and set the time to 10 minutes. Select START/STOP to begin. 6. When the cooking is complete, a food thermometer inserted into the pork should register at least 145°F (63°C). Let the pork stand for 5 minutes and serve.

Kheema Meatloaf

Prep time: 10 minutes | Cook time: 15 minutes | Serves 4

1 pound (454 g) 85% lean ground beef
2 large eggs, lightly beaten
1 cup diced yellow onion
¼ cup chopped fresh cilantro
1 tablespoon minced fresh ginger
1 tablespoon minced garlic
2 teaspoons garam masala
1 teaspoon kosher salt
1 teaspoon ground turmeric
1 teaspoon cayenne pepper
½ teaspoon ground cinnamon
⅛ teaspoon ground cardamom

1. In a large bowl, gently mix the ground beef, eggs, onion, cilantro, ginger, garlic, garam masala, salt, turmeric, cayenne, cinnamon, and cardamom until thoroughly combined. 2. Place the seasoned meat in a baking pan. Place the pan in the air fryer basket. Set the air fryer to 350°F (177°C) for 15 minutes. Use a meat thermometer to ensure the meat loaf has reached an internal temperature of 160°F / 71°C (medium). 3. Drain the fat and liquid from the pan and let stand for 5 minutes before slicing. 4. Slice and serve hot.

Italian Sausage Links

Prep time: 10 minutes | Cook time: 24 minutes | Serves 4

1 bell pepper (any color), sliced
1 medium onion, sliced
1 tablespoon avocado oil
1 teaspoon Italian seasoning
Sea salt and freshly ground black pepper, to taste
1 pound (454 g) Italian sausage links

1. Place the bell pepper and onion in a medium bowl, and toss with the avocado oil, Italian seasoning, and salt and pepper to taste. 2. Set the air fryer to 400°F (204°C). Put the vegetables in the air fryer basket and cook for 12 minutes. 3. Push the vegetables to the side of the basket and arrange the sausage links in the bottom of the basket in a single layer. Spoon the vegetables over the sausages. Cook for 12 minutes, tossing halfway through, until an instant-read thermometer inserted into the sausage reads 160°F (71°C).

Broccoli and Pork Teriyaki

Prep time: 10 minutes | Cook time: 13 minutes |
Serves 4

1 head broccoli, trimmed into florets
1 tablespoon extra-virgin olive oil
¼ teaspoon sea salt
¼ teaspoon freshly ground black pepper
1 pound (454 g) pork tenderloin, trimmed and cut into 1-inch pieces
½ cup teriyaki sauce, divided
Olive oil spray
2 cups cooked brown rice
Sesame seeds, for garnish

1. Insert the crisper plate into the basket and the basket into the unit. Preheat the unit by selecting AIR ROAST, setting the temperature to 400°F (204°C), and setting the time to 3 minutes. Select START/STOP to begin. 2. In a large bowl, toss together the broccoli, olive oil, salt, and pepper. 3. In a medium bowl, toss together the pork and 3 tablespoons of teriyaki sauce to coat the meat. 4. Once the unit is preheated, spray the crisper plate with olive oil. Put the broccoli and pork into the basket. Spray them with olive oil and drizzle with 1 tablespoon of teriyaki sauce. 5. Select AIR ROAST, set the temperature to 400°F (204°C), and set the time to 13 minutes. Select START/STOP to begin. 6. After 10 to 12 minutes, the broccoli is tender and light golden brown and a food thermometer inserted into the pork should register 145°F (63°C). Remove the basket and drizzle the broccoli and pork with the remaining ¼ cup of teriyaki sauce and toss to coat. Reinsert the basket to resume cooking for 1 minute. 7. When the cooking is complete, serve immediately over the hot cooked rice, if desired, garnished with the sesame seeds.

Cajun Bacon Pork Loin Fillet

Prep time: 30 minutes | Cook time: 20 minutes |
Serves 6

1½ pounds (680 g) pork loin fillet or pork tenderloin
3 tablespoons olive oil
2 tablespoons Cajun spice mix
Salt, to taste
6 slices bacon
Olive oil spray

1. Cut the pork in half so that it will fit in the air fryer basket. 2. Place both pieces of meat in a resealable plastic bag. Add the oil, Cajun seasoning, and salt to taste, if using. Seal the bag and massage to coat all of the meat with the oil and seasonings. Marinate in the refrigerator for at least 1 hour or up to 24 hours. 3. Remove the pork from the bag and wrap 3 bacon slices around each piece. Spray the air fryer basket with olive oil spray. Place the meat in the air fryer. Set the air fryer to 350°F (177°C) for 15 minutes. Increase the temperature to 400°F (204°C) for 5 minutes. Use a meat thermometer to ensure the meat has reached an internal temperature of 145°F (63°C). 4. Let the meat rest for 10 minutes. Slice into 6 medallions and serve.

Cantonese BBQ Pork

Prep time: 30 minutes | Cook time: 15 minutes |
Serves 4

¼ cup honey
2 tablespoons dark soy sauce
1 tablespoon sugar
1 tablespoon Shaoxing wine (rice cooking wine)
1 tablespoon hoisin sauce
2 teaspoons minced garlic
2 teaspoons minced fresh ginger
1 teaspoon Chinese five-spice powder
1 pound (454 g) fatty pork shoulder, cut into long, 1-inch-thick pieces

1. In a small microwave-safe bowl, combine the honey, soy sauce, sugar, wine, hoisin, garlic, ginger, and five-spice powder. Microwave in 10-second intervals, stirring in between, until the honey has dissolved. 2. Use a fork to pierce the pork slices to allow the marinade to penetrate better. Place the pork in a large bowl or resealable plastic bag and pour in half the marinade; set aside the remaining marinade to use for the sauce. Toss to coat. Marinate the pork at room temperature for 30 minutes, or cover and refrigerate for up 24 hours. 3. Place the pork in a single layer in the air fryer basket. Set the air fryer to 400°F (204°C) for 15 minutes, turning and basting the pork halfway through the cooking time. 4. While the pork is cooking, microwave the reserved marinade on high for 45 to 60 seconds, stirring every 15 seconds, to thicken it slightly to the consistency of a sauce. 5. Transfer the pork to a cutting board and let rest for 10 minutes. Brush with the sauce and serve.

Jalapeño Popper Pork Chops

Prep time: 15 minutes | Cook time: 6 to 8 minutes |
Serves 4

1¾ pounds (794 g) bone-in, center-cut loin pork chops
Sea salt and freshly ground black pepper, to taste
6 ounces (170 g) cream cheese, at room temperature
4 ounces (113 g) sliced bacon, cooked and crumbled
4 ounces (113 g) Cheddar cheese, shredded
1 jalapeño, seeded and diced
1 teaspoon garlic powder

1. Cut a pocket into each pork chop, lengthwise along the side, making sure not to cut it all the way through. Season the outside of the chops with salt and pepper. 2. In a small bowl, combine the cream cheese, bacon, Cheddar cheese, jalapeño, and garlic powder. Divide this mixture among the pork chops, stuffing it into the pocket of each chop. 3. Set the air fryer to 400°F (204°C). Place the pork chops in the air fryer basket in a single layer, working in batches if necessary. Air fry for 3 minutes. Flip the chops and cook for 3 to 5 minutes more, until an instant-read thermometer reads 145°F (63°C). 4. Allow the chops to rest for 5 minutes, then serve warm.

Rosemary Roast Beef

Prep time: 30 minutes | Cook time: 30 to 35 minutes | Serves 8

1 (2 pounds / 907 g) top round beef roast, tied with kitchen string

Sea salt and freshly ground black pepper, to taste

2 teaspoons minced garlic

2 tablespoons finely chopped fresh rosemary

¼ cup avocado oil

1. Season the roast generously with salt and pepper. 2. In a small bowl, whisk together the garlic, rosemary, and avocado oil. Rub this all over the roast. Cover loosely with aluminum foil or plastic wrap and refrigerate for at least 12 hours or up to 2 days. 3. Remove the roast from the refrigerator and allow to sit at room temperature for about 1 hour. 4. Set the air fryer to 325°F (163°C). Place the roast in the air fryer basket and roast for 15 minutes. Flip the roast and cook for 15 to 20 minutes more, until the meat is browned and an instant-read thermometer reads 120°F (49°C) at the thickest part (for medium-rare). 5. Transfer the meat to a cutting board, and let it rest for 15 minutes before thinly slicing and serving.

Spicy Tomato Beef Meatballs

Prep time: 10 minutes | Cook time: 15 minutes | Serves 4

3 scallions, minced

1 garlic clove, minced

1 egg yolk

¼ cup saltine cracker crumbs

Pinch salt

Freshly ground black pepper, to taste

1 pound (454 g) 95% lean ground beef

Olive oil spray

1¼ cups any tomato pasta sauce (from a 16 ounces / 454 g jar)

2 tablespoons Dijon mustard

1. In a large bowl, combine the scallions, garlic, egg yolk, cracker crumbs, salt, and pepper and mix well. 2. Add the ground beef and gently but thoroughly mix with your hands until combined. Form the meat mixture into 1½-inch round meatballs. 3. Insert the crisper plate into the basket and the basket into the unit. Preheat the unit by selecting BAKE, setting the temperature to 400°F (204°C), and setting the time to 3 minutes. Select START/STOP to begin. 4. Once the unit is preheated, spray the crisper plate with olive oil. Working in batches, spray the meatballs with olive oil and place them into the basket in a single layer, without touching. 5. Select BAKE, set the temperature to 400°F (204°C), and set the time to 11 minutes. Select START/STOP to begin. 6. When the cooking is complete, a food thermometer inserted into the meatballs should register 165°F (74°C). Transfer the meatballs to a 6-inch metal bowl. 7. Repeat steps 4, 5, and 6 with the remaining meatballs. 8. Top the meatballs with the pasta sauce and Dijon mustard, and mix gently. Place the bowl into the basket. 9. Select BAKE, set the temperature to 400°F (204°C), and set the time to 4 minutes. Select START/STOP to begin. 10. When the cooking is complete, serve hot.

Cheese Pork Chops

Prep time: 15 minutes | Cook time: 9 to 14 minutes | Serves 4

2 large eggs

½ cup finely grated Parmesan cheese

½ cup finely ground blanched almond flour or finely crushed pork rinds

1 teaspoon paprika

½ teaspoon dried oregano

½ teaspoon garlic powder

Salt and freshly ground black pepper, to taste

1¼ pounds (567 g) (1-inch-thick) boneless pork chops

Avocado oil spray

1. Beat the eggs in a shallow bowl. In a separate bowl, combine the Parmesan cheese, almond flour, paprika, oregano, garlic powder, and salt and pepper to taste. 2. Dip the pork chops into the eggs, then coat them with the Parmesan mixture, gently pressing the coating onto the meat. Spray the breaded pork chops with oil. 3. Set the air fryer to 400°F (204°C). Place the pork chops in the air fryer basket in a single layer, working in batches if necessary. Cook for 6 minutes. Flip the chops and spray them with more oil. Cook for another 3 to 8 minutes, until an instant-read thermometer reads 145°F (63°C). 4. Allow the pork chops to rest for at least 5 minutes, then serve.

Provolone Stuffed Beef and Pork Meatballs

Prep time: 15 minutes | Cook time: 12 minutes | Serves 4 to 6

1 tablespoon olive oil

1 small onion, finely chopped

1 to 2 cloves garlic, minced

¾ pound (340 g) ground beef

¾ pound (340 g) ground pork

¾ cup bread crumbs

¼ cup grated Parmesan cheese

¼ cup finely chopped fresh parsley

½ teaspoon dried oregano

1½ teaspoons salt

Freshly ground black pepper, to taste

2 eggs, lightly beaten

5 ounces (142 g) sharp or aged provolone cheese, cut into 1-inch cubes

1. Preheat a skillet over medium-high heat. Add the oil and cook the onion and garlic until tender, but not browned. 2. Transfer the onion and garlic to a large bowl and add the beef, pork, bread crumbs, Parmesan cheese, parsley, oregano, salt, pepper and eggs. Mix well until all the ingredients are combined. Divide the mixture into 12 evenly sized balls. Make one meatball at a time, by pressing a hole in the meatball mixture with the finger and pushing a piece of provolone cheese into the hole. Mold the meat back into a ball, enclosing the cheese. 3. Preheat the air fryer to 380°F (193°C). 4. Working in two batches, transfer six of the meatballs to the air fryer basket and air fry for 12 minutes, shaking the basket and turning the meatballs twice during the cooking process. Repeat with the remaining 6 meatballs. Serve warm.

Spice-Coated Steaks with Cucumber and Snap Pea Salad

Prep time: 15 minutes | Cook time: 15 to 20 minutes | Serves 4

1 (1½-pound / 680-g) boneless top sirloin steak, trimmed and halved crosswise
1½ teaspoons chili powder
1½ teaspoons ground cumin
¾ teaspoon ground coriander
⅛ teaspoon cayenne pepper
⅛ teaspoon ground cinnamon
1¼ teaspoons plus ⅛ teaspoon salt, divided
½ teaspoon plus ⅛ teaspoon ground black pepper, divided
1 teaspoon plus 1½ tablespoons extra-virgin olive oil, divided
3 tablespoons mayonnaise
1½ tablespoons white wine vinegar
1 tablespoon minced fresh dill
1 small garlic clove, minced
8 ounces (227 g) sugar snap peas, strings removed and cut in half on bias
½ English cucumber, halved lengthwise and sliced thin
2 radishes, trimmed, halved and sliced thin
2 cups baby arugula

1. Preheat the air fryer to 400ºF (204ºC). 2. In a bowl, mix chili powder, cumin, coriander, cayenne pepper, cinnamon, 1¼ teaspoons salt and ½ teaspoon pepper until well combined. 3. Add the steaks to another bowl and pat dry with paper towels. Brush with 1 teaspoon oil and transfer to the bowl of spice mixture. Roll over to coat thoroughly. 4. Arrange the coated steaks in the air fryer basket, spaced evenly apart. Air fry for 15 to 20 minutes, or until an instant-read thermometer inserted in the thickest part of the meat registers at least 145ºF (63ºC). Flip halfway through to ensure even cooking. 5. Transfer the steaks to a clean work surface and wrap with aluminum foil. Let stand while preparing salad. 6. Make the salad: In a large bowl, stir together 1½ tablespoons olive oil, mayonnaise, vinegar, dill, garlic, ⅛ teaspoon salt, and ⅛ teaspoon pepper. Add snap peas, cucumber, radishes and arugula. Toss to blend well. 7. Slice the steaks and serve with the salad.

Roast Beef with Horseradish Cream

Prep time: 5 minutes | Cook time: 35 to 45 minutes | Serves 6

2 pounds (907 g) beef roast top round or eye of round
1 tablespoon salt
2 teaspoons garlic powder
1 teaspoon freshly ground black pepper
1 teaspoon dried thyme
Horseradish Cream:
⅓ cup heavy cream
⅓ cup sour cream
⅓ cup prepared horseradish
2 teaspoons fresh lemon juice
Salt and freshly ground black pepper, to taste

1. Preheat the air fryer to 400ºF (204ºC). 2. Season the beef with the salt, garlic powder, black pepper, and thyme. Place the beef fat-side down in the basket of the air fryer and lightly coat with olive oil. Pausing halfway through the cooking time to turn the meat, air fry for 35 to 45 minutes, until a thermometer inserted into the thickest part indicates the desired doneness, 125ºF (52ºC) (rare) to 150ºF (66ºC) (medium). Let the beef rest for 10 minutes before slicing. 3. To make the horseradish cream: In a small bowl, combine the heavy cream, sour cream, horseradish, and lemon juice. Whisk until thoroughly combined. Season to taste with salt and freshly ground black pepper. Serve alongside the beef.

Pork Medallions with Radicchio and Endive Salad

Prep time: 25 minutes | Cook time: 7 minutes | Serves 4

1 (8-ounce / 227-g) pork tenderloin
Salt and freshly ground black pepper, to taste
¼ cup flour
2 eggs, lightly beaten
¾ cup cracker meal
1 teaspoon paprika
1 teaspoon dry mustard
1 teaspoon garlic powder
1 teaspoon dried thyme
1 teaspoon salt
vegetable or canola oil, in spray bottle
Vinaigrette:
¼ cup white balsamic vinegar
2 tablespoons agave syrup (or honey or maple syrup)
1 tablespoon Dijon mustard
juice of ½ lemon
2 tablespoons chopped chervil or flat-leaf parsley
salt and freshly ground black pepper
½ cup extra-virgin olive oil
Radicchio and Endive Salad:
1 heart romaine lettuce, torn into large pieces
½ head radicchio, coarsely chopped
2 heads endive, sliced
½ cup cherry tomatoes, halved
3 ounces (85 g) fresh Mozzarella, diced
Salt and freshly ground black pepper, to taste

1. Slice the pork tenderloin into 1-inch slices. Using a meat pounder, pound the pork slices into thin ½-inch medallions. Generously season the pork with salt and freshly ground black pepper on both sides. 2. Set up a dredging station using three shallow dishes. Put the flour in one dish and the beaten eggs in a second dish. Combine the cracker meal, paprika, dry mustard, garlic powder, thyme and salt in a third dish. 3. Preheat the air fryer to 400ºF (204ºC). 4. Dredge the pork medallions in flour first and then into the beaten egg. Let the excess egg drip off and coat both sides of the medallions with the cracker meal crumb mixture. Spray both sides of the coated medallions with vegetable or canola oil. 5. Air fry the medallions in two batches at 400ºF (204ºC) for 5 minutes. Once you have air-fried all the medallions, flip them all over and return the first batch of medallions back into the air fryer on top of the second batch. Air fry at 400ºF (204ºC) for an additional 2 minutes. 6. While the medallions are cooking, make the salad and dressing. Whisk the white balsamic vinegar, agave syrup, Dijon mustard, lemon juice, chervil, salt and pepper together in a small bowl. Whisk in the olive oil slowly until combined and thickened. 7. Combine the romaine lettuce, radicchio, endive, cherry tomatoes, and Mozzarella cheese in a large salad bowl. Drizzle the dressing over the vegetables and toss to combine. Season with salt and freshly ground black pepper. 8. Serve the pork medallions warm on or beside the salad.

Pork Meatballs

Prep time: 10 minutes | Cook time: 12 minutes | Makes 18 meatballs

1 pound (454 g) ground pork	¼ teaspoon crushed red pepper
1 large egg, whisked	flakes
½ teaspoon garlic powder	1 medium scallion, trimmed
½ teaspoon salt	and sliced
½ teaspoon ground ginger	

1. Combine all ingredients in a large bowl. Spoon out 2 tablespoons mixture and roll into a ball. Repeat to form eighteen meatballs total. 2. Place meatballs into ungreased air fryer basket. Adjust the temperature to 400ºF (204ºC) and air fry for 12 minutes, shaking the basket three times throughout cooking. Meatballs will be browned and have an internal temperature of at least 145ºF (63ºC) when done. Serve warm.

Smoky Pork Tenderloin

Prep time: 5 minutes | Cook time: 19 to 22 minutes | Serves 6

1½ pounds (680 g) pork	1 teaspoon garlic powder
tenderloin	1 teaspoon sea salt
1 tablespoon avocado oil	1 teaspoon freshly ground black
1 teaspoon chili powder	pepper
1 teaspoon smoked paprika	

1. Pierce the tenderloin all over with a fork and rub the oil all over the meat. 2. In a small dish, stir together the chili powder, smoked paprika, garlic powder, salt, and pepper. 3. Rub the spice mixture all over the tenderloin. 4. Set the air fryer to 400ºF (204ºC). Place the pork in the air fryer basket and air fry for 10 minutes. Flip the tenderloin and cook for 9 to 12 minutes more, until an instant-read thermometer reads at least 145ºF (63ºC). 5. Allow the tenderloin to rest for 5 minutes, then slice and serve.

Herbed Beef

Prep time: 5 minutes | Cook time: 22 minutes | Serves 6

1 teaspoon dried dill	2 pounds (907 g) beef steak
1 teaspoon dried thyme	3 tablespoons butter
1 teaspoon garlic powder	

1. Preheat the air fryer to 360ºF (182ºC). 2. Combine the dill, thyme, and garlic powder in a small bowl, and massage into the steak. 3. Air fry the steak in the air fryer for 20 minutes, then remove, shred, and return to the air fryer. 4. Add the butter and air fry the shredded steak for a further 2 minutes at 365ºF (185ºC). Make sure the beef is coated in the butter before serving.

Sausage and Zucchini Lasagna

Prep time: 25 minutes | Cook time: 56 minutes | Serves 4

1 zucchini	¾ cup ricotta cheese
Avocado oil spray	1 cup shredded fontina cheese,
6 ounces (170 g) hot Italian	divided
sausage, casings removed	½ cup finely grated Parmesan
2 ounces (57 g) mushrooms,	cheese
stemmed and sliced	Sea salt and freshly ground
1 teaspoon minced garlic	black pepper, to taste
1 cup keto-friendly marinara	Fresh basil, for garnish
sauce	

1. Cut the zucchini into long thin slices using a mandoline slicer or sharp knife. Spray both sides of the slices with oil. 2. Place the slices in a single layer in the air fryer basket, working in batches if necessary. Set the air fryer to 325ºF (163ºC) and air fry for 4 to 6 minutes, until most of the moisture has been released from the zucchini. 3. Place a large skillet over medium-high heat. Crumble the sausage into the hot skillet and cook for 6 minutes, breaking apart the meat with the back of a spoon. Remove the sausage from the skillet, leaving any fats that remain. Add the mushrooms to the skillet and cook for 10 minutes, until the liquid nearly evaporates. Add the garlic and cook for 1 minute more. Stir in the marinara and cook for 2 more minutes. 4. In a medium bowl, combine the ricotta cheese, ½ cup of fontina cheese, Parmesan cheese, and salt and pepper to taste. 5. Spread ¼ cup of the meat sauce in the bottom of a deep pan (or other pan that fits inside your air fryer). Top with half of the zucchini slices. Add half of the cheese mixture. Top the cheese with half of the remaining meat sauce. Layer the remaining zucchini over the meat sauce and top with the remaining cheese mixture. Top the lasagna with the remaining ½ cup of fontina cheese. 6. Cover the lasagna with aluminum foil or parchment paper and place it in the air fryer. Bake for 25 minutes. Remove the foil and cook for 8 to 10 minutes more. 7. Allow the lasagna to rest for 15 minutes before cutting and serving. Garnish with basil.

Avocado Buttered Flank Steak

Prep time: 5 minutes | Cook time: 12 minutes | Serves 1

1 flank steak	2 avocados
Salt and ground black pepper,	2 tablespoons butter, melted
to taste	½ cup chimichurri sauce

1. Rub the flank steak with salt and pepper to taste and leave to sit for 20 minutes. 2. Preheat the air fryer to 400ºF (204ºC). 3. Halve the avocados and take out the pits. Spoon the flesh into a bowl and mash with a fork. Mix in the melted butter and chimichurri sauce, making sure everything is well combined. 4. Put the steak in the air fryer basket and air fry for 6 minutes. Flip over and allow to air fry for another 6 minutes. 5. Serve the steak with the avocado butter.

New York Strip with Honey-Mustard Butter

Prep time: 5 minutes | Cook time: 14 minutes |

Serves 4

2 pounds (907 g) New York Strip	½ stick butter, softened
1 teaspoon cayenne pepper	Sea salt and freshly ground black pepper, to taste
1 tablespoon honey	Cooking spray
1 tablespoon Dijon mustard	

1. Preheat the air fryer to 400ºF (204ºC) and spritz with cooking spray. 2. Sprinkle the New York Strip with cayenne pepper, salt, and black pepper on a clean work surface. 3. Arrange the New York Strip in the preheated air fryer and spritz with cooking spray. 4. Air fry for 14 minutes or until browned and reach your desired doneness. Flip the New York Strip halfway through. 5. Meanwhile, combine the honey, mustard, and butter in a small bowl. Stir to mix well. 6. Transfer the air fried New York Strip onto a plate and baste with the honey-mustard butter before serving.

Ritzy Skirt Steak Fajitas

Prep time: 15 minutes | Cook time: 30 minutes |

Serves 4

2 tablespoons olive oil	1 green pepper, sliced
¼ cup lime juice	Salt and freshly ground black pepper, to taste
1 clove garlic, minced	
½ teaspoon ground cumin	8 flour tortillas
½ teaspoon hot sauce	Toppings:
½ teaspoon salt	Shredded lettuce
2 tablespoons chopped fresh cilantro	Crumbled Queso Fresco (or grated Cheddar cheese)
1 pound (454 g) skirt steak	Sliced black olives
1 onion, sliced	Diced tomatoes
1 teaspoon chili powder	Sour cream
1 red pepper, sliced	Guacamole

1. Combine the olive oil, lime juice, garlic, cumin, hot sauce, salt and cilantro in a shallow dish. Add the skirt steak and turn it over several times to coat all sides. Pierce the steak with a needle-style meat tenderizer or paring knife. Marinate the steak in the refrigerator for at least 3 hours, or overnight. When you are ready to cook, remove the steak from the refrigerator and let it sit at room temperature for 30 minutes. 2. Preheat the air fryer to 400ºF (204ºC). 3. Toss the onion slices with the chili powder and a little olive oil and transfer them to the air fryer basket. Air fry for 5 minutes. Add the red and green peppers to the air fryer basket with the onions, season with salt and pepper and air fry for 8 more minutes, until the onions and peppers are soft. Transfer the vegetables to a dish and cover with aluminum foil to keep warm. 4. Put the skirt steak in the air fryer basket and pour the marinade over the top. Air fry at 400ºF (204ºC) for 12 minutes. Flip the steak over

and air fry for an additional 5 minutes. Transfer the cooked steak to a cutting board and let the steak rest for a few minutes. If the peppers and onions need to be heated, return them to the air fryer for just 1 to 2 minutes. 5. Thinly slice the steak at an angle, cutting against the grain of the steak. Serve the steak with the onions and peppers, the warm tortillas and the fajita toppings on the side.

Parmesan-Crusted Pork Chops

Prep time: 5 minutes | Cook time: 12 minutes |

Serves 4

1 large egg	½ teaspoon salt
½ cup grated Parmesan cheese	¼ teaspoon ground black pepper
4 (4 ounces / 113 g) boneless pork chops	

1. Whisk egg in a medium bowl and place Parmesan in a separate medium bowl. 2. Sprinkle pork chops on both sides with salt and pepper. Dip each pork chop into egg, then press both sides into Parmesan. 3. Place pork chops into ungreased air fryer basket. Adjust the temperature to 400ºF (204ºC) and air fry for 12 minutes, turning chops halfway through cooking. Pork chops will be golden and have an internal temperature of at least 145ºF (63ºC) when done. Serve warm.

Korean Beef Tacos

Prep time: 30 minutes | Cook time: 12 minutes |

Serves 6

2 tablespoons gochujang (Korean red chile paste)	1½ pounds (680 g) thinly sliced beef (chuck, rib eye, or sirloin)
2 cloves garlic, minced	1 medium red onion, sliced
2 teaspoons minced fresh ginger	12 (6-inch) flour tortillas, warmed; or lettuce leaves
2 tablespoons toasted sesame oil	
1 tablespoon soy sauce	½ cup chopped green onions
2 tablespoons sesame seeds	¼ cup chopped fresh cilantro (optional)
2 teaspoons sugar	½ cup kimchi (optional)
½ teaspoon kosher salt	

1. In a small bowl, combine the gochujang, garlic, ginger, sesame oil, soy sauce, sesame seeds, sugar, and salt. Whisk until well combined. Place the beef and red onion in a resealable plastic bag and pour the marinade over. Seal the bag and massage to coat all of the meat and onion. Marinate at room temperature for 30 minutes or in the refrigerator for up to 24 hours. 2. Place the meat and onion in the air fryer basket, leaving behind as much of the marinade as possible; discard the marinade. Set the air fryer to 400ºF (204ºC) for 12 minutes, shaking halfway through the cooking time. 3. To serve, place meat and onion in the tortillas. Top with the green onions and the cilantro and kimchi, if using, and serve.

Indian Mint and Chile Kebabs

Prep time: 30 minutes | Cook time: 15 minutes | Serves 4

1 pound (454 g) ground lamb	½ teaspoon ground turmeric
½ cup finely minced onion	½ teaspoon cayenne pepper
¼ cup chopped fresh mint	¼ teaspoon ground cardamom
¼ cup chopped fresh cilantro	¼ teaspoon ground cinnamon
1 tablespoon minced garlic	1 teaspoon kosher salt

1. In the bowl of a stand mixer fitted with the paddle attachment, combine the lamb, onion, mint, cilantro, garlic, turmeric, cayenne, cardamom, cinnamon, and salt. Mix on low speed until you have a sticky mess of spiced meat. If you have time, let the mixture stand at room temperature for 30 minutes (or cover and refrigerate for up to a day or two, until you're ready to make the kebabs). 2. Divide the meat into eight equal portions. Form each into a long sausage shape. Place the kebabs in a single layer in the air fryer basket. Set the air fryer to 350ºF (177ºC) for 10 minutes. Increase the air fryer temperature to 400ºF (204ºC) and cook for 3 to 4 minutes more to brown the kebabs. Use a meat thermometer to ensure the kebabs have reached an internal temperature of 160ºF / 71ºC (medium).

Bacon, Cheese and Pear Stuffed Pork

Prep time: 10 minutes | Cook time: 24 minutes | Serves 3

4 slices bacon, chopped	⅛ teaspoon black pepper
1 tablespoon butter	1 pear, finely diced
½ cup finely diced onion	⅓ cup crumbled blue cheese
⅓ cup chicken stock	3 boneless center-cut pork
1½ cups seasoned stuffing	chops (2-inch thick)
cubes	Olive oil
1 egg, beaten	Salt and freshly ground black
½ teaspoon dried thyme	pepper, to taste
½ teaspoon salt	

1. Preheat the air fryer to 400ºF (204ºC). 2. Place the bacon into the air fryer basket and air fry for 6 minutes, stirring halfway through the cooking time. Remove the bacon and set it aside on a paper towel. Pour out the grease from the bottom of the air fryer. 3. Make the stuffing: Melt the butter in a medium saucepan over medium heat on the stovetop. Add the onion and sauté for a few minutes, until it starts to soften. Add the chicken stock and simmer for 1 minute. Remove the pan from the heat and add the stuffing cubes. Stir until the stock has been absorbed. Add the egg, dried thyme, salt and freshly ground black pepper, and stir until combined. Fold in the diced pear and crumbled blue cheese. 4. Place the pork chops on a cutting board. Using the palm of your hand to hold the chop flat and steady, slice into the side of the pork chop to make a pocket in the center of the chop. Leave about an inch of chop uncut and make sure you don't cut all the way through the pork chop. Brush both sides of the pork chops with olive oil and season with salt and freshly ground black pepper. Stuff each pork chop with a third of the stuffing, packing the stuffing tightly inside the pocket. 5. Preheat the air fryer to 360ºF (182ºC). 6. Spray or brush the sides of the air fryer basket with oil. Place the pork chops in the air fryer basket with the open stuffed edge of the pork chop facing the outside edges of the basket. 7. Air fry the pork chops for 18 minutes, turning the pork chops over halfway through the cooking time. When the chops are done, let them rest for 5 minutes and then transfer to a serving platter.

Bacon-Wrapped Pork Tenderloin

Prep time: 30 minutes | Cook time: 22 to 25 minutes | Serves 6

½ cup minced onion	¼ teaspoon freshly ground
½ cup hard apple cider, or apple	black pepper
juice	2 pounds (907 g) pork
¼ cup honey	tenderloin
1 tablespoon minced garlic	1 to 2 tablespoons oil
¼ teaspoon salt	8 uncooked bacon slices

1. In a medium bowl, stir together the onion, hard cider, honey, garlic, salt, and pepper. Transfer to a large resealable bag or airtight container and add the pork. Seal the bag. Refrigerate to marinate for at least 2 hours. 2. Preheat the air fryer to 400ºF (204ºC). Line the air fryer basket with parchment paper. 3. Remove the pork from the marinade and place it on the parchment. Spritz with oil. 4. Cook for 15 minutes. 5. Wrap the bacon slices around the pork and secure them with toothpicks. Turn the pork roast and spritz with oil. Cook for 7 to 10 minutes more until the internal temperature reaches 145ºF (63ºC), depending on how well-done you like pork loin. It will continue cooking after it's removed from the fryer, so let it sit for 5 minutes before serving.

Cinnamon-Beef Kofta

Prep time: 10 minutes | Cook time: 13 minutes per batch | Makes 12 koftas

1½ pounds (680 g) lean ground	1 teaspoon ground cumin
beef	¾ teaspoon salt
1 teaspoon onion powder	¼ teaspoon cayenne
¾ teaspoon ground cinnamon	12 (3½- to 4-inch-long)
¾ teaspoon ground dried	cinnamon sticks
turmeric	Cooking spray

1. Preheat the air fryer to 375ºF (191ºC). Spritz the air fryer basket with cooking spray. 2. Combine all the ingredients, except for the cinnamon sticks, in a large bowl. Toss to mix well. 3. Divide and shape the mixture into 12 balls, then wrap each ball around each cinnamon stick and leave a quarter of the length uncovered. 4. Arrange the beef-cinnamon sticks in the preheated air fryer and spritz with cooking spray. Work in batches to avoid overcrowding. 5. Air fry for 13 minutes or until the beef is browned. Flip the sticks halfway through. 6. Serve immediately.

Pork Tenderloin with Avocado Lime Sauce

Prep time: 30 minutes | Cook time: 15 minutes | Serves 4

Marinade:

½ cup lime juice

Grated zest of 1 lime

2 teaspoons stevia glycerite, or ¼ teaspoon liquid stevia

3 cloves garlic, minced

1½ teaspoons fine sea salt

1 teaspoon chili powder, or more for more heat

1 teaspoon smoked paprika

1 pound (454 g) pork tenderloin

Avocado Lime Sauce:

1 medium-sized ripe avocado, roughly chopped

½ cup full-fat sour cream (or coconut cream for dairy-free)

Grated zest of 1 lime

Juice of 1 lime

2 cloves garlic, roughly chopped

½ teaspoon fine sea salt

¼ teaspoon ground black pepper

Chopped fresh cilantro leaves, for garnish

Lime slices, for serving

Pico de gallo, for serving

1. In a medium-sized casserole dish, stir together all the marinade ingredients until well combined. Add the tenderloin and coat it well in the marinade. Cover and place in the fridge to marinate for 2 hours or overnight. 2. Spray the air fryer basket with avocado oil. Preheat the air fryer to 400ºF (204ºC). 3. Remove the pork from the marinade and place it in the air fryer basket. Air fry for 13 to 15 minutes, until the internal temperature of the pork is 145ºF (63ºC), flipping after 7 minutes. Remove the pork from the air fryer and place it on a cutting board. Allow it to rest for 8 to 10 minutes, then cut it into ½-inch-thick slices. 4. While the pork cooks, make the avocado lime sauce: Place all the sauce ingredients in a food processor and purée until smooth. Taste and adjust the seasoning to your liking. 5. Place the pork slices on a serving platter and spoon the avocado lime sauce on top. Garnish with cilantro leaves and serve with lime slices and pico de gallo. 6. Store leftovers in an airtight container in the fridge for up to 4 days. Reheat in a preheated 400ºF (204ºC) air fryer for 5 minutes, or until heated through.

Parmesan-Crusted Steak

Prep time: 30 minutes | Cook time: 12 minutes | Serves 6

½ cup (1 stick) unsalted butter, at room temperature

1 cup finely grated Parmesan cheese

¼ cup finely ground blanched

almond flour

1½ pounds (680 g) New York strip steak

Sea salt and freshly ground black pepper, to taste

1. Place the butter, Parmesan cheese, and almond flour in a food processor. Process until smooth. Transfer to a sheet of parchment paper and form into a log. Wrap tightly in plastic wrap. Freeze for 45 minutes or refrigerate for at least 4 hours. 2. While the butter

is chilling, season the steak liberally with salt and pepper. Let the steak rest at room temperature for about 45 minutes. 3. Place the grill pan or basket in your air fryer, set it to 400ºF (204ºC), and let it preheat for 5 minutes. 4. Working in batches, if necessary, place the steak on the grill pan and air fry for 4 minutes. Flip and cook for 3 minutes more, until the steak is brown on both sides. 5. Remove the steak from the air fryer and arrange an equal amount of the Parmesan butter on top of each steak. Return the steak to the air fryer and continue cooking for another 5 minutes, until an instant-read thermometer reads 120ºF (49ºC) for medium-rare and the crust is golden brown (or to your desired doneness). 6. Transfer the cooked steak to a plate; let rest for 10 minutes before serving.

Mongolian-Style Beef

Prep time: 10 minutes | Cook time: 10 minutes | Serves 4

Oil, for spraying

¼ cup cornstarch

1 pound (454 g) flank steak, thinly sliced

¾ cup packed light brown sugar

½ cup soy sauce

2 teaspoons toasted sesame oil

1 tablespoon minced garlic

½ teaspoon ground ginger

½ cup water

Cooked white rice or ramen noodles, for serving

1. Line the air fryer basket with parchment and spray lightly with oil. 2. Place the cornstarch in a bowl and dredge the steak until evenly coated. Shake off any excess cornstarch. 3. Place the steak in the prepared basket and spray lightly with oil. 4. Roast at 390ºF (199ºC) for 5 minutes, flip, and cook for another 5 minutes. 5. In a small saucepan, combine the brown sugar, soy sauce, sesame oil, garlic, ginger, and water and bring to a boil over medium-high heat, stirring frequently. Remove from the heat. 6. Transfer the meat to the sauce and toss until evenly coated. Let sit for about 5 minutes so the steak absorbs the flavors. Serve with white rice or ramen noodles.

Super Bacon with Meat

Prep time: 5 minutes | Cook time: 1 hour | Serves 4

30 slices thick-cut bacon

4 ounces (113 g) Cheddar cheese, shredded

12 ounces (340 g) steak

10 ounces (283 g) pork sausage

Salt and ground black pepper, to taste

1. Preheat the air fryer to 400ºF (204ºC). 2. Lay out 30 slices of bacon in a woven pattern and bake for 20 minutes until crisp. Put the cheese in the center of the bacon. 3. Combine the steak and sausage to form a meaty mixture. 4. Lay out the meat in a rectangle of similar size to the bacon strips. Season with salt and pepper. 5. Roll the meat into a tight roll and refrigerate. 6. Preheat the air fryer to 400ºF (204ºC). 7. Make a 7×7 bacon weave and roll the bacon weave over the meat, diagonally. 8. Bake for 60 minutes or until the internal temperature reaches at least 165ºF (74ºC). 9. Let rest for 5 minutes before serving.

Garlic Balsamic London Broil

Prep time: 30 minutes | Cook time: 8 to 10 minutes |

Serves 8

2 pounds (907 g) London broil
3 large garlic cloves, minced
3 tablespoons balsamic vinegar
3 tablespoons whole-grain mustard

2 tablespoons olive oil
Sea salt and ground black pepper, to taste
½ teaspoon dried hot red pepper flakes

1. Score both sides of the cleaned London broil. 2. Thoroughly combine the remaining ingredients; massage this mixture into the meat to coat it on all sides. Let it marinate for at least 3 hours. 3. Set the air fryer to 400ºF (204ºC); Then cook the London broil for 15 minutes. Flip it over and cook another 10 to 12 minutes. Bon appétit!

Teriyaki Rump Steak with Broccoli and Capsicum

Prep time: 5 minutes | Cook time: 13 minutes |

Serves 4

½ pound (227 g) rump steak
⅓ cup teriyaki marinade
1½ teaspoons sesame oil
½ head broccoli, cut into florets

2 red capsicums, sliced
Fine sea salt and ground black pepper, to taste
Cooking spray

1. Toss the rump steak in a large bowl with teriyaki marinade. Wrap the bowl in plastic and refrigerate to marinate for at least an hour. 2. Preheat the air fryer to 400ºF (204ºC) and spritz with cooking spray. 3. Discard the marinade and transfer the steak in the preheated air fryer. Spritz with cooking spray. 4. Air fry for 13 minutes or until well browned. Flip the steak halfway through. 5. Meanwhile, heat the sesame oil in a nonstick skillet over medium heat. Add the broccoli and capsicum. Sprinkle with salt and ground black pepper. Sauté for 5 minutes or until the broccoli is tender. 6. Transfer the air fried rump steak on a plate and top with the sautéed broccoli and capsicum. Serve hot.

Spinach and Beef Braciole

Prep time: 25 minutes | Cook time: 1 hour 32 minutes | Serves 4

½ onion, finely chopped
1 teaspoon olive oil
⅓ cup red wine
2 cups crushed tomatoes
1 teaspoon Italian seasoning
½ teaspoon garlic powder
¼ teaspoon crushed red pepper

flakes
2 tablespoons chopped fresh parsley
2 top round steaks (about 1½ pounds / 680 g)
salt and freshly ground black pepper

2 cups fresh spinach, chopped
1 clove minced garlic
½ cup roasted red peppers, julienned

½ cup grated pecorino cheese
¼ cup pine nuts, toasted and roughly chopped
2 tablespoons olive oil

1. Preheat the air fryer to 400ºF (204ºC). 2. Toss the onions and olive oil together in a baking pan or casserole dish. Air fry at 400ºF (204ºC) for 5 minutes, stirring a couple times during the cooking process. Add the red wine, crushed tomatoes, Italian seasoning, garlic powder, red pepper flakes and parsley and stir. Cover the pan tightly with aluminum foil, lower the air fryer temperature to 350ºF (177ºC) and continue to air fry for 15 minutes. 3. While the sauce is simmering, prepare the beef. Using a meat mallet, pound the beef until it is ¼-inch thick. Season both sides of the beef with salt and pepper. Combine the spinach, garlic, red peppers, pecorino cheese, pine nuts and olive oil in a medium bowl. Season with salt and freshly ground black pepper. Disperse the mixture over the steaks. Starting at one of the short ends, roll the beef around the filling, tucking in the sides as you roll to ensure the filling is completely enclosed. Secure the beef rolls with toothpicks. 4. Remove the baking pan with the sauce from the air fryer and set it aside. Preheat the air fryer to 400ºF (204ºC). 5. Brush or spray the beef rolls with a little olive oil and air fry at 400ºF (204ºC) for 12 minutes, rotating the beef during the cooking process for even browning. When the beef is browned, submerge the rolls into the sauce in the baking pan, cover the pan with foil and return it to the air fryer. Reduce the temperature of the air fryer to 250ºF (121ºC) and air fry for 60 minutes. 6. Remove the beef rolls from the sauce. Cut each roll into slices and serve, ladling some sauce overtop.

Pork Kebab with Yogurt Sauce

Prep time: 25 minutes | Cook time: 12 minutes |

Serves 4

2 teaspoons olive oil
½ pound (227 g) ground pork
½ pound (227 g) ground beef
1 egg, whisked
Sea salt and ground black pepper, to taste
1 teaspoon paprika
2 garlic cloves, minced
1 teaspoon dried marjoram
1 teaspoon mustard seeds

½ teaspoon celery seeds
Yogurt Sauce:
2 tablespoons olive oil
2 tablespoons fresh lemon juice
Sea salt, to taste
¼ teaspoon red pepper flakes, crushed
½ cup full-fat yogurt
1 teaspoon dried dill weed

1. Spritz the sides and bottom of the air fryer basket with 2 teaspoons of olive oil. 2. In a mixing dish, thoroughly combine the ground pork, beef, egg, salt, black pepper, paprika, garlic, marjoram, mustard seeds, and celery seeds. 3. Form the mixture into kebabs and transfer them to the greased basket. Cook at 365ºF (185ºC) for 11 to 12 minutes, turning them over once or twice. 4. In the meantime, mix all the sauce ingredients and place in the refrigerator until ready to serve. Serve the pork kebabs with the yogurt sauce on the side. Enjoy!

Poblano Pepper Cheeseburgers

Prep time: 5 minutes | Cook time: 30 minutes | Serves 4

2 poblano chile peppers

1½ pounds (680 g) 85% lean ground beef

1 clove garlic, minced

1 teaspoon salt

½ teaspoon freshly ground black pepper

4 slices Cheddar cheese (about 3 ounces / 85 g)

4 large lettuce leaves

1. Preheat the air fryer to 400°F (204°C). 2. Arrange the poblano peppers in the basket of the air fryer. Pausing halfway through the cooking time to turn the peppers, air fry for 20 minutes, or until they are softened and beginning to char. Transfer the peppers to a large bowl and cover with a plate. When cool enough to handle, peel off the skin, remove the seeds and stems, and slice into strips. Set aside. 3. Meanwhile, in a large bowl, combine the ground beef with the garlic, salt, and pepper. Shape the beef into 4 patties. 4. Lower the heat on the air fryer to 360°F (182°C). Arrange the burgers in a single layer in the basket of the air fryer. Pausing halfway through the cooking time to turn the burgers, air fry for 10 minutes, or until a thermometer inserted into the thickest part registers 160°F (71°C). 5. Top the burgers with the cheese slices and continue baking for a minute or two, just until the cheese has melted. Serve the burgers on a lettuce leaf topped with the roasted poblano peppers.

Swedish Meatloaf

Prep time: 10 minutes | Cook time: 35 minutes | Serves 8

1½ pounds (680 g) ground beef (85% lean)

¼ pound (113 g) ground pork

1 large egg (omit for egg-free)

½ cup minced onions

¼ cup tomato sauce

2 tablespoons dry mustard

2 cloves garlic, minced

2 teaspoons fine sea salt

1 teaspoon ground black pepper, plus more for garnish

Sauce:

½ cup (1 stick) unsalted butter

½ cup shredded Swiss or mild Cheddar cheese (about 2 ounces / 57 g)

2 ounces (57 g) cream cheese (¼ cup), softened

⅓ cup beef broth

⅛ teaspoon ground nutmeg

Halved cherry tomatoes, for serving (optional)

1. Preheat the air fryer to 390°F (199°C). 2. In a large bowl, combine the ground beef, ground pork, egg, onions, tomato sauce, dry mustard, garlic, salt, and pepper. Using your hands, mix until well combined. 3. Place the meatloaf mixture in a loaf pan and place it in the air fryer. Bake for 35 minutes, or until cooked through and the internal temperature reaches 145°F (63°C). Check the meatloaf after 25 minutes; if it's getting too brown on the top, cover it loosely with foil to prevent burning. 4. While the meatloaf cooks, make the sauce: Heat the butter in a saucepan over medium-high heat until it sizzles and brown flecks appear, stirring constantly to keep the butter from burning. Turn the heat down to low and whisk in the Swiss cheese, cream cheese, broth, and nutmeg. Simmer for at least 10 minutes. The longer it simmers, the more the flavors open up. 5. When the meatloaf is done, transfer it to a serving tray and pour the sauce over it. Garnish with ground black pepper and serve with cherry tomatoes, if desired. Allow the meatloaf to rest for 10 minutes before slicing so it doesn't crumble apart. 6. Store leftovers in an airtight container in the fridge for 3 days or in the freezer for up to a month. Reheat in a preheated 350°F (177°C) air fryer for 4 minutes, or until heated through.

Chapter 6 Fish and Seafood

Sole and Cauliflower Fritters

Prep time: 5 minutes | Cook time: 24 minutes |
Serves 2

½ pound (227 g) sole fillets
½ pound (227 g) mashed
cauliflower
½ cup red onion, chopped
1 bell pepper, finely chopped
1 egg, beaten
2 garlic cloves, minced
2 tablespoons fresh parsley,
chopped
1 tablespoon olive oil
1 tablespoon coconut aminos
½ teaspoon scotch bonnet
pepper, minced
½ teaspoon paprika
Salt and white pepper, to taste
Cooking spray

1. Preheat the air fryer to 395ºF (202ºC). Spray the air fryer basket with cooking spray. 2. Place the sole fillets in the basket and air fry for 10 minutes, flipping them halfway through. 3. When the fillets are done, transfer them to a large bowl. Mash the fillets into flakes. Add the remaining ingredients and stir to combine. 4. Make the fritters: Scoop out 2 tablespoons of the fish mixture and shape into a patty about ½ inch thick with your hands. Repeat with the remaining fish mixture. 5. Arrange the patties in the air fryer basket and bake for 14 minutes, flipping the patties halfway through, or until they are golden brown and cooked through. 6. Cool for 5 minutes and serve on a plate.

Scallops with Asparagus and Peas

Prep time: 10 minutes | Cook time: 7 to 10 minutes |
Serves 4

Cooking oil spray
1 pound (454 g) asparagus,
ends trimmed, cut into 2-inch
pieces
1 cup sugar snap peas
1 pound (454 g) sea scallops
1 tablespoon freshly squeezed
lemon juice
2 teaspoons extra-virgin olive
oil
½ teaspoon dried thyme
Salt and freshly ground black
pepper, to taste

1. Insert the crisper plate into the basket and the basket into the unit. Preheat the unit by selecting AIR FRY, setting the temperature to 400ºF (204ºC), and setting the time to 3 minutes. Select START/STOP to begin. 2. Once the unit is preheated, spray the crisper plate with cooking oil. Place the asparagus and sugar snap peas into the basket. 3. Select AIR FRY, set the temperature to 400ºF (204ºC), and set the time to 10 minutes. Select START/STOP to begin. 4. Meanwhile, check the scallops for a small muscle attached to the

side. Pull it off and discard. In a medium bowl, toss together the scallops, lemon juice, olive oil, and thyme. Season with salt and pepper. 5. After 3 minutes, the vegetables should be just starting to get tender. Place the scallops on top of the vegetables. Reinsert the basket to resume cooking. After 3 minutes more, remove the basket and shake it. Again reinsert the basket to resume cooking. 6. When the cooking is complete, the scallops should be firm when tested with your finger and opaque in the center, and the vegetables tender. Serve immediately.

Shrimp with Smoky Tomato Dressing

Prep time: 5 minutes | Cook time: 8 minutes | Serves 2

3 tablespoons mayonnaise
1 tablespoon ketchup
1 tablespoon minced garlic
1 teaspoon Sriracha
½ teaspoon smoked paprika
½ teaspoon kosher salt
1 pound (454 g) large raw
shrimp (21 to 25 count), peeled
(tails left on) and deveined
Vegetable oil spray
½ cup chopped scallions

1. In a large bowl, combine the mayonnaise, ketchup, garlic, Sriracha, paprika, and salt. Add the shrimp and toss to coat with the sauce. 2. Spray the air fryer basket with vegetable oil spray. Place the shrimp in the basket. Set the air fryer to 350ºF (177ºC) for 8 minutes, tossing and spraying the shrimp with vegetable oil spray halfway through the cooking time. 3. Sprinkle with the chopped scallions before serving.

Baked Salmon with Tomatoes and Olives

Prep time: 5 minutes | Cook time: 8 minutes | Serves 4

2 tablespoons olive oil
4 (1½-inch-thick) salmon fillets
½ teaspoon salt
¼ teaspoon cayenne
1 teaspoon chopped fresh dill
2 Roma tomatoes, diced
¼ cup sliced Kalamata olives
4 lemon slices

1. Preheat the air fryer to 380°F(193ºC). 2. Brush the olive oil on both sides of the salmon fillets, and then season them lightly with salt, cayenne, and dill. 3. Place the fillets in a single layer in the basket of the air fryer, then layer the tomatoes and olives over the top. Top each fillet with a lemon slice. 4. Bake for 8 minutes, or until the salmon has reached an internal temperature of 145°F(63ºC).

Butter-Wine Baked Salmon

Prep time: 5 minutes | Cook time: 10 minutes |
Serves 4

4 tablespoons butter, melted

2 cloves garlic, minced

Sea salt and ground black
pepper, to taste

¼ cup dry white wine

1 tablespoon lime juice

1 teaspoon smoked paprika

½ teaspoon onion powder

4 salmon steaks

Cooking spray

1. Place all the ingredients except the salmon and oil in a shallow dish and stir to mix well. 2. Add the salmon steaks, turning to coat well on both sides. Transfer the salmon to the refrigerator to marinate for 30 minutes. 3. Preheat the air fryer to 360ºF (182ºC). 4. Place the salmon steaks in the air fryer basket, discarding any excess marinade. Spray the salmon steaks with cooking spray. 5. Air fry for about 10 minutes, flipping the salmon steaks halfway through, or until cooked to your preferred doneness. 6. Divide the salmon steaks among four plates and serve.

Golden Shrimp

Prep time: 20 minutes | Cook time: 7 minutes |
Serves 4

2 egg whites

½ cup coconut flour

1 cup Parmigiano-Reggiano,
grated

½ teaspoon celery seeds

½ teaspoon porcini powder

½ teaspoon onion powder

1 teaspoon garlic powder

½ teaspoon dried rosemary

½ teaspoon sea salt

½ teaspoon ground black
pepper

1½ pounds (680 g) shrimp,
deveined

1. Whisk the egg with coconut flour and Parmigiano-Reggiano. Add in seasonings and mix to combine well. 2. Dip your shrimp in the batter. Roll until they are covered on all sides. 3. Cook in the preheated air fryer at 390ºF (199ºC) for 5 to 7 minutes or until golden brown. Work in batches. Serve with lemon wedges if desired.

Coconut Cream Mackerel

Prep time: 10 minutes | Cook time: 6 minutes |
Serves 4

2 pounds (907 g) mackerel fillet

1 cup coconut cream

1 teaspoon ground coriander

1 teaspoon cumin seeds

1 garlic clove, peeled, chopped

1. Chop the mackerel roughly and sprinkle it with coconut cream, ground coriander, cumin seeds, and garlic. 2. Then put the fish in the air fryer and cook at 400ºF (204ºC) for 6 minutes.

Tortilla Shrimp Tacos

Prep time: 10 minutes | Cook time: 6 minutes |
Serves 4

Spicy Mayo:

3 tablespoons mayonnaise

1 tablespoon Louisiana-style
hot pepper sauce

Cilantro-Lime Slaw:

2 cups shredded green cabbage

½ small red onion, thinly sliced

1 small jalapeño, thinly sliced

2 tablespoons chopped fresh
cilantro

Juice of 1 lime

¼ teaspoon kosher salt

Shrimp:

1 large egg, beaten

1 cup crushed tortilla chips

24 jumbo shrimp (about 1
pound / 454 g), peeled and
deveined

⅛ teaspoon kosher salt

Cooking spray

8 corn tortillas, for serving

1. For the spicy mayo: In a small bowl, mix the mayonnaise and hot pepper sauce. 2. For the cilantro-lime slaw: In a large bowl, toss together the cabbage, onion, jalapeño, cilantro, lime juice, and salt to combine. Cover and refrigerate to chill. 3. For the shrimp: Place the egg in a shallow bowl and the crushed tortilla chips in another. Season the shrimp with the salt. Dip the shrimp in the egg, then in the crumbs, pressing gently to adhere. Place on a work surface and spray both sides with oil. 4. Preheat the air fryer to 360ºF (182ºC). 5. Working in batches, arrange a single layer of the shrimp in the air fryer basket. Air fry for 6 minutes, flipping halfway, until golden and cooked through in the center. 6. To serve, place 2 tortillas on each plate and top each with 3 shrimp. Top each taco with ¼ cup slaw, then drizzle with spicy mayo.

Confetti Salmon Burgers

Prep time: 10 minutes | Cook time: 12 minutes |
Serves 4

14 ounces (397 g) cooked fresh
or canned salmon, flaked with a
fork

¼ cup minced scallion, white
and light green parts only

¼ cup minced red bell pepper

¼ cup minced celery

2 small lemons

1 teaspoon crab boil seasoning
such as Old Bay

½ teaspoon kosher salt

½ teaspoon black pepper

1 egg, beaten

½ cup fresh bread crumbs

Vegetable oil, for spraying

1. In a large bowl, combine the salmon, vegetables, the zest and juice of 1 of the lemons, crab boil seasoning, salt, and pepper. Add the egg and bread crumbs and stir to combine. Form the mixture into 4 patties weighing approximately 5 ounces (142 g) each. Chill until firm, about 15 minutes. 2. Preheat the air fryer to 400ºF (204ºC). 3. Spray the salmon patties with oil on all sides and spray the air fryer basket to prevent sticking. Air fry for 12 minutes, flipping halfway through, until the burgers are browned and cooked through. Cut the remaining lemon into 4 wedges and serve with the burgers.

Crab Cake Sandwich

Prep time: 15 minutes | Cook time: 10 minutes | Serves 4

Crab Cakes:
½ cup panko bread crumbs
1 large egg, beaten
1 large egg white
1 tablespoon mayonnaise
1 teaspoon Dijon mustard
¼ cup minced fresh parsley
1 tablespoon fresh lemon juice
½ teaspoon Old Bay seasoning
⅛ teaspoon sweet paprika
⅛ teaspoon kosher salt
Freshly ground black pepper, to taste

10 ounces (283 g) lump crab meat
Cooking spray
Cajun Mayo:
¼ cup mayonnaise
1 tablespoon minced dill pickle
1 teaspoon fresh lemon juice
¾ teaspoon Cajun seasoning
For Serving:
4 Boston lettuce leaves
4 whole wheat potato buns or gluten-free buns

1. For the crab cakes: In a large bowl, combine the panko, whole egg, egg white, mayonnaise, mustard, parsley, lemon juice, Old Bay, paprika, salt, and pepper to taste and mix well. Fold in the crab meat, being careful not to over mix. Gently shape into 4 round patties, about ½ cup each, ¾ inch thick. Spray both sides with oil. 2. Preheat the air fryer to 370ºF (188ºC). 3. Working in batches, place the crab cakes in the air fryer basket. Air fry for about 10 minutes, flipping halfway, until the edges are golden. 4. Meanwhile, for the Cajun mayo: In a small bowl, combine the mayonnaise, pickle, lemon juice, and Cajun seasoning. 5. To serve: Place a lettuce leaf on each bun bottom and top with a crab cake and a generous tablespoon of Cajun mayonnaise. Add the bun top and serve.

Parmesan-Crusted Hake with Garlic Sauce

Prep time: 5 minutes | Cook time: 10 minutes | Serves 3

Fish:
6 tablespoons mayonnaise
1 tablespoon fresh lime juice
1 teaspoon Dijon mustard
1 cup grated Parmesan cheese
Salt, to taste
¼ teaspoon ground black pepper, or more to taste

3 hake fillets, patted dry
Nonstick cooking spray
Garlic Sauce:
¼ cup plain Greek yogurt
2 tablespoons olive oil
2 cloves garlic, minced
½ teaspoon minced tarragon leaves

1. Preheat the air fryer to 395ºF (202ºC). 2. Mix the mayo, lime juice, and mustard in a shallow bowl and whisk to combine. In another shallow bowl, stir together the grated Parmesan cheese, salt, and pepper. 3. Dredge each fillet in the mayo mixture, then roll them in the cheese mixture until they are evenly coated on both sides. 4. Spray the air fryer basket with nonstick cooking spray. Arrange the fillets in the basket and air fry for 10 minutes, or until

the fish flakes easily with a fork. Flip the fillets halfway through the cooking time. 5. Meanwhile, in a small bowl, whisk all the ingredients for the sauce until well incorporated. 6. Serve the fish warm alongside the sauce.

Mediterranean-Style Cod

Prep time: 5 minutes | Cook time: 12 minutes | Serves 4

4 (6 ounces / 170 g) cod fillets
3 tablespoons fresh lemon juice
1 tablespoon olive oil
¼ teaspoon salt

6 cherry tomatoes, halved
¼ cup pitted and sliced kalamata olives

1. Place cod into an ungreased round nonstick baking dish. Pour lemon juice into dish and drizzle cod with olive oil. Sprinkle with salt. Place tomatoes and olives around baking dish in between fillets. 2. Place dish into air fryer basket. Adjust the temperature to 350ºF (177ºC) and bake for 12 minutes, carefully turning cod halfway through cooking. Fillets will be lightly browned, easily flake, and have an internal temperature of at least 145ºF (63ºC) when done. Serve warm.

Thai Shrimp Skewers with Peanut Dipping Sauce

Prep time: 15 minutes | Cook time: 6 minutes | Serves 2

Salt and pepper, to taste
12 ounces (340 g) extra-large shrimp, peeled and deveined
1 tablespoon vegetable oil
1 teaspoon honey
½ teaspoon grated lime zest plus 1 tablespoon juice, plus lime wedges for serving

6 (6-inch) wooden skewers
3 tablespoons creamy peanut butter
3 tablespoons hot tap water
1 tablespoon chopped fresh cilantro
1 teaspoon fish sauce

1. Preheat the air fryer to 400ºF (204ºC). 2. Dissolve 2 tablespoons salt in 1 quart cold water in a large container. Add shrimp, cover, and refrigerate for 15 minutes. 3. Remove shrimp from brine and pat dry with paper towels. Whisk oil, honey, lime zest, and ¼ teaspoon pepper together in a large bowl. Add shrimp and toss to coat. Thread shrimp onto skewers, leaving about ¼ inch between each shrimp (3 or 4 shrimp per skewer). 4. Arrange 3 skewers in air fryer basket, parallel to each other and spaced evenly apart. Arrange remaining 3 skewers on top, perpendicular to the bottom layer. Air fry until shrimp are opaque throughout, 6 to 8 minutes, flipping and rotating skewers halfway through cooking. 5. Whisk peanut butter, hot tap water, lime juice, cilantro, and fish sauce together in a bowl until smooth. Serve skewers with peanut dipping sauce and lime wedges.

Tuna Steak

Prep time: 10 minutes | Cook time: 12 minutes |
Serves 4

1 pound (454 g) tuna steaks, boneless and cubed	1 tablespoon avocado oil
1 tablespoon mustard	1 tablespoon apple cider vinegar

1. Mix avocado oil with mustard and apple cider vinegar. 2. Then brush tuna steaks with mustard mixture and put in the air fryer basket. 3. Cook the fish at 360ºF (182ºC) for 6 minutes per side.

Seasoned Breaded Shrimp

Prep time: 15 minutes | Cook time: 10 to 15 minutes | Serves 4

2 teaspoons Old Bay seasoning, divided	deveined, with tails on
½ teaspoon garlic powder	2 large eggs
½ teaspoon onion powder	½ cup whole-wheat panko bread crumbs
1 pound (454 g) large shrimp,	Cooking spray

1. Preheat the air fryer to 380ºF (193ºC). 2. Spray the air fryer basket lightly with cooking spray. 3. In a medium bowl, mix together 1 teaspoon of Old Bay seasoning, garlic powder, and onion powder. Add the shrimp and toss with the seasoning mix to lightly coat. 4. In a separate small bowl, whisk the eggs with 1 teaspoon water. 5. In a shallow bowl, mix together the remaining 1 teaspoon Old Bay seasoning and the panko bread crumbs. 6. Dip each shrimp in the egg mixture and dredge in the bread crumb mixture to evenly coat. 7. Place the shrimp in the air fryer basket, in a single layer. Lightly spray the shrimp with cooking spray. You many need to cook the shrimp in batches. 8. Air fry for 10 to 15 minutes, or until the shrimp is cooked through and crispy, shaking the basket at 5-minute intervals to redistribute and evenly cook. 9. Serve immediately.

Tuna and Fruit Kebabs

Prep time: 15 minutes | Cook time: 8 to 12 minutes |
Serves 4

1 pound (454 g) tuna steaks, cut into 1-inch cubes	1 tablespoon honey
½ cup canned pineapple chunks, drained, juice reserved	2 teaspoons grated fresh ginger
½ cup large red grapes	1 teaspoon olive oil
	Pinch cayenne pepper

1. Thread the tuna, pineapple, and grapes on 8 bamboo or 4 metal skewers that fit in the air fryer. 2. In a small bowl, whisk the honey, 1 tablespoon of reserved pineapple juice, the ginger, olive oil, and cayenne. Brush this mixture over the kebabs. Let them stand for 10

minutes. 3. Air fry the kebabs at 370ºF (188ºC) for 8 to 12 minutes, or until the tuna reaches an internal temperature of at least 145ºF (63ºC) on a meat thermometer, and the fruit is tender and glazed, brushing once with the remaining sauce. Discard any remaining marinade. Serve immediately.

Calamari with Hot Sauce

Prep time: 10 minutes | Cook time: 6 minutes |
Serves 2

10 ounces (283 g) calamari, trimmed	2 tablespoons keto hot sauce
	1 tablespoon avocado oil

1. Slice the calamari and sprinkle with avocado oil. 2. Put the calamari in the air fryer and cook at 400ºF (204ºC) for 3 minutes per side. 3. Then transfer the calamari in the serving plate and sprinkle with hot sauce.

Lime Lobster Tails

Prep time: 10 minutes | Cook time: 6 minutes |
Serves 4

4 lobster tails, peeled	½ teaspoon dried basil
2 tablespoons lime juice	½ teaspoon coconut oil, melted

1. Mix lobster tails with lime juice, dried basil, and coconut oil. 2. Put the lobster tails in the air fryer and cook at 380ºF (193ºC) for 6 minutes.

Scallops in Lemon-Butter Sauce

Prep time: 10 minutes | Cook time: 6 minutes |
Serves 2

8 large dry sea scallops (about ¾ pound / 340 g)	2 tablespoons chopped flat-leaf parsley
Salt and freshly ground black pepper, to taste	1 tablespoon fresh lemon juice
2 tablespoons olive oil	2 teaspoons capers, drained and chopped
2 tablespoons unsalted butter, melted	1 teaspoon grated lemon zest
	1 clove garlic, minced

1. Preheat the air fryer to 400ºF (204ºC). 2. Use a paper towel to pat the scallops dry. Sprinkle lightly with salt and pepper. Brush with the olive oil. Arrange the scallops in a single layer in the air fryer basket. Pausing halfway through the cooking time to turn the scallops, air fry for about 6 minutes until firm and opaque. 3. Meanwhile, in a small bowl, combine the oil, butter, parsley, lemon juice, capers, lemon zest, and garlic. Drizzle over the scallops just before serving.

Creamy Haddock

Prep time: 10 minutes | Cook time: 8 minutes |
Serves 4

1 pound (454 g) haddock fillet
1 teaspoon cayenne pepper
1 teaspoon salt
1 teaspoon coconut oil
½ cup heavy cream

1. Grease a baking pan with coconut oil. 2. Then put haddock fillet inside and sprinkle it with cayenne pepper, salt, and heavy cream. 3. Put the baking pan in the air fryer basket and cook at 375ºF (191ºC) for 8 minutes.

Roasted Salmon Fillets

Prep time: 5 minutes | Cook time: 10 minutes |
Serves 2

2 (8 ounces / 227 g) skin-on salmon fillets, 1½ inches thick
1 teaspoon vegetable oil
Salt and pepper, to taste
Vegetable oil spray

1. Preheat the air fryer to 400ºF (204ºC). 2. Make foil sling for air fryer basket by folding 1 long sheet of aluminum foil so it is 4 inches wide. Lay sheet of foil widthwise across basket, pressing foil into and up sides of basket. Fold excess foil as needed so that edges of foil are flush with top of basket. Lightly spray foil and basket with vegetable oil spray. 3. Pat salmon dry with paper towels, rub with oil, and season with salt and pepper. Arrange fillets skin side down on sling in prepared basket, spaced evenly apart. Air fry salmon until center is still translucent when checked with the tip of a paring knife and registers 125ºF (52ºC) (for medium-rare), 10 to 14 minutes, using sling to rotate fillets halfway through cooking. 4. Using the sling, carefully remove salmon from air fryer. Slide fish spatula along underside of fillets and transfer to individual serving plates, leaving skin behind. Serve.

Parmesan Lobster Tails

Prep time: 5 minutes | Cook time: 7 minutes | Serves 4

4 (4 ounces / 113 g) lobster tails
2 tablespoons salted butter, melted
1½ teaspoons Cajun seasoning, divided
¼ teaspoon salt
¼ teaspoon ground black pepper
¼ cup grated Parmesan cheese
½ ounce (14 g) plain pork rinds, finely crushed

1. Cut lobster tails open carefully with a pair of scissors and gently pull meat away from shells, resting meat on top of shells. 2. Brush lobster meat with butter and sprinkle with 1 teaspoon Cajun seasoning, ¼ teaspoon per tail. 3. In a small bowl, mix remaining Cajun seasoning, salt, pepper, Parmesan, and pork rinds. Gently

press ¼ mixture onto meat on each lobster tail. 4. Carefully place tails into ungreased air fryer basket. Adjust the temperature to 400ºF (204ºC) and air fry for 7 minutes. Lobster tails will be crispy and golden on top and have an internal temperature of at least 145ºF (63ºC) when done. Serve warm.

Chili Prawns

Prep time: 10 minutes | Cook time: 8 minutes |
Serves 2

8 prawns, cleaned
Salt and black pepper, to taste
½ teaspoon ground cayenne pepper
½ teaspoon garlic powder
½ teaspoon ground cumin
½ teaspoon red chili flakes
Cooking spray

1. Preheat the air fryer to 340ºF (171ºC). Spritz the air fryer basket with cooking spray. 2. Toss the remaining ingredients in a large bowl until the prawns are well coated. 3. Spread the coated prawns evenly in the basket and spray them with cooking spray. 4. Air fry for 8 minutes, flipping the prawns halfway through, or until the prawns are pink. 5. Remove the prawns from the basket to a plate.

Trout Amandine with Lemon Butter Sauce

Prep time: 20 minutes | Cook time:8 minutes |
Serves 4

Trout Amandine:
⅔ cup toasted almonds
⅓ cup grated Parmesan cheese
1 teaspoon salt
½ teaspoon freshly ground black pepper
2 tablespoons butter, melted
4 (4 ounces / 113 g) trout fillets, or salmon fillets
Cooking spray
Lemon Butter Sauce:
8 tablespoons (1 stick) butter, melted
2 tablespoons freshly squeezed lemon juice
½ teaspoon Worcestershire sauce
½ teaspoon salt
½ teaspoon freshly ground black pepper
¼ teaspoon hot sauce

1. In a blender or food processor, pulse the almonds for 5 to 10 seconds until finely processed. Transfer to a shallow bowl and whisk in the Parmesan cheese, salt, and pepper. Place the melted butter in another shallow bowl. 2. One at a time, dip the fish in the melted butter, then the almond mixture, coating thoroughly. 3. Preheat the air fryer to 300ºF (149ºC). Line the air fryer basket with parchment paper. 4. Place the coated fish on the parchment and spritz with oil. 5. Bake for 4 minutes. Flip the fish, spritz it with oil, and bake for 4 minutes more until the fish flakes easily with a fork. 6. In a small bowl, whisk the butter, lemon juice, Worcestershire sauce, salt, pepper, and hot sauce until blended. 7. Serve with the fish.

BBQ Shrimp with Creole Butter Sauce

Prep time: 10 minutes | Cook time: 12 to 15 minutes | Serves 4

6 tablespoons unsalted butter	1 teaspoon Creole seasoning
⅓ cup Worcestershire sauce	1½ pounds (680 g) large
3 cloves garlic, minced	uncooked shrimp, peeled and
Juice of 1 lemon	deveined
1 teaspoon paprika	2 tablespoons fresh parsley

1. Preheat the air fryer to 370ºF (188ºC). 2. In a large microwave-safe bowl, combine the butter, Worcestershire, and garlic. Microwave on high for 1 to 2 minutes until the butter is melted. Stir in the lemon juice, paprika, and Creole seasoning. Add the shrimp and toss until thoroughly coated. 3. Transfer the mixture to a casserole dish or pan that fits in your air fryer. Pausing halfway through the cooking time to turn the shrimp, air fry for 12 to 15 minutes, until the shrimp are cooked through. Top with the parsley just before serving.

Parmesan Mackerel with Coriander

Prep time: 10 minutes | Cook time: 7 minutes | Serves 2

12 ounces (340 g) mackerel fillet	grated
	1 teaspoon ground coriander
2 ounces (57 g) Parmesan,	1 tablespoon olive oil

1. Sprinkle the mackerel fillet with olive oil and put it in the air fryer basket. 2. Top the fish with ground coriander and Parmesan. 3. Cook the fish at 390ºF (199ºC) for 7 minutes.

Southern-Style Catfish

Prep time: 10 minutes | Cook time: 12 minutes | Serves 4

4 (7 ounces / 198 g) catfish fillets	almond flour
	2 teaspoons Old Bay seasoning
⅓ cup heavy whipping cream	½ teaspoon salt
1 tablespoon lemon juice	¼ teaspoon ground black
1 cup blanched finely ground	pepper

1. Place catfish fillets into a large bowl with cream and pour in lemon juice. Stir to coat. 2. In a separate large bowl, mix flour and Old Bay seasoning. 3. Remove each fillet and gently shake off excess cream. Sprinkle with salt and pepper. Press each fillet gently into flour mixture on both sides to coat. 4. Place fillets into ungreased air fryer basket. Adjust the temperature to 400ºF (204ºC) and air fry for 12 minutes, turning fillets halfway through cooking. Catfish will be golden brown and have an internal temperature of at least 145ºF (63ºC) when done. Serve warm.

Tuna Nuggets in Hoisin Sauce

Prep time: 15 minutes | Cook time: 5 to 7 minutes | Serves 4

½ cup hoisin sauce	½ small onion, quartered and
2 tablespoons rice wine vinegar	thinly sliced
2 teaspoons sesame oil	8 ounces (227 g) fresh tuna, cut
1 teaspoon garlic powder	into 1-inch cubes
2 teaspoons dried lemongrass	Cooking spray
¼ teaspoon red pepper flakes	3 cups cooked jasmine rice

1. Mix the hoisin sauce, vinegar, sesame oil, and seasonings together. 2. Stir in the onions and tuna nuggets. 3. Spray a baking pan with nonstick spray and pour in tuna mixture. 4. Roast at 390ºF (199ºC) for 3 minutes. Stir gently. 5. Cook 2 minutes and stir again, checking for doneness. Tuna should be barely cooked through, just beginning to flake and still very moist. If necessary, continue cooking and stirring in 1-minute intervals until done. 6. Serve warm over hot jasmine rice.

Mouthwatering Cod over Creamy Leek Noodles

Prep time: 10 minutes | Cook time: 24 minutes | Serves 4

1 small leek, sliced into long thin noodles (about 2 cups)	Coating:
	¼ cup grated Parmesan cheese
½ cup heavy cream	2 tablespoons mayonnaise
2 cloves garlic, minced	2 tablespoons unsalted butter,
1 teaspoon fine sea salt, divided	softened
4 (4 ounces / 113 g) cod fillets (about 1 inch thick)	1 tablespoon chopped fresh thyme, or ½ teaspoon dried
½ teaspoon ground black pepper	thyme leaves, plus more for garnish

1. Preheat the air fryer to 350ºF (177ºC). 2. Place the leek noodles in a casserole dish or a pan that will fit in your air fryer. 3. In a small bowl, stir together the cream, garlic, and ½ teaspoon of the salt. Pour the mixture over the leeks and cook in the air fryer for 10 minutes, or until the leeks are very tender. 4. Pat the fish dry and season with the remaining ½ teaspoon of salt and the pepper. When the leeks are ready, open the air fryer and place the fish fillets on top of the leeks. Air fry for 8 to 10 minutes, until the fish flakes easily with a fork (the thicker the fillets, the longer this will take). 5. While the fish cooks, make the coating: In a small bowl, combine the Parmesan, mayo, butter, and thyme. 6. When the fish is ready, remove it from the air fryer and increase the heat to 425ºF (218ºC) (or as high as your air fryer can go). Spread the fillets with a ½-inch-thick to ¾-inch-thick layer of the coating. 7. Place the fish back in the air fryer and air fry for 3 to 4 minutes, until the coating browns. 8. Garnish with fresh or dried thyme, if desired. Store leftovers in an airtight container in the refrigerator for up to 3 days. Reheat in a casserole dish in a preheated 350ºF (177ºC) air fryer for 6 minutes, or until heated through.

Sweet Tilapia Fillets

Prep time: 5 minutes | Cook time: 14 minutes |

Serves 4

2 tablespoons erythritol	4 tilapia fillets, boneless
1 tablespoon apple cider vinegar	1 teaspoon olive oil

1. Mix apple cider vinegar with olive oil and erythritol. 2. Then rub the tilapia fillets with the sweet mixture and put in the air fryer basket in one layer. 3. Cook the fish at 360°F (182°C) for 7 minutes per side.

Maple Balsamic Glazed Salmon

Prep time: 5 minutes | Cook time: 10 minutes |

Serves 4

4 (6 ounces / 170 g) fillets of salmon	Vegetable oil
	¼ cup pure maple syrup
Salt and freshly ground black pepper, to taste	3 tablespoons balsamic vinegar
	1 teaspoon Dijon mustard

1. Preheat the air fryer to 400°F (204°C). 2. Season the salmon well with salt and freshly ground black pepper. Spray or brush the bottom of the air fryer basket with vegetable oil and place the salmon fillets inside. Air fry the salmon for 5 minutes. 3. While the salmon is air frying, combine the maple syrup, balsamic vinegar and Dijon mustard in a small saucepan over medium heat and stir to blend well. Let the mixture simmer while the fish is cooking. It should start to thicken slightly, but keep your eye on it so it doesn't burn. 4. Brush the glaze on the salmon fillets and air fry for an additional 5 minutes. The salmon should feel firm to the touch when finished and the glaze should be nicely browned on top. Brush a little more glaze on top before removing and serving with rice and vegetables, or a nice green salad.

Cheesy Tuna Patties

Prep time: 5 minutes | Cook time: 17 to 18 minutes |

Serves 4

Tuna Patties:	pepper, to taste
1 pound (454 g) canned tuna, drained	1 tablespoon sesame oil
	Cheese Sauce:
1 egg, whisked	1 tablespoon butter
2 tablespoons shallots, minced	1 cup beer
1 garlic clove, minced	2 tablespoons grated Colby
1 cup grated Romano cheese	cheese
Sea salt and ground black	

1. Mix together the canned tuna, whisked egg, shallots, garlic,

cheese, salt, and pepper in a large bowl and stir to incorporate. 2. Divide the tuna mixture into four equal portions and form each portion into a patty with your hands. Refrigerate the patties for 2 hours. 3. When ready, brush both sides of each patty with sesame oil. 4. Preheat the air fryer to 360°F (182°C). 5. Place the patties in the air fryer basket and bake for 14 minutes, flipping the patties halfway through, or until lightly browned and cooked through. 6. Meanwhile, melt the butter in a pan over medium heat. 7. Pour in the beer and whisk constantly, or until it begins to bubble. 8. Add the grated Colby cheese and mix well. Continue cooking for 3 to 4 minutes, or until the cheese melts. Remove the patties from the basket to a plate. Drizzle them with the cheese sauce and serve immediately.

Salmon Fritters with Zucchini

Prep time: 15 minutes | Cook time: 12 minutes |

Serves 4

2 tablespoons almond flour	diced
1 zucchini, grated	1 teaspoon avocado oil
1 egg, beaten	½ teaspoon ground black
6 ounces (170 g) salmon fillet,	pepper

1. Mix almond flour with zucchini, egg, salmon, and ground black pepper. 2. Then make the fritters from the salmon mixture. 3. Sprinkle the air fryer basket with avocado oil and put the fritters inside. 4. Cook the fritters at 375°F (191°C) for 6 minutes per side.

Roasted Fish with Almond-Lemon Crumbs

Prep time: 10 minutes | Cook time: 7 to 8 minutes |

Serves 4

½ cup raw whole almonds	Freshly ground black pepper, to
1 scallion, finely chopped	taste
Grated zest and juice of 1 lemon	4 (6 ounces / 170 g each) skinless fish fillets
½ tablespoon extra-virgin olive oil	Cooking spray
	1 teaspoon Dijon mustard
¾ teaspoon kosher salt, divided	

1. In a food processor, pulse the almonds to coarsely chop. Transfer to a small bowl and add the scallion, lemon zest, and olive oil. Season with ¼ teaspoon of the salt and pepper to taste and mix to combine. 2. Spray the top of the fish with oil and squeeze the lemon juice over the fish. Season with the remaining ½ teaspoon salt and pepper to taste. Spread the mustard on top of the fish. Dividing evenly, press the almond mixture onto the top of the fillets to adhere. 3. Preheat the air fryer to 375°F (191°C). 4. Working in batches, place the fillets in the air fryer basket in a single layer. Air fry for 7 to 8 minutes, until the crumbs start to brown and the fish is cooked through. 5. Serve immediately.

Shrimp Dejonghe Skewers

Prep time: 10 minutes | Cook time: 15 minutes | Serves 4

2 teaspoons sherry	1 teaspoon kosher salt
3 tablespoons unsalted butter, melted	Pinch of cayenne pepper
1 cup panko bread crumbs	1½ pounds (680 g) shrimp, peeled and deveined
3 cloves garlic, minced	Vegetable oil, for spraying
⅓ cup minced flat-leaf parsley, plus more for garnish	Lemon wedges, for serving

1. Stir the sherry and melted butter together in a shallow bowl or pie plate and whisk until combined. Set aside. Whisk together the panko, garlic, parsley, salt, and cayenne pepper on a large plate or shallow bowl. 2. Thread the shrimp onto metal skewers designed for the air fryer or bamboo skewers, 3 to 4 per skewer. Dip 1 shrimp skewer in the butter mixture, then dredge in the panko mixture until each shrimp is lightly coated. Place the skewer on a plate or rimmed baking sheet and repeat the process with the remaining skewers. 3. Preheat the air fryer to 350ºF (177ºC). Arrange 4 skewers in the air fryer basket. Spray the skewers with oil and air fry for 8 minutes, until the bread crumbs are golden brown and the shrimp are cooked through. Transfer the cooked skewers to a serving plate and keep warm while cooking the remaining 4 skewers in the air fryer. 4. Sprinkle the cooked skewers with additional fresh parsley and serve with lemon wedges if desired.

Oyster Po'Boy

Prep time: 20 minutes | Cook time: 5 minutes | Serves 4

¾ cup all-purpose flour	1 (12-inch) French baguette, quartered and sliced horizontally
¼ cup yellow cornmeal	
1 tablespoon Cajun seasoning	
1 teaspoon salt	Tartar Sauce, as needed
2 large eggs, beaten	2 cups shredded lettuce, divided
1 teaspoon hot sauce	2 tomatoes, cut into slices
1 pound (454 g) pre-shucked oysters	Cooking spray

1. In a shallow bowl, whisk the flour, cornmeal, Cajun seasoning, and salt until blended. In a second shallow bowl, whisk together the eggs and hot sauce. 2. One at a time, dip the oysters in the cornmeal mixture, the eggs, and again in the cornmeal, coating thoroughly. 3. Preheat the air fryer to 400ºF (204ºC). Line the air fryer basket with parchment paper. 4. Place the oysters on the parchment and spritz with oil. 5. Air fry for 2 minutes. Shake the basket, spritz the oysters with oil, and air fry for 3 minutes more until lightly browned and crispy. 6. Spread each sandwich half with Tartar Sauce. Assemble the po'boys by layering each sandwich with fried oysters, ½ cup shredded lettuce, and 2 tomato slices. 7. Serve immediately.

Tuna with Herbs

Prep time: 20 minutes | Cook time: 17 minutes | Serves 4

1 tablespoon butter, melted	Sea salt and ground black pepper, to taste
1 medium-sized leek, thinly sliced	
1 tablespoon chicken stock	½ teaspoon dried rosemary
1 tablespoon dry white wine	½ teaspoon dried basil
1 pound (454 g) tuna	½ teaspoon dried thyme
½ teaspoon red pepper flakes, crushed	2 small ripe tomatoes, puréed
	1 cup Parmesan cheese, grated

1. Melt ½ tablespoon of butter in a sauté pan over medium-high heat. Now, cook the leek and garlic until tender and aromatic. Add the stock and wine to deglaze the pan. 2. Preheat the air fryer to 370ºF (188ºC). 3. Grease a casserole dish with the remaining ½ tablespoon of melted butter. Place the fish in the casserole dish. Add the seasonings. Top with the sautéed leek mixture. Add the tomato purée. Cook for 10 minutes in the preheated air fryer. Top with grated Parmesan cheese; cook an additional 7 minutes until the crumbs are golden. Bon appétit!

Fish Sandwich with Tartar Sauce

Prep time: 10 minutes | Cook time: 17 minutes | Serves 2

Tartar Sauce:	pepper
½ cup mayonnaise	Fish:
2 tablespoons dried minced onion	2 tablespoons all-purpose flour
1 dill pickle spear, finely chopped	1 egg, lightly beaten
	1 cup panko
2 teaspoons pickle juice	2 teaspoons lemon pepper
¼ teaspoon salt	2 tilapia fillets
⅛ teaspoon ground black	Cooking spray
	2 hoagie rolls

1. Preheat the air fryer to 400ºF (204ºC). 2. In a small bowl, combine the mayonnaise, dried minced onion, pickle, pickle juice, salt, and pepper. 3. Whisk to combine and chill in the refrigerator while you make the fish. 4. Place a parchment liner in the air fryer basket. 5. Scoop the flour out onto a plate; set aside. 6. Put the beaten egg in a medium shallow bowl. 7. On another plate, mix to combine the panko and lemon pepper. 8. Dredge the tilapia fillets in the flour, then dip in the egg, and then press into the panko mixture. 9. Place the prepared fillets on the liner in the air fryer in a single layer. 10. Spray lightly with cooking spray and air fry for 8 minutes. Carefully flip the fillets, spray with more cooking spray, and air fry for an additional 9 minutes, until golden and crispy. 11. Place each cooked fillet in a hoagie roll, top with a little bit of tartar sauce, and serve.

Cajun Catfish Cakes with Cheese

Prep time: 5 minutes | Cook time: 35 minutes |

Serves 4

2 catfish fillets	½ cup buttermilk
3 ounces (85 g) butter	1 teaspoon baking powder
1 cup shredded Parmesan cheese	1 teaspoon baking soda
	1 teaspoon Cajun seasoning
1 cup shredded Swiss cheese	

1. Bring a pot of salted water to a boil. Add the catfish fillets to the boiling water and let them boil for 5 minutes until they become opaque. 2. Remove the fillets from the pot to a mixing bowl and flake them into small pieces with a fork. 3. Add the remaining ingredients to the bowl of fish and stir until well incorporated. 4. Divide the fish mixture into 12 equal portions and shape each portion into a patty. 5. Preheat the air fryer to 380ºF (193ºC). 6. Arrange the patties in the air fryer basket and air fry in batches for 15 minutes until golden brown and cooked through. Flip the patties halfway through the cooking time. 7. Let the patties sit for 5 minutes and serve.

Almond Catfish

Prep time: 10 minutes | Cook time: 12 minutes |

Serves 4

2 pounds (907 g) catfish fillet	1 teaspoon salt
½ cup almond flour	1 teaspoon avocado oil
2 eggs, beaten	

1. Sprinkle the catfish fillet with salt and dip in the eggs. 2. Then coat the fish in the almond flour and put in the air fryer basket. Sprinkle the fish with avocado oil. 3. Cook the fish for 6 minutes per side at 380ºF (193ºC).

Paprika Crab Burgers

Prep time: 30 minutes | Cook time: 14 minutes |

Serves 3

2 eggs, beaten	10 ounces (283 g) crab meat
1 shallot, chopped	1 teaspoon smoked paprika
2 garlic cloves, crushed	½ teaspoon ground black pepper
1 tablespoon olive oil	
1 teaspoon yellow mustard	Sea salt, to taste
1 teaspoon fresh cilantro, chopped	¾ cup Parmesan cheese

1. In a mixing bowl, thoroughly combine the eggs, shallot, garlic,

olive oil, mustard, cilantro, crab meat, paprika, black pepper, and salt. Mix until well combined. 2. Shape the mixture into 6 patties. Roll the crab patties over grated Parmesan cheese, coating well on all sides. Place in your refrigerator for 2 hours. 3. Spritz the crab patties with cooking oil on both sides. Cook in the preheated air fryer at 360ºF (182ºC) for 14 minutes. Serve on dinner rolls if desired. Bon appétit!

Pecan-Crusted Tilapia

Prep time: 10minutes | Cook time: 10 minutes |

Serves 4

1¼ cups pecans	tablespoons water
¾ cup panko bread crumbs	4 (6 ounces/ 170 g) tilapia fillets
½ cup all-purpose flour	Vegetable oil, for spraying
2 tablespoons Cajun seasoning	Lemon wedges, for serving
2 eggs, beaten with 2	

1. Grind the pecans in the food processor until they resemble coarse meal. Combine the ground pecans with the panko on a plate. On a second plate, combine the flour and Cajun seasoning. Dry the tilapia fillets using paper towels and dredge them in the flour mixture, shaking off any excess. Dip the fillets in the egg mixture and then dredge them in the pecan and panko mixture, pressing the coating onto the fillets. Place the breaded fillets on a plate or rack. 2. Preheat the air fryer to 375ºF (191ºC). Spray both sides of the breaded fillets with oil. Carefully transfer 2 of the fillets to the air fryer basket and air fry for 9 to 10 minutes, flipping once halfway through, until the flesh is opaque and flaky. Repeat with the remaining fillets. 3. Serve immediately with lemon wedges.

Lemony Salmon

Prep time: 30 minutes | Cook time: 10 minutes |

Serves 4

1½ pounds (680 g) salmon steak	Fresh chopped chives, for garnish
½ teaspoon grated lemon zest	½ cup dry white wine
Freshly cracked mixed peppercorns, to taste	½ teaspoon fresh cilantro, chopped
⅓ cup lemon juice	Fine sea salt, to taste

1. To prepare the marinade, place all ingredients, except for salmon steak and chives, in a deep pan. Bring to a boil over medium-high flame until it has reduced by half. Allow it to cool down. 2. After that, allow salmon steak to marinate in the refrigerator approximately 40 minutes. Discard the marinade and transfer the fish steak to the preheated air fryer. 3. Air fry at 400ºF (204ºC) for 9 to 10 minutes. To finish, brush hot fish steaks with the reserved marinade, garnish with fresh chopped chives, and serve right away!

Crab Cakes

Prep time: 10 minutes | Cook time: 10 minutes |
Serves 4

2 (6 ounces / 170 g) cans lump
crab meat
¼ cup blanched finely ground
almond flour
1 large egg
2 tablespoons full-fat
mayonnaise

½ teaspoon Dijon mustard
½ tablespoon lemon juice
½ medium green bell pepper,
seeded and chopped
¼ cup chopped green onion
½ teaspoon Old Bay seasoning

1. In a large bowl, combine all ingredients. Form into four balls and flatten into patties. Place patties into the air fryer basket. 2. Adjust the temperature to 350ºF (177ºC) and air fry for 10 minutes. 3. Flip patties halfway through the cooking time. Serve warm.

Tandoori Shrimp

Prep time: 25 minutes | Cook time: 6 minutes |
Serves 4

1 pound (454 g) jumbo raw
shrimp (21 to 25 count), peeled
and deveined
1 tablespoon minced fresh
ginger
3 cloves garlic, minced
¼ cup chopped fresh cilantro or
parsley, plus more for garnish

1 teaspoon ground turmeric
1 teaspoon garam masala
1 teaspoon smoked paprika
1 teaspoon kosher salt
½ to 1 teaspoon cayenne pepper
2 tablespoons olive oil (for
Paleo) or melted ghee
2 teaspoons fresh lemon juice

1. In a large bowl, combine the shrimp, ginger, garlic, cilantro, turmeric, garam masala, paprika, salt, and cayenne. Toss well to coat. Add the oil or ghee and toss again. Marinate at room temperature for 15 minutes, or cover and refrigerate for up to 8 hours. 2. Place the shrimp in a single layer in the air fryer basket. Set the air fryer to 325ºF (163ºC) for 6 minutes. Transfer the shrimp to a serving platter. Cover and let the shrimp finish cooking in the residual heat, about 5 minutes. 3. Sprinkle the shrimp with the lemon juice and toss to coat. Garnish with additional cilantro and serve.

Shrimp Curry

Prep time: 30 minutes | Cook time: 10 minutes |
Serves 4

¾ cup unsweetened full-fat
coconut milk
¼ cup finely chopped yellow
onion
2 teaspoons garam masala

1 tablespoon minced fresh
ginger
1 tablespoon minced garlic
1 teaspoon ground turmeric
1 teaspoon salt

¼ to ½ teaspoon cayenne
pepper
1 pound (454 g) raw shrimp
(21 to 25 count), peeled and

deveined
2 teaspoons chopped fresh
cilantro

1. In a large bowl, stir together the coconut milk, onion, garam masala, ginger, garlic, turmeric, salt and cayenne, until well blended. 2. Add the shrimp and toss until coated with sauce on all sides. Marinate at room temperature for 30 minutes. 3. Transfer the shrimp and marinade to a baking pan. Place the pan in the air fryer basket. Set the air fryer to 375ºF (191ºC) for 10 minutes, stirring halfway through the cooking time. 4. Transfer the shrimp to a serving bowl or platter. Sprinkle with the cilantro and serve.

Lemony Shrimp

Prep time: 10 minutes | Cook time: 7 to 8 minutes |
Serves 4

1 pound (454 g) shrimp,
deveined
4 tablespoons olive oil
1½ tablespoons lemon juice
1½ tablespoons fresh parsley,
roughly chopped

2 cloves garlic, finely minced
1 teaspoon crushed red pepper
flakes, or more to taste
Garlic pepper, to taste
Sea salt flakes, to taste

1. Preheat the air fryer to 385ºF (196ºC). 2. Toss all the ingredients in a large bowl until the shrimp are coated on all sides. 3. Arrange the shrimp in the air fryer basket and air fry for 7 to 8 minutes, or until the shrimp are pink and cooked through. 4. Serve warm.

Lemony Shrimp and Zucchini

Prep time: 15 minutes | Cook time: 7 to 8 minutes |
Serves 4

1¼ pounds (567 g) extra-
large raw shrimp, peeled and
deveined
2 medium zucchini (about 8
ounces / 227 g each), halved
lengthwise and cut into ½-inch-
thick slices
1½ tablespoons olive oil

½ teaspoon garlic salt
1½ teaspoons dried oregano
⅛ teaspoon crushed red pepper
flakes (optional)
Juice of ½ lemon
1 tablespoon chopped fresh
mint
1 tablespoon chopped fresh dill

1. Preheat the air fryer to 350ºF (177ºC). 2. In a large bowl, combine the shrimp, zucchini, oil, garlic salt, oregano, and pepper flakes (if using) and toss to coat. 3. Working in batches, arrange a single layer of the shrimp and zucchini in the air fryer basket. Air fry for 7 to 8 minutes, shaking the basket halfway, until the zucchini is golden and the shrimp are cooked through. 4. Transfer to a serving dish and tent with foil while you air fry the remaining shrimp and zucchini. 5. Top with the lemon juice, mint, and dill and serve.

Bacon Halibut Steak

Prep time: 15 minutes | Cook time: 10 minutes | Serves 4

24 ounces (680 g) halibut steaks (6 ounces / 170 g each fillet)

1 teaspoon avocado oil

1 teaspoon ground black pepper

4 ounces bacon, sliced

1. Sprinkle the halibut steaks with avocado oil and ground black pepper. 2. Then wrap the fish in the bacon slices and put in the air fryer. 3. Cook the fish at 390ºF (199ºC) for 5 minutes per side.

Scallops Gratiné with Parmesan

Prep time: 10 minutes | Cook time: 9 minutes | Serves 2

Scallops:

½ cup half-and-half

½ cup grated Parmesan cheese

¼ cup thinly sliced green onions

¼ cup chopped fresh parsley

3 cloves garlic, minced

½ teaspoon kosher salt

½ teaspoon black pepper

1 pound (454 g) sea scallops

Topping:

¼ cup crushed pork rinds or panko bread crumbs

¼ cup grated Parmesan cheese

Vegetable oil spray

For Serving:

Lemon wedges

Crusty French bread (optional)

1. For the scallops: In a baking pan, combine the half-and-half, cheese, green onions, parsley, garlic, salt, and pepper. Stir in the scallops. 2. For the topping: In a small bowl, combine the pork rinds or bread crumbs and cheese. Sprinkle evenly over the scallops. Spray the topping with vegetable oil spray. 3. Place the pan in the air fryer basket. Set the air fryer to 325ºF (163ºC) for 6 minutes. Set the air fryer to 400ºF (204ºC) for 3 minutes until the topping has browned. 4. To serve: Squeeze the lemon wedges over the gratin and serve with crusty French bread, if desired.

Dark Chocolate and Cranberry Granola Bars

Prep time: 5 minutes | Cook time: 15 minutes |

Serves 6

2 cups certified gluten-free quick oats	3 tablespoons unsweetened shredded coconut
2 tablespoons sugar-free dark chocolate chunks	½ cup raw honey
2 tablespoons unsweetened dried cranberries	1 teaspoon ground cinnamon
	⅛ teaspoon salt
	2 tablespoons olive oil

1. Preheat the air fryer to 360°F(182°C). Line an 8-by-8-inch baking dish with parchment paper that comes up the side so you can lift it out after cooking. 2. In a large bowl, mix together all of the ingredients until well combined. 3. Press the oat mixture into the pan in an even layer. 4. Place the pan into the air fryer basket and bake for 15 minutes. 5. Remove the pan from the air fryer, and lift the granola cake out of the pan using the edges of the parchment paper. 6. Allow to cool for 5 minutes before slicing into 6 equal bars. 7. Serve immediately, or wrap in plastic wrap and store at room temperature for up to 1 week.

Beef and Mango Skewers

Prep time: 10 minutes | Cook time: 4 to 7 minutes |

Serves 4

¾ pound (340 g) beef sirloin tip, cut into 1-inch cubes	½ teaspoon dried marjoram
2 tablespoons balsamic vinegar	Pinch of salt
1 tablespoon olive oil	Freshly ground black pepper, to taste
1 tablespoon honey	1 mango

1. Preheat the air fryer to 390°F (199°C). 2. Put the beef cubes in a medium bowl and add the balsamic vinegar, olive oil, honey, marjoram, salt, and pepper. Mix well, then massage the marinade into the beef with your hands. Set aside. 3. To prepare the mango, stand it on end and cut the skin off, using a sharp knife. Then carefully cut around the oval pit to remove the flesh. Cut the mango into 1-inch cubes. 4. Thread metal skewers alternating with three beef cubes and two mango cubes. 5. Roast the skewers in the air fryer basket for 4 to 7 minutes, or until the beef is browned and at least 145°F (63°C). 6. Serve hot.

Browned Ricotta with Capers and Lemon

Prep time: 10 minutes | Cook time: 8 to 10 minutes |

Serves 4 to 6

1½ cups whole milk ricotta cheese	1 teaspoon finely chopped fresh rosemary
2 tablespoons extra-virgin olive oil	Pinch crushed red pepper flakes
2 tablespoons capers, rinsed	Salt and freshly ground black pepper, to taste
Zest of 1 lemon, plus more for garnish	1 tablespoon grated Parmesan cheese

1. Preheat the air fryer to 380°F (193°C). 2. In a mixing bowl, stir together the ricotta cheese, olive oil, capers, lemon zest, rosemary, red pepper flakes, salt, and pepper until well combined. 3. Spread the mixture evenly in a baking dish and place it in the air fryer basket. 4. Air fry for 8 to 10 minutes until the top is nicely browned. 5. Remove from the basket and top with a sprinkle of grated Parmesan cheese. 6. Garnish with the lemon zest and serve warm.

Taco-Spiced Chickpeas

Prep time: 5 minutes | Cook time: 17 minutes |

Serves 3

Oil, for spraying	½ teaspoon ground cumin
1 (15½-ounce / 439-g) can chickpeas, drained	½ teaspoon salt
1 teaspoon chili powder	½ teaspoon granulated garlic
	2 teaspoons lime juice

1. Line the air fryer basket with parchment and spray lightly with oil. Place the chickpeas in the prepared basket. 2. Air fry at 390°F (199°C) for 17 minutes, shaking or stirring the chickpeas and spraying lightly with oil every 5 to 7 minutes. 3. In a small bowl, mix together the chili powder, cumin, salt, and garlic. 4. When 2 to 3 minutes of cooking time remain, sprinkle half of the seasoning mix over the chickpeas. Finish cooking. 5. Transfer the chickpeas to a medium bowl and toss with the remaining seasoning mix and the lime juice. Serve immediately.

Crispy Phyllo Artichoke Triangles

Prep time: 15 minutes | Cook time: 9 to 12 minutes | Makes 18 triangles

¼ cup Ricotta cheese	cheese
1 egg white	½ teaspoon dried thyme
⅓ cup minced and drained	6 sheets frozen phyllo dough,
artichoke hearts	thawed
3 tablespoons grated Mozzarella	2 tablespoons melted butter

1. Preheat the air fryer to 400ºF (204ºC). 2. In a small bowl, combine the Ricotta cheese, egg white, artichoke hearts, Mozzarella cheese, and thyme, and mix well. 3. Cover the phyllo dough with a damp kitchen towel while you work so it doesn't dry out. Using one sheet at a time, place on the work surface and cut into thirds lengthwise. 4. Put about 1½ teaspoons of the filling on each strip at the base. Fold the bottom right-hand tip of phyllo over the filling to meet the other side in a triangle, then continue folding in a triangle. Brush each triangle with butter to seal the edges. Repeat with the remaining phyllo dough and filling. 5. Place the triangles in the air fryer basket. Bake, 6 at a time, for about 3 to 4 minutes, or until the phyllo is golden brown and crisp. 6. Serve hot.

Garlic-Parmesan Croutons

Prep time: 3 minutes | Cook time: 12 minutes | Serves 4

Oil, for spraying	3 tablespoons olive oil
4 cups cubed French bread	1 tablespoon granulated garlic
1 tablespoon grated Parmesan	½ teaspoon unsalted salt
cheese	

1. Line the air fryer basket with parchment and spray lightly with oil. 2. In a large bowl, mix together the bread, Parmesan cheese, olive oil, garlic, and salt, tossing with your hands to evenly distribute the seasonings. Transfer the coated bread cubes to the prepared basket. 3. Air fry at 350ºF (177ºC) for 10 to 12 minutes, stirring once after 5 minutes, or until crisp and golden brown.

Stuffed Fried Mushrooms

Prep time: 20 minutes | Cook time: 10 to 11 minutes | Serves 10

½ cup panko bread crumbs	cream cheese, at room
½ teaspoon freshly ground	temperature
black pepper	20 cremini or button
½ teaspoon onion powder	mushrooms, stemmed
½ teaspoon cayenne pepper	1 to 2 tablespoons oil
1 (8-ounce / 227-g) package	

1. In a medium bowl, whisk the bread crumbs, black pepper, onion powder, and cayenne until blended. 2. Add the cream cheese and mix until well blended. Fill each mushroom top with 1 teaspoon of the cream cheese mixture 3. Preheat the air fryer to 360ºF (182ºC). Line the air fryer basket with a piece of parchment paper. 4. Place the mushrooms on the parchment and spritz with oil. 5. Cook for 5 minutes. Shake the basket and cook for 5 to 6 minutes more until the filling is firm and the mushrooms are soft.

Asian Rice Logs

Prep time: 30 minutes | Cook time: 5 minutes | Makes 8 rice logs

1½ cups cooked jasmine or	⅓ cup plain bread crumbs
sushi rice	¾ cup panko bread crumbs
¼ teaspoon salt	2 tablespoons sesame seeds
2 teaspoons five-spice powder	Orange Marmalade Dipping
2 teaspoons diced shallots	Sauce:
1 tablespoon tamari sauce	½ cup all-natural orange
1 egg, beaten	marmalade
1 teaspoon sesame oil	1 tablespoon soy sauce
2 teaspoons water	

1. Make the rice according to package instructions. While the rice is cooking, make the dipping sauce by combining the marmalade and soy sauce and set aside. 2. Stir together the cooked rice, salt, five-spice powder, shallots, and tamari sauce. 3. Divide rice into 8 equal pieces. With slightly damp hands, mold each piece into a log shape. Chill in freezer for 10 to 15 minutes. 4. Mix the egg, sesame oil, and water together in a shallow bowl. 5. Place the plain bread crumbs on a sheet of wax paper. 6. Mix the panko bread crumbs with the sesame seeds and place on another sheet of wax paper. 7. Roll the rice logs in plain bread crumbs, then dip in egg wash, and then dip in the panko and sesame seeds. 8. Cook the logs at 390ºF (199ºC) for approximately 5 minutes, until golden brown. 9. Cool slightly before serving with Orange Marmalade Dipping Sauce.

Red Pepper Tapenade

Prep time: 5 minutes | Cook time: 5 minutes | Serves 4

1 large red bell pepper	and roughly chopped
2 tablespoons plus 1 teaspoon	1 garlic clove, minced
olive oil, divided	½ teaspoon dried oregano
½ cup Kalamata olives, pitted	1 tablespoon lemon juice

1. Preheat the air fryer to 380°F(193ºC). 2. Brush the outside of a whole red pepper with 1 teaspoon olive oil and place it inside the air fryer basket. Roast for 5 minutes. 3. Meanwhile, in a medium bowl combine the remaining 2 tablespoons of olive oil with the olives, garlic, oregano, and lemon juice. 4. Remove the red pepper from the air fryer, then gently slice off the stem and remove the seeds. Roughly chop the roasted pepper into small pieces. 5. Add the red pepper to the olive mixture and stir all together until combined. 6. Serve with pita chips, crackers, or crusty bread.

Spiced Nuts

Prep time: 5 minutes | Cook time: 25 minutes | Makes 3 cups

1 egg white, lightly beaten	¼ teaspoon ground allspice
¼ cup sugar	Pinch ground cayenne pepper
1 teaspoon salt	1 cup pecan halves
½ teaspoon ground cinnamon	1 cup cashews
¼ teaspoon ground cloves	1 cup almonds

1. Combine the egg white with the sugar and spices in a bowl. 2. Preheat the air fryer to 300°F (149°C). 3. Spray or brush the air fryer basket with vegetable oil. Toss the nuts together in the spiced egg white and transfer the nuts to the air fryer basket. 4. Air fry for 25 minutes, stirring the nuts in the basket a few times during the cooking process. Taste the nuts (carefully because they will be very hot) to see if they are crunchy and nicely toasted. Air fry for a few more minutes if necessary. 5. Serve warm or cool to room temperature and store in an airtight container for up to two weeks.

Crispy Chili Chickpeas

Prep time: 5 minutes | Cook time: 15 minutes | Serves 4

1 (15 ounces / 425 g) can cooked chickpeas, drained and rinsed	¼ teaspoon salt
	⅛ teaspoon chili powder
	⅛ teaspoon garlic powder
1 tablespoon olive oil	⅛ teaspoon paprika

1. Preheat the air fryer to 380°F (193°C). 2. In a medium bowl, toss all of the ingredients together until the chickpeas are well coated. 3. Pour the chickpeas into the air fryer and spread them out in a single layer. 4. Roast for 15 minutes, stirring once halfway through the cook time.

Authentic Scotch Eggs

Prep time: 15 minutes | Cook time: 11 to 13 minutes | Serves 6

1½ pounds (680 g) bulk lean chicken or turkey sausage	divided
	½ cup all-purpose flour
3 raw eggs, divided	6 hardboiled eggs, peeled
1½ cups dried bread crumbs,	Cooking oil spray

1. In a large bowl, combine the chicken sausage, 1 raw egg, and ½ cup of bread crumbs and mix well. Divide the mixture into 6 pieces and flatten each into a long oval. 2. In a shallow bowl, beat the remaining 2 raw eggs. 3. Place the flour in a small bowl. 4. Place the remaining 1 cup of bread crumbs in a second small bowl. 5. Roll each hardboiled egg in the flour and wrap one of the chicken sausage pieces around each egg to encircle it completely. 6. One at a time, roll the encased eggs in the flour, dip in the beaten eggs, and finally dip in the bread crumbs to coat. 7. Insert the crisper plate into the basket and the basket into the unit. Preheat the unit by selecting AIR FRY, setting the temperature to 375°F (191°C), and setting the time to 3 minutes. Select START/STOP to begin. 8. Once the unit is preheated, spray the crisper plate with cooking oil. Place the eggs in a single layer into the basket and spray them with oil. 9. Select AIR FRY, set the temperature to 375°F (191°C), and set the time to 13 minutes. Select START/STOP to begin. 10. After about 6 minutes, use tongs to turn the eggs and spray them with more oil. Resume cooking for 5 to 7 minutes more, or until the chicken is thoroughly cooked and the Scotch eggs are browned. 11. When the cooking is complete, serve warm.

Cheese Wafers

Prep time: 30 minutes | Cook time: 5 to 6 minutes per batch | Makes 4 dozen

4 ounces (113 g) sharp Cheddar cheese, grated	¼ teaspoon salt
	½ cup crisp rice cereal
¼ cup butter	Oil for misting or cooking spray
½ cup flour	

1. Cream the butter and grated cheese together. You can do it by hand, but using a stand mixer is faster and easier. 2. Sift flour and salt together. Add it to the cheese mixture and mix until well blended. 3. Stir in cereal. 4. Place dough on wax paper and shape into a long roll about 1 inch in diameter. Wrap well with the wax paper and chill for at least 4 hours. 5. When ready to cook, preheat the air fryer to 360°F (182°C). 6. Cut cheese roll into ¼-inch slices. 7. Spray the air fryer basket with oil or cooking spray and place slices in a single layer, close but not touching. 8. Cook for 5 to 6 minutes or until golden brown. When done, place them on paper towels to cool. 9. Repeat previous step to cook remaining cheese bites.

Jalapeño Poppers

Prep time: 10 minutes | Cook time: 20 minutes | Serves 4

Oil, for spraying	parsley
8 ounces (227 g) cream cheese	½ teaspoon granulated garlic
¾ cup gluten-free bread crumbs, divided	½ teaspoon salt
	10 jalapeño peppers, halved and seeded
2 tablespoons chopped fresh	

1. Line the air fryer basket with parchment and spray lightly with oil. 2. In a medium bowl, mix together the cream cheese, half of the bread crumbs, the parsley, garlic, and salt. 3. Spoon the mixture into the jalapeño halves. Gently press the stuffed jalapeños in the remaining bread crumbs. 4. Place the stuffed jalapeños in the prepared basket. 5. Air fry at 370°F (188°C) for 20 minutes, or until the cheese is melted and the bread crumbs are crisp and golden brown.

Spicy Tortilla Chips

Prep time: 5 minutes | Cook time: 8 to 12 minutes | Serves 4

½ teaspoon ground cumin	Pinch cayenne pepper
½ teaspoon paprika	8 (6-inch) corn tortillas, each
½ teaspoon chili powder	cut into 6 wedges
½ teaspoon salt	Cooking spray

1. Preheat the air fryer to 375ºF (191ºC). Lightly spritz the air fryer basket with cooking spray. 2. Stir together the cumin, paprika, chili powder, salt, and pepper in a small bowl. 3. Working in batches, arrange the tortilla wedges in the air fryer basket in a single layer. Lightly mist them with cooking spray. Sprinkle some seasoning mixture on top of the tortilla wedges. 4. Air fry for 4 to 6 minutes, shaking the basket halfway through, or until the chips are lightly browned and crunchy. 5. Repeat with the remaining tortilla wedges and seasoning mixture. 6. Let the tortilla chips cool for 5 minutes and serve.

Cheesy Hash Brown Bruschetta

Prep time: 5 minutes | Cook time: 6 to 8 minutes | Serves 4

4 frozen hash brown patties	2 tablespoons grated Parmesan
1 tablespoon olive oil	cheese
⅓ cup chopped cherry tomatoes	1 tablespoon balsamic vinegar
3 tablespoons diced fresh	1 tablespoon minced fresh basil
Mozzarella	

1. Preheat the air fryer to 400ºF (204ºC). 2. Place the hash brown patties in the air fryer in a single layer. Air fry for 6 to 8 minutes, or until the potatoes are crisp, hot, and golden brown. 3. Meanwhile, combine the olive oil, tomatoes, Mozzarella, Parmesan, vinegar, and basil in a small bowl. 4. When the potatoes are done, carefully remove from the basket and arrange on a serving plate. Top with the tomato mixture and serve.

Ranch Oyster Snack Crackers

Prep time: 3 minutes | Cook time: 12 minutes | Serves 6

Oil, for spraying	½ teaspoon granulated garlic
¼ cup olive oil	½ teaspoon salt
2 teaspoons dry ranch seasoning	1 (9 ounces / 255 g) bag oyster
1 teaspoon chili powder	crackers
½ teaspoon dried dill	

1. Preheat the air fryer to 325ºF (163ºC). Line the air fryer basket with parchment and spray lightly with oil. 2. In a large bowl, mix together the olive oil, ranch seasoning, chili powder, dill, garlic, and salt. Add the crackers and toss until evenly coated. 3. Place the mixture in the prepared basket. 4. Cook for 10 to 12 minutes, shaking or stirring every 3 to 4 minutes, or until crisp and golden brown.

Asiago Shishito Peppers

Prep time: 5 minutes | Cook time: 10 minutes | Serves 4

Oil, for spraying	½ teaspoon salt
6 ounces (170 g) shishito	½ teaspoon lemon pepper
peppers	⅓ cup grated Asiago cheese,
1 tablespoon olive oil	divided

1. Line the air fryer basket with parchment and spray lightly with oil. 2. Rinse the shishitos and pat dry with paper towels. 3. In a large bowl, mix together the shishitos, olive oil, salt, and lemon pepper. Place the shishitos in the prepared basket. 4. Roast at 350ºF (177ºC) for 10 minutes, or until blistered but not burned. 5. Sprinkle with half of the cheese and cook for 1 more minute. 6. Transfer to a serving plate. Immediately sprinkle with the remaining cheese and serve.

Garlicky and Cheesy French Fries

Prep time: 5 minutes | Cook time: 20 to 25 minutes | Serves 4

3 medium russet potatoes,	½ teaspoon salt
rinsed, dried, and cut into thin	¼ teaspoon freshly ground
wedges or classic fry shapes	black pepper
2 tablespoons extra-virgin olive	Cooking oil spray
oil	2 tablespoons finely chopped
1 tablespoon granulated garlic	fresh parsley (optional)
⅓ cup grated Parmesan cheese	

1. In a large bowl combine the potato wedges or fries and the olive oil. Toss to coat. 2. Sprinkle the potatoes with the granulated garlic, Parmesan cheese, salt, and pepper, and toss again. 3. Insert the crisper plate into the basket and the basket into the unit. Preheat the unit by selecting AIR FRY, setting the temperature to 400ºF (204ºC), and setting the time to 3 minutes. Select START/STOP to begin. 4. Once the unit is preheated, spray the crisper plate with cooking oil. Place the potatoes into the basket. 5. Select AIR FRY, set the temperature to 400ºF (204ºC), and set the time to 20 to 25 minutes. Select START/STOP to begin. 6. After about 10 minutes, remove the basket and shake it so the fries at the bottom come up to the top. Reinsert the basket to resume cooking. 7. When the cooking is complete, top the fries with the parsley (if using) and serve hot.

Black Bean Corn Dip

Prep time: 10 minutes | Cook time: 10 minutes |

Serves 4

½ (15 ounces / 425 g) can black beans, drained and rinsed

½ (15 ounces / 425 g) can corn, drained and rinsed

¼ cup chunky salsa

2 ounces (57 g) reduced-fat cream cheese, softened

¼ cup shredded reduced-fat Cheddar cheese

½ teaspoon ground cumin

½ teaspoon paprika

Salt and freshly ground black pepper, to taste

1. Preheat the air fryer to 325ºF (163ºC). 2. In a medium bowl, mix together the black beans, corn, salsa, cream cheese, Cheddar cheese, cumin, and paprika. Season with salt and pepper and stir until well combined. 3. Spoon the mixture into a baking dish. 4. Place baking dish in the air fryer basket and bake until heated through, about 10 minutes. 5. Serve hot.

Garlic-Roasted Tomatoes and Olives

Prep time: 5 minutes | Cook time: 20 minutes |

Serves 6

2 cups cherry tomatoes

4 garlic cloves, roughly chopped

½ red onion, roughly chopped

1 cup black olives

1 cup green olives

1 tablespoon fresh basil, minced

1 tablespoon fresh oregano, minced

2 tablespoons olive oil

¼ to ½ teaspoon salt

1. Preheat the air fryer to 380°F(193ºC). 2. In a large bowl, combine all of the ingredients and toss together so that the tomatoes and olives are coated well with the olive oil and herbs. 3. Pour the mixture into the air fryer basket, and roast for 10 minutes. Stir the mixture well, then continue roasting for an additional 10 minutes. 4. Remove from the air fryer, transfer to a serving bowl, and enjoy.

Greek Street Tacos

Prep time: 10 minutes | Cook time: 3 minutes |

Makes 8 small tacos

8 small flour tortillas (4-inch diameter)

8 tablespoons hummus

4 tablespoons crumbled feta

cheese

4 tablespoons chopped kalamata or other olives (optional)

Olive oil for misting

1. Place 1 tablespoon of hummus or tapenade in the center of each tortilla. Top with 1 teaspoon of feta crumbles and 1 teaspoon of

chopped olives, if using. 2. Using your finger or a small spoon, moisten the edges of the tortilla all around with water. 3. Fold tortilla over to make a half-moon shape. Press center gently. Then press the edges firmly to seal in the filling. 4. Mist both sides with olive oil. 5. Place in air fryer basket very close but try not to overlap. 6. Air fry at 390ºF (199ºC) for 3 minutes, just until lightly browned and crispy.

Bacon-Wrapped Pickle Spears

Prep time: 10 minutes | Cook time: 8 minutes |

Serves 4

8 to 12 slices bacon

¼ cup (2 ounces / 57 g) cream cheese, softened

¼ cup shredded Mozzarella

cheese

8 dill pickle spears

½ cup ranch dressing

1. Lay the bacon slices on a flat surface. In a medium bowl, combine the cream cheese and Mozzarella. Stir until well blended. Spread the cheese mixture over the bacon slices. 2. Place a pickle spear on a bacon slice and roll the bacon around the pickle in a spiral, ensuring the pickle is fully covered. (You may need to use more than one slice of bacon per pickle to fully cover the spear.) Tuck in the ends to ensure the bacon stays put. Repeat to wrap all the pickles. 3. Place the wrapped pickles in the air fryer basket in a single layer. Set the air fryer to 400ºF (204ºC) for 8 minutes, or until the bacon is cooked through and crisp on the edges. 4. Serve the pickle spears with ranch dressing on the side.

Eggplant Fries

Prep time: 10 minutes | Cook time: 7 to 8 minutes |

per batch | Serves 4

1 medium eggplant

1 teaspoon ground coriander

1 teaspoon cumin

1 teaspoon garlic powder

½ teaspoon salt

1 cup crushed panko bread crumbs

1 large egg

2 tablespoons water

Oil for misting or cooking spray

1. Peel and cut the eggplant into fat fries, ⅜ to ½-inch thick. 2. Preheat the air fryer to 390ºF (199ºC). 3. In a small cup, mix together the coriander, cumin, garlic, and salt. 4. Combine 1 teaspoon of the seasoning mix and panko crumbs in a shallow dish. 5. Place eggplant fries in a large bowl, sprinkle with remaining seasoning, and stir well to combine. 6. Beat eggs and water together and pour over eggplant fries. Stir to coat. 7. Remove eggplant from egg wash, shaking off excess, and roll in panko crumbs. 8. Spray with oil. 9. Place half of the fries in air fryer basket. You should have only a single layer, but it's fine if they overlap a little. 10. Cook for 5 minutes. Shake basket, mist lightly with oil, and cook 2 to 3 minutes longer, until browned and crispy. 11. Repeat step 10 to cook remaining eggplant.

Cheesy Zucchini Tots

Prep time: 15 minutes | Cook time: 6 minutes |
Serves 8

2 medium zucchini (about 12 ounces / 340 g), shredded
1 large egg, whisked
½ cup grated pecorino romano cheese

½ cup panko bread crumbs
¼ teaspoon black pepper
1 clove garlic, minced
Cooking spray

1. Using your hands, squeeze out as much liquid from the zucchini as possible. In a large bowl, mix the zucchini with the remaining ingredients except the oil until well incorporated. 2. Make the zucchini tots: Use a spoon or cookie scoop to place tablespoonfuls of the zucchini mixture onto a lightly floured cutting board and form into 1-inch logs. 3. Preheat air fryer to 375ºF (191ºC). Spritz the air fryer basket with cooking spray. 4. Place the tots in the basket. You may need to cook in batches to avoid overcrowding. 5. Air fry for 6 minutes until golden brown. 6. Remove from the basket to a serving plate and repeat with the remaining zucchini tots. 7. Serve immediately.

Mushroom Tarts

Prep time: 15 minutes | Cook time: 38 minutes |
Makes 15 tarts

2 tablespoons extra-virgin olive oil, divided
1 small white onion, sliced
8 ounces (227 g) shiitake mushrooms, sliced
¼ teaspoon sea salt
¼ teaspoon freshly ground black pepper

¼ cup dry white wine
1 sheet frozen puff pastry, thawed
1 cup shredded Gruyère cheese
Cooking oil spray
1 tablespoon thinly sliced fresh chives

1. Insert the crisper plate into the basket and the basket into the unit. Preheat the unit by selecting BAKE, setting the temperature to 300ºF (149ºC), and setting the time to 3 minutes. Select START/STOP to begin. 2. In a heatproof bowl that fits into the basket, stir together 1 tablespoon of olive oil, the onion, and the mushrooms. 3. Once the unit is preheated, place the bowl into the basket. 4. Select BAKE, set the temperature to 300ºF (149ºC), and set the time to 7 minutes. Select START/STOP to begin. 5. After about 2½ minutes, stir the vegetables. Resume cooking. After another 2½ minutes, the vegetables should be browned and tender. Season with the salt and pepper and add the wine. Resume cooking until the liquid evaporates, about 2 minutes. 6. When the cooking is complete, place the bowl on a heatproof surface. 7. Increase the air fryer temperature to 390ºF (199ºC) and set the time to 3 minutes. Select START/STOP to begin. 8. Unfold the puff pastry and cut it into 15 (3-by-3-inch) squares. Using a fork, pierce the dough and brush both sides with the remaining 1 tablespoon of olive oil. 9. Evenly distribute half the cheese among the puff pastry squares, leaving a ½-inch border around the edges. Divide the mushroom-onion mixture among the pastry squares and top with the remaining cheese. 10. Once the unit is preheated, spray the crisper plate with cooking oil. Working in batches, place 5 tarts into the basket; do not stack or overlap. 11. Select BAKE, set the temperature to 390ºF (199ºC), and set the time to 8 minutes. Select START/STOP to begin. 12. After 6 minutes, check the tarts; if not yet golden brown, resume cooking for about 2 minutes more. 13. When the cooking is complete, remove the tarts and transfer to a wire rack to cool. Repeat steps 10, 11, and 12 with the remaining tarts. 14. Serve garnished with the chives.

Pickle Chips

Prep time: 30 minutes | Cook time: 12 minutes |
Serves 4

Oil, for spraying
2 cups sliced dill or sweet pickles, drained
1 cup buttermilk

2 cups all-purpose flour
2 large eggs, beaten
2 cups panko bread crumbs
¼ teaspoon salt

1. Line the air fryer basket with parchment and spray lightly with oil. 2. In a shallow bowl, combine the pickles and buttermilk and let soak for at least 1 hour, then drain. 3. Place the flour, beaten eggs, and bread crumbs in separate bowls. 4. Coat each pickle chip lightly in the flour, dip in the eggs, and dredge in the bread crumbs. Be sure each one is evenly coated. 5. Place the pickle chips in the prepared basket, sprinkle with the salt, and spray lightly with oil. You may need to work in batches, depending on the size of your air fryer. 6. Air fry at 390ºF (199ºC) for 5 minutes, flip, and cook for another 5 to 7 minutes, or until crispy. Serve hot.

String Bean Fries

Prep time: 15 minutes | Cook time: 5 to 6 minutes |
Serves 4

½ pound (227 g) fresh string beans
2 eggs
4 teaspoons water
½ cup white flour
½ cup bread crumbs

¼ teaspoon salt
¼ teaspoon ground black pepper
¼ teaspoon dry mustard (optional)
Oil for misting or cooking spray

1. Preheat the air fryer to 360ºF (182ºC). 2. Trim stem ends from string beans, wash, and pat dry. 3. In a shallow dish, beat eggs and water together until well blended. 4. Place flour in a second shallow dish. 5. In a third shallow dish, stir together the bread crumbs, salt, pepper, and dry mustard if using. 6. Dip each string bean in egg mixture, flour, egg mixture again, then bread crumbs. 7. When you finish coating all the string beans, open air fryer and place them in basket. 8. Cook for 3 minutes. 9. Stop and mist string beans with oil or cooking spray. 10. Cook for 2 to 3 more minutes or until string beans are crispy and nicely browned.

Carrot Chips

Prep time: 15 minutes | Cook time: 8 to 10 minutes | Serves 4

1 tablespoon olive oil, plus more for greasing the basket
4 to 5 medium carrots, trimmed and thinly sliced
1 teaspoon seasoned salt

1. Preheat the air fryer to 390ºF (199ºC). Grease the air fryer basket with the olive oil. 2. Toss the carrot slices with 1 tablespoon of olive oil and salt in a medium bowl until thoroughly coated. 3. Arrange the carrot slices in the greased basket. You may need to work in batches to avoid overcrowding. 4. Air fry for 8 to 10 minutes until the carrot slices are crisp-tender. Shake the basket once during cooking. 5. Transfer the carrot slices to a bowl and repeat with the remaining carrots. 6. Allow to cool for 5 minutes and serve.

Poutine with Waffle Fries

Prep time: 10 minutes | Cook time: 15 to 17 minutes | Serves 4

2 cups frozen waffle cut fries
2 teaspoons olive oil
1 red bell pepper, chopped
2 green onions, sliced
1 cup shredded Swiss cheese
½ cup bottled chicken gravy

1. Preheat the air fryer to 380ºF (193ºC). 2. Toss the waffle fries with the olive oil and place in the air fryer basket. Air fry for 10 to 12 minutes, or until the fries are crisp and light golden brown, shaking the basket halfway through the cooking time. 3. Transfer the fries to a baking pan and top with the pepper, green onions, and cheese. Air fry for 3 minutes, or until the vegetables are crisp and tender. 4. Remove the pan from the air fryer and drizzle the gravy over the fries. Air fry for 2 minutes, or until the gravy is hot. 5. Serve immediately.

Air Fried Pot Stickers

Prep time: 10 minutes | Cook time: 18 to 20 minutes | Makes 30 pot stickers

½ cup finely chopped cabbage
¼ cup finely chopped red bell pepper
2 green onions, finely chopped
1 egg, beaten
2 tablespoons cocktail sauce
2 teaspoons low-sodium soy sauce
30 wonton wrappers
1 tablespoon water, for brushing the wrappers

1. Preheat the air fryer to 360ºF (182ºC). 2. In a small bowl, combine the cabbage, pepper, green onions, egg, cocktail sauce, and soy sauce, and mix well. 3. Put about 1 teaspoon of the mixture in the center of each wonton wrapper. Fold the wrapper in half, covering the filling; dampen the edges with water, and seal. You can crimp the edges of the wrapper with your fingers so they look like the pot stickers you get in restaurants. Brush them with water. 4. Place the pot stickers in the air fryer basket and air fry in 2 batches for 9 to 10 minutes, or until the pot stickers are hot and the bottoms are lightly browned. 5. Serve hot.

Pepperoni Pizza Dip

Prep time: 10 minutes | Cook time: 10 minutes | Serves 6

6 ounces (170 g) cream cheese, softened
¾ cup shredded Italian cheese blend
¼ cup sour cream
1½ teaspoons dried Italian seasoning
¼ teaspoon garlic salt
¼ teaspoon onion powder
¾ cup pizza sauce
½ cup sliced miniature pepperoni
¼ cup sliced black olives
1 tablespoon thinly sliced green onion
Cut-up raw vegetables, toasted baguette slices, pita chips, or tortilla chips, for serving

1. In a small bowl, combine the cream cheese, ¼ cup of the shredded cheese, the sour cream, Italian seasoning, garlic salt, and onion powder. Stir until smooth and the ingredients are well blended. 2. Spread the mixture in a baking pan. Top with the pizza sauce, spreading to the edges. Sprinkle with the remaining ½ cup shredded cheese. Arrange the pepperoni slices on top of the cheese. Top with the black olives and green onion. 3. Place the pan in the air fryer basket. Set the air fryer to 350ºF (177ºC) for 10 minutes, or until the pepperoni is beginning to brown on the edges and the cheese is bubbly and lightly browned. 4. Let stand for 5 minutes before serving with vegetables, toasted baguette slices, pita chips, or tortilla chips.

Veggie Shrimp Toast

Prep time: 15 minutes | Cook time: 3 to 6 minutes | Serves 4

8 large raw shrimp, peeled and finely chopped
1 egg white
2 garlic cloves, minced
3 tablespoons minced red bell pepper
1 medium celery stalk, minced
2 tablespoons cornstarch
¼ teaspoon Chinese five-spice powder
3 slices firm thin-sliced no-sodium whole-wheat bread

1. Preheat the air fryer to 350ºF (177ºC). 2. In a small bowl, stir together the shrimp, egg white, garlic, red bell pepper, celery, cornstarch, and five-spice powder. Top each slice of bread with one-third of the shrimp mixture, spreading it evenly to the edges. With a sharp knife, cut each slice of bread into 4 strips. 3. Place the shrimp toasts in the air fryer basket in a single layer. You may need to cook them in batches. Air fry for 3 to 6 minutes, until crisp and golden brown. 4. Serve hot.

Corn Dog Muffins

Prep time: 10 minutes | Cook time: 8 to 10 minutes per batch | Makes 8 muffins

1¼ cups sliced kosher hotdogs (3 or 4, depending on size)
½ cup flour
½ cup yellow cornmeal
2 teaspoons baking powder
½ cup skim milk
1 egg
2 tablespoons canola oil
8 foil muffin cups, paper liners removed
Cooking spray
Mustard or your favorite dipping sauce

1. Slice each hotdog in half lengthwise, then cut in ¼-inch half-moon slices. Set aside. 2. Preheat the air fryer to 390ºF (199ºC). 3. In a large bowl, stir together flour, cornmeal, and baking powder. 4. In a small bowl, beat together the milk, egg, and oil until just blended. 5. Pour egg mixture into dry ingredients and stir with a spoon to mix well. 6. Stir in sliced hot dogs. 7. Spray the foil cups lightly with cooking spray. 8. Divide mixture evenly into muffin cups. 9. Place 4 muffin cups in the air fryer basket and cook for 5 minutes. 10. Reduce temperature to 360ºF (182ºC) and cook 3 to 5 minutes or until toothpick inserted in center of muffin comes out clean. 11. Repeat steps 9 and 10 to bake remaining corn dog muffins. 12. Serve with mustard or other sauces for dipping.

Pork and Cabbage Egg Rolls

Prep time: 15 minutes | Cook time: 12 minutes | Makes 12 egg rolls

Cooking oil spray
2 garlic cloves, minced
12 ounces (340 g) ground pork
1 teaspoon sesame oil
¼ cup soy sauce
2 teaspoons grated peeled fresh
ginger
2 cups shredded green cabbage
4 scallions, green parts (white parts optional), chopped
24 egg roll wrappers

1. Spray a skillet with the cooking oil and place it over medium-high heat. Add the garlic and cook for 1 minute until fragrant. 2. Add the ground pork to the skillet. Using a spoon, break the pork into smaller chunks. 3. In a small bowl, whisk the sesame oil, soy sauce, and ginger until combined. Add the sauce to the skillet. Stir to combine and continue cooking for about 5 minutes until the pork is browned and thoroughly cooked. 4. Stir in the cabbage and scallions. Transfer the pork mixture to a large bowl. 5. Lay the egg roll wrappers on a flat surface. Dip a basting brush in water and glaze each egg roll wrapper along the edges with the wet brush. This will soften the dough and make it easier to roll. 6. Stack 2 egg roll wrappers (it works best if you double-wrap the egg rolls). Scoop 1 to 2 tablespoons of the pork mixture into the center of each wrapper stack. 7. Roll one long side of the wrappers up over the filling. Press firmly on the area with the filling, tucking it in lightly to secure it in place. Fold in the left and right sides. Continue rolling to close. Use the basting brush to wet the seam and seal the egg roll. Repeat with the remaining ingredients. 8. Insert the crisper plate into the basket and the basket into the unit. Preheat the unit by selecting AIR FRY, setting the temperature to 400ºF (204ºC), and setting the time to 3 minutes. Select START/STOP to begin. 9. Once the unit is preheated, spray the crisper plate with cooking oil. Place the egg rolls into the basket. It is okay to stack them. Spray them with cooking oil. 10. Select AIR FRY, set the temperature to 400ºF (204ºC), and set the time to 12 minutes. Insert the basket into the unit. Select START/STOP to begin. 11. After 8 minutes, use tongs to flip the egg rolls. Reinsert the basket to resume cooking. 12. When the cooking is complete, serve the egg rolls hot.

Cheesy Steak Fries

Prep time: 5 minutes | Cook time: 20 minutes | Serves 5

1 (28-ounce / 794-g) bag frozen steak fries
Cooking spray
Salt and pepper, to taste
½ cup beef gravy
1 cup shredded Mozzarella cheese
2 scallions, green parts only, chopped

1. Preheat the air fryer to 400ºF (204ºC). 2. Place the frozen steak fries in the air fryer. Air fry for 10 minutes. Shake the basket and spritz the fries with cooking spray. Sprinkle with salt and pepper. Air fry for an additional 8 minutes. 3. Pour the beef gravy into a medium, microwave-safe bowl. Microwave for 30 seconds, or until the gravy is warm. 4. Sprinkle the fries with the cheese. Air fry for an additional 2 minutes, until the cheese is melted. 5. Transfer the fries to a serving dish. Drizzle the fries with gravy and sprinkle the scallions on top for a green garnish. Serve.

Greens Chips with Curried Yogurt Sauce

Prep time: 10 minutes | Cook time: 5 to 6 minutes | Serves 4

1 cup low-fat Greek yogurt
1 tablespoon freshly squeezed lemon juice
1 tablespoon curry powder
½ bunch curly kale, stemmed, ribs removed and discarded,
leaves cut into 2- to 3-inch pieces
½ bunch chard, stemmed, ribs removed and discarded, leaves cut into 2- to 3-inch pieces
1½ teaspoons olive oil

1. In a small bowl, stir together the yogurt, lemon juice, and curry powder. Set aside. 2. In a large bowl, toss the kale and chard with the olive oil, working the oil into the leaves with your hands. This helps break up the fibers in the leaves so the chips are tender. 3. Air fry the greens in batches at 390ºF (199ºC) for 5 to 6 minutes, until crisp, shaking the basket once during cooking. Serve with the yogurt sauce.

Shrimp Pirogues

Prep time: 15 minutes | Cook time: 4 to 5 minutes | Serves 8

12 ounces (340 g) small, peeled, and deveined raw shrimp
3 ounces (85 g) cream cheese, room temperature
2 tablespoons plain yogurt
1 teaspoon lemon juice

1 teaspoon dried dill weed, crushed
Salt, to taste
4 small hothouse cucumbers, each approximately 6 inches long

1. Pour 4 tablespoons water in bottom of air fryer drawer. 2. Place shrimp in air fryer basket in single layer and air fry at 390°F (199°C) for 4 to 5 minutes, just until done. Watch carefully because shrimp cooks quickly, and overcooking makes it tough. 3. Chop shrimp into small pieces, no larger than ½ inch. Refrigerate while mixing the remaining ingredients. 4. With a fork, mash and whip the cream cheese until smooth. 5. Stir in the yogurt and beat until smooth. Stir in lemon juice, dill weed, and chopped shrimp. 6. Taste for seasoning. If needed, add ¼ to ½ teaspoon salt to suit your taste. 7. Store in refrigerator until serving time. 8. When ready to serve, wash and dry cucumbers and split them lengthwise. Scoop out the seeds and turn cucumbers upside down on paper towels to drain for 10 minutes. 9. Just before filling, wipe centers of cucumbers dry. Spoon the shrimp mixture into the pirogues and cut in half crosswise. Serve immediately.

Hush Puppies

Prep time: 45 minutes | Cook time: 10 minutes | Serves 12

1 cup self-rising yellow cornmeal
½ cup all-purpose flour
1 teaspoon sugar
1 teaspoon salt
1 teaspoon freshly ground black pepper

1 large egg
⅓ cup canned creamed corn
1 cup minced onion
2 teaspoons minced jalapeño pepper
2 tablespoons olive oil, divided

1. Thoroughly combine the cornmeal, flour, sugar, salt, and pepper in a large bowl. 2. Whisk together the egg and corn in a small bowl. Pour the egg mixture into the bowl of cornmeal mixture and stir to combine. Stir in the minced onion and jalapeño. Cover the bowl with plastic wrap and place in the refrigerator for 30 minutes. 3. Preheat the air fryer to 375°F (191°C). Line the air fryer basket with parchment paper and lightly brush it with 1 tablespoon of olive oil. 4. Scoop out the cornmeal mixture and form into 24 balls, about 1 inch. 5. Arrange the balls in the parchment paper-lined basket, leaving space between each ball. 6. Air fry in batches for 5 minutes. Shake the basket and brush the balls with the remaining 1 tablespoon of olive oil. Continue cooking for 5 minutes until golden brown. 7. Remove the balls (hush puppies) from the basket and serve on a plate.

Cinnamon Apple Chips

Prep time: 5 minutes | Cook time: 7 to 8 hours | Serves 4

4 medium apples, any type, cored and cut into ⅓-inch-thick slices (thin slices yield crunchy

chips)
¼ teaspoon ground cinnamon
¼ teaspoon ground nutmeg

1. Place the apple slices in a large bowl. Sprinkle the cinnamon and nutmeg onto the apple slices and toss to coat. 2. Insert the crisper plate into the basket and the basket into the unit. Preheat the unit by selecting DEHYDRATE, setting the temperature to 135°F (57°C), and setting the time to 3 minutes. Select START/STOP to begin. 3. Once the unit is preheated, place the apple chips into the basket. It is okay to stack them. 4. Select DEHYDRATE, set the temperature to 135°F (57°C), and set the time to 7 or 8 hours. Select START/STOP to begin. 5. When the cooking is complete, cool the apple chips. Serve or store at room temperature in an airtight container for up to 1 week.

Air Fryer Popcorn with Garlic Salt

Prep time: 3 minutes | Cook time: 10 minutes | Serves 2

2 tablespoons olive oil
¼ cup popcorn kernels

1 teaspoon garlic salt

1. Preheat the air fryer to 380°F(193°C). 2. Tear a square of aluminum foil the size of the bottom of the air fryer and place into the air fryer. 3. Drizzle olive oil over the top of the foil, and then pour in the popcorn kernels. 4. Roast for 8 to 10 minutes, or until the popcorn stops popping. 5. Transfer the popcorn to a large bowl and sprinkle with garlic salt before serving.

Parmesan Cauliflower

Prep time: 15 minutes | Cook time: 15 minutes | Makes 5 cups

8 cups small cauliflower florets (about 1¼ pounds / 567 g)
3 tablespoons olive oil
1 teaspoon garlic powder

½ teaspoon salt
½ teaspoon turmeric
¼ cup shredded Parmesan cheese

1. Preheat the air fryer to 390°F (199°C). 2. In a bowl, combine the cauliflower florets, olive oil, garlic powder, salt, and turmeric and toss to coat. 3. Transfer to the air fryer basket and air fry for 15 minutes, or until the florets are crisp-tender. Shake the basket twice during cooking. 4. Remove from the basket to a plate. Sprinkle with the shredded Parmesan cheese and toss well. Serve warm.

Crunchy Basil White Beans

Prep time: 2 minutes | Cook time: 19 minutes |

Serves 2

1 (15 ounces / 425 g) can cooked white beans

2 tablespoons olive oil

1 teaspoon fresh sage, chopped

¼ teaspoon garlic powder

¼ teaspoon salt, divided

1 teaspoon chopped fresh basil

1. Preheat the air fryer to 380°F(193°C). 2. In a medium bowl, mix together the beans, olive oil, sage, garlic, ⅛ teaspoon salt, and basil. 3. Pour the white beans into the air fryer and spread them out in a single layer. 4. Bake for 10 minutes. Stir and continue cooking for an additional 5 to 9 minutes, or until they reach your preferred level of crispiness. 5. Toss with the remaining ⅛ teaspoon salt before serving.

Lemony Pear Chips

Prep time: 15 minutes | Cook time: 9 to 13 minutes |

Serves 4

2 firm Bosc pears, cut crosswise into ⅛-inch-thick slices

1 tablespoon freshly squeezed

lemon juice

½ teaspoon ground cinnamon

⅛ teaspoon ground cardamom

1. Preheat the air fryer to 380°F (193°C). 2. Separate the smaller stem-end pear rounds from the larger rounds with seeds. Remove the core and seeds from the larger slices. Sprinkle all slices with lemon juice, cinnamon, and cardamom. 3. Put the smaller chips into the air fryer basket. Air fry for 3 to 5 minutes, or until light golden brown, shaking the basket once during cooking. Remove from the air fryer. 4. Repeat with the larger slices, air frying for 6 to 8 minutes, or until light golden brown, shaking the basket once during cooking. 5. Remove the chips from the air fryer. Cool and serve or store in an airtight container at room temperature up for to 2 days.

Apple Wedges

Prep time: 10 minutes | Cook time: 8 to 9 minutes |

Serves 4

¼ cup panko bread crumbs

¼ cup pecans

1½ teaspoons cinnamon

1½ teaspoons brown sugar

¼ cup cornstarch

1 egg white

2 teaspoons water

1 medium apple

Oil for misting or cooking spray

1. In a food processor, combine panko, pecans, cinnamon, and brown sugar. Process to make small crumbs. 2. Place cornstarch in a plastic bag or bowl with lid. In a shallow dish, beat together the egg white and water until slightly foamy. 3. Preheat the air fryer to 390°F (199°C). 4. Cut apple into small wedges. The thickest edge should be no more than ⅜ to ½-inch thick. Cut away the core, but do not peel. 5. Place apple wedges in cornstarch, reseal bag or bowl, and shake to coat. 6. Dip wedges in egg wash, shake off excess, and roll in crumb mixture. Spray with oil. 7. Place apples in air fryer basket in single layer and cook for 5 minutes. Shake basket and break apart any apples that have stuck together. Mist lightly with oil and cook 3 to 4 minutes longer, until crispy.

Kale Chips with Tex-Mex Dip

Prep time: 10 minutes | Cook time: 5 to 6 minutes |

Serves 8

1 cup Greek yogurt

1 tablespoon chili powder

⅓ cup low-sodium salsa, well drained

1 bunch curly kale

1 teaspoon olive oil

¼ teaspoon coarse sea salt

1. In a small bowl, combine the yogurt, chili powder, and drained salsa; refrigerate. 2. Rinse the kale thoroughly, and pat dry. Remove the stems and ribs from the kale, using a sharp knife. Cut or tear the leaves into 3-inch pieces. 3. Toss the kale with the olive oil in a large bowl. 4. Air fry the kale in small batches at 390°F (199°C) until the leaves are crisp. This should take 5 to 6 minutes. Shake the basket once during cooking time. 5. As you remove the kale chips, sprinkle them with a bit of the sea salt. 6. When all of the kale chips are done, serve with the dip.

Caramelized Onion Dip

Prep time: 5 minutes | Cook time: 30 minutes |

Serves 8 to 10

1 tablespoon butter

1 medium yellow onion, halved and thinly sliced

¼ teaspoon kosher salt, plus additional for seasoning

4 ounces (113 g) cream cheese, softened

½ cup sour cream

¼ teaspoon onion powder

1 tablespoon chopped fresh chives

Black pepper, to taste

Thick-cut potato chips or vegetable chips

1. Place the butter in a baking pan. Place the pan in the air fryer basket. Set the air fryer to 200°F (93°C) for 1 minute, or until the butter is melted. Add the onions and salt to the pan. 2. Set the air fryer to 200°F (93°C) for 15 minutes, or until onions are softened. Set the air fryer to 375°F (191°C) for 15 minutes, until onions are a deep golden brown, stirring two or three times during the cooking time. Let cool completely. 3. In a medium bowl, stir together the cooked onions, cream cheese, sour cream, onion powder, and chives. Season with salt and pepper. Cover and refrigerate for 2 hours to allow the flavors to blend. 4. Serve the dip with potato chips or vegetable chips.

Sweet Potato Fries with Mayonnaise

Prep time: 5 minutes | Cook time: 20 minutes |
Serves 2 to 3

1 large sweet potato (about 1 pound / 454 g), scrubbed	¼ cup light mayonnaise
1 teaspoon vegetable or canola oil	½ teaspoon sriracha sauce
Salt, to taste	1 tablespoon spicy brown mustard
Dipping Sauce:	1 tablespoon sweet Thai chili sauce

1. Preheat the air fryer to 200ºF (93ºC). 2. On a flat work surface, cut the sweet potato into fry-shaped strips about ¼ inch wide and ¼ inch thick. You can use a mandoline to slice the sweet potato quickly and uniformly. 3. In a medium bowl, drizzle the sweet potato strips with the oil and toss well. 4. Transfer to the air fryer basket and air fry for 10 minutes, shaking the basket twice during cooking. 5. Remove the air fryer basket and sprinkle with the salt and toss to coat. 6. Increase the air fryer temperature to 400ºF (204ºC) and air fry for an additional 10 minutes, or until the fries are crispy and tender. Shake the basket a few times during cooking. 7. Meanwhile, whisk together all the ingredients for the sauce in a small bowl. 8. Remove the sweet potato fries from the basket to a plate and serve warm alongside the dipping sauce.

Zucchini Fries with Roasted Garlic Aïoli

Prep time: 20 minutes | Cook time: 12 minutes |
Serves 4

1 tablespoon vegetable oil	Zucchini Fries:
½ head green or savoy cabbage, finely shredded	½ cup flour
Roasted Garlic Aïoli:	2 eggs, beaten
1 teaspoon roasted garlic	1 cup seasoned bread crumbs
½ cup mayonnaise	Salt and pepper, to taste
2 tablespoons olive oil	1 large zucchini, cut into ½-inch sticks
Juice of ½ lemon	Olive oil
Salt and pepper, to taste	

1. Make the aïoli: Combine the roasted garlic, mayonnaise, olive oil and lemon juice in a bowl and whisk well. Season the aïoli with salt and pepper to taste. 2. Prepare the zucchini fries. Create a dredging station with three shallow dishes. Place the flour in the first shallow dish and season well with salt and freshly ground black pepper. Put the beaten eggs in the second shallow dish. In the third shallow dish, combine the bread crumbs, salt and pepper. Dredge the zucchini sticks, coating with flour first, then dipping them into the eggs to coat, and finally tossing in bread crumbs. Shake the dish with the bread crumbs and pat the crumbs onto the zucchini sticks gently with your hands so they stick evenly. 3. Place the zucchini fries on a flat surface and let them sit at least 10 minutes before air frying to let them dry out a little. Preheat the air fryer to 400ºF (204ºC). 4. Spray the zucchini sticks with olive oil, and place them into the air fryer basket. You can air fry the zucchini in two layers, placing the second layer in the opposite direction to the first. Air fry for 12 minutes turning and rotating the fries halfway through the cooking time. Spray with additional oil when you turn them over. 5. Serve zucchini fries warm with the roasted garlic aïoli.

Crispy Mozzarella Sticks

Prep time: 8 minutes | Cook time: 5 minutes | Serves 4

½ cup all-purpose flour	½ teaspoon garlic salt
1 egg, beaten	6 Mozzarella sticks, halved crosswise
½ cup panko bread crumbs	Olive oil spray
½ cup grated Parmesan cheese	
1 teaspoon Italian seasoning	

1. Put the flour in a small bowl. 2. Put the beaten egg in another small bowl. 3. In a medium bowl, stir together the panko, Parmesan cheese, Italian seasoning, and garlic salt. 4. Roll a Mozzarella-stick half in the flour, dip it into the egg, and then roll it in the panko mixture to coat. Press the coating lightly to make sure the bread crumbs stick to the cheese. Repeat with the remaining 11 Mozzarella sticks. 5. Insert the crisper plate into the basket and the basket into the unit. Preheat the unit by selecting AIR FRY, setting the temperature to 400ºF (204ºC), and setting the time to 3 minutes. Select START/STOP to begin. 6. Once the unit is preheated, spray the crisper plate with olive oil and place a parchment paper liner in the basket. Place the Mozzarella sticks into the basket and lightly spray them with olive oil. 7. Select AIR FRY, set the temperature to 400ºF (204ºC), and set the time to 5 minutes. Select START/STOP to begin. 8. When the cooking is complete, the Mozzarella sticks should be golden and crispy. Let the sticks stand for 1 minute before transferring them to a serving plate. Serve warm.

Chapter 8 Vegetables and Sides

Spinach and Cheese Stuffed Tomatoes

Prep time: 20 minutes | Cook time: 15 minutes |

Serves 2

4 ripe beefsteak tomatoes	1 (5.2-ounce / 147-g) package
¾ teaspoon black pepper	garlic-and-herb Boursin cheese
½ teaspoon kosher salt	3 tablespoons sour cream
1 (10-ounce / 283-g) package	½ cup finely grated Parmesan
frozen chopped spinach, thawed	cheese
and squeezed dry	

1. Cut the tops off the tomatoes. Using a small spoon, carefully remove and discard the pulp. Season the insides with ½ teaspoon of the black pepper and ¼ teaspoon of the salt. Invert the tomatoes onto paper towels and allow to drain while you make the filling. 2. Meanwhile, in a medium bowl, combine the spinach, Boursin cheese, sour cream, ¼ cup of the Parmesan, and the remaining ¼ teaspoon salt and ¼ teaspoon pepper. Stir until ingredients are well combined. Divide the filling among the tomatoes. Top with the remaining ¼ cup Parmesan. 3. Place the tomatoes in the air fryer basket. Set the air fryer to 350ºF (177ºC) for 15 minutes, or until the filling is hot.

Garlic-Parmesan Crispy Baby Potatoes

Prep time: 10 minutes | Cook time: 15 minutes |

Serves 4

Oil, for spraying	½ teaspoon salt
1 pound (454 g) baby potatoes	¼ teaspoon freshly ground
½ cup grated Parmesan cheese,	black pepper
divided	¼ teaspoon paprika
3 tablespoons olive oil	2 tablespoons chopped fresh
2 teaspoons granulated garlic	parsley, for garnish
½ teaspoon onion powder	

1. Line the air fryer basket with parchment and spray lightly with oil. 2. Rinse the potatoes, pat dry with paper towels, and place in a large bowl. 3. In a small bowl, mix together ¼ cup of Parmesan cheese, the olive oil, garlic, onion powder, salt, black pepper, and paprika. Pour the mixture over the potatoes and toss to coat. 4. Transfer the potatoes to the prepared basket and spread them out in an even layer, taking care to keep them from touching. You may need to work in batches, depending on the size of your air fryer. 5. Air fry at 400ºF (204ºC) for 15 minutes, stirring after 7 to 8 minutes, or until easily pierced with a fork. Continue to cook for

another 1 to 2 minutes, if needed. 6. Sprinkle with the parsley and the remaining Parmesan cheese and serve.

Buttery Green Beans

Prep time: 5 minutes | Cook time: 8 to 10 minutes |

Serves 6

1 pound (454 g) green beans,	black pepper, to taste
trimmed	¼ cup (4 tablespoons) unsalted
1 tablespoon avocado oil	butter, melted
1 teaspoon garlic powder	¼ cup freshly grated Parmesan
Sea salt and freshly ground	cheese

1. In a large bowl, toss together the green beans, avocado oil, and garlic powder and season with salt and pepper. 2. Set the air fryer to 400ºF (204ºC). Arrange the green beans in a single layer in the air fryer basket. Air fry for 8 to 10 minutes, tossing halfway through. 3. Transfer the beans to a large bowl and toss with the melted butter. Top with the Parmesan cheese and serve warm.

Cabbage Wedges with Caraway Butter

Prep time: 30 minutes | Cook time: 35 to 40 minutes

| Serves 6

1 tablespoon caraway seeds	cabbage, cut into 6 wedges
½ cup (1 stick) unsalted butter,	1 tablespoon avocado oil
at room temperature	½ teaspoon sea salt
½ teaspoon grated lemon zest	¼ teaspoon freshly ground
1 small head green or red	black pepper

1. Place the caraway seeds in a small dry skillet over medium-high heat. Toast the seeds for 2 to 3 minutes, then remove them from the heat and let cool. Lightly crush the seeds using a mortar and pestle or with the back of a knife. 2. Place the butter in a small bowl and stir in the crushed caraway seeds and lemon zest. Form the butter into a log and wrap it in parchment paper or plastic wrap. Refrigerate for at least 1 hour or freeze for 20 minutes. 3. Brush or spray the cabbage wedges with the avocado oil, and sprinkle with the salt and pepper. 4. Set the air fryer to 375ºF (191ºC). Place the cabbage in a single layer in the air fryer basket and roast for 20 minutes. Flip and cook for 15 to 20 minutes more, until the cabbage is tender and lightly charred. Plate the cabbage and dot with caraway butter. Tent with foil for 5 minutes to melt the butter, and serve.

Garlic Herb Radishes

Prep time: 10 minutes | Cook time: 10 minutes | Serves 4

1 pound (454 g) radishes	½ teaspoon dried parsley
2 tablespoons unsalted butter, melted	¼ teaspoon dried oregano
½ teaspoon garlic powder	¼ teaspoon ground black pepper

1. Remove roots from radishes and cut into quarters. 2. In a small bowl, add butter and seasonings. Toss the radishes in the herb butter and place into the air fryer basket. 3. Adjust the temperature to 350ºF (177ºC) and set the timer for 10 minutes. 4. Halfway through the cooking time, toss the radishes in the air fryer basket. Continue cooking until edges begin to turn brown. 5. Serve warm.

Buttery Mushrooms

Prep time: 10 minutes | Cook time: 10 minutes | Serves 4

8 ounces (227 g) cremini mushrooms, halved	¼ teaspoon salt
2 tablespoons salted butter, melted	¼ teaspoon ground black pepper

1. In a medium bowl, toss mushrooms with butter, then sprinkle with salt and pepper. Place into ungreased air fryer basket. Adjust the temperature to 400ºF (204ºC) and air fry for 10 minutes, shaking the basket halfway through cooking. Mushrooms will be tender when done. Serve warm.

Tofu Bites

Prep time: 15 minutes | Cook time: 30 minutes | Serves 4

1 packaged firm tofu, cubed and pressed to remove excess water	1 teaspoon hot sauce
1 tablespoon soy sauce	2 tablespoons sesame seeds
1 tablespoon ketchup	1 teaspoon garlic powder
1 tablespoon maple syrup	Salt and ground black pepper, to taste
½ teaspoon vinegar	Cooking spray
1 teaspoon liquid smoke	

1. Preheat the air fryer to 375ºF (191ºC). 2. Spritz a baking dish with cooking spray. 3. Combine all the ingredients to coat the tofu completely and allow the marinade to absorb for half an hour. 4. Transfer the tofu to the baking dish, then air fry for 15 minutes. Flip the tofu over and air fry for another 15 minutes on the other side. 5. Serve immediately.

Cauliflower with Lime Juice

Prep time: 10 minutes | Cook time: 7 minutes | Serves 4

2 cups chopped cauliflower florets	2 teaspoons chili powder
2 tablespoons coconut oil, melted	½ teaspoon garlic powder
	1 medium lime
	2 tablespoons chopped cilantro

1. In a large bowl, toss cauliflower with coconut oil. Sprinkle with chili powder and garlic powder. Place seasoned cauliflower into the air fryer basket. 2. Adjust the temperature to 350ºF (177ºC) and set the timer for 7 minutes. 3. Cauliflower will be tender and begin to turn golden at the edges. Place into a serving bowl. 4. Cut the lime into quarters and squeeze juice over cauliflower. Garnish with cilantro.

Scalloped Potatoes

Prep time: 5 minutes | Cook time: 20 minutes | Serves 4

2 cup sliced frozen potatoes, thawed	Freshly ground black pepper, to taste
3 cloves garlic, minced	¾ cup heavy cream
Pinch salt	

1. Preheat the air fryer to 380ºF (193ºC). 2. Toss the potatoes with the garlic, salt, and black pepper in a baking pan until evenly coated. Pour the heavy cream over the top. 3. Place the baking pan in the air fryer basket and bake for 15 minutes, or until the potatoes are tender and top is golden brown. Check for doneness and bake for another 5 minutes as needed. 4. Serve hot.

Mushrooms with Goat Cheese

Prep time: 10 minutes | Cook time: 10 minutes | Serves 4

3 tablespoons vegetable oil	½ teaspoon black pepper
1 pound (454 g) mixed mushrooms, trimmed and sliced	4 ounces (113 g) goat cheese, diced
1 clove garlic, minced	2 teaspoons chopped fresh thyme leaves (optional)
¼ teaspoon dried thyme	

1. In a baking pan, combine the oil, mushrooms, garlic, dried thyme, and pepper. Stir in the goat cheese. Place the pan in the air fryer basket. Set the air fryer to 400ºF (204ºC) for 10 minutes, stirring halfway through the cooking time. 2. Sprinkle with fresh thyme, if desired.

Cauliflower Steaks Gratin

Prep time: 10 minutes | Cook time: 13 minutes |

Serves 2

1 head cauliflower	thyme leaves
1 tablespoon olive oil	3 tablespoons grated
Salt and freshly ground black	Parmigiano-Reggiano cheese
pepper, to taste	2 tablespoons panko bread
½ teaspoon chopped fresh	crumbs

1. Preheat the air fryer to 370ºF (188ºC). 2. Cut two steaks out of the center of the cauliflower. To do this, cut the cauliflower in half and then cut one slice about 1-inch thick off each half. The rest of the cauliflower will fall apart into florets, which you can roast on their own or save for another meal. 3. Brush both sides of the cauliflower steaks with olive oil and season with salt, freshly ground black pepper and fresh thyme. Place the cauliflower steaks into the air fryer basket and air fry for 6 minutes. Turn the steaks over and air fry for another 4 minutes. Combine the Parmesan cheese and panko bread crumbs and sprinkle the mixture over the tops of both steaks and air fry for another 3 minutes until the cheese has melted and the bread crumbs have browned. Serve this with some sautéed bitter greens and air-fried blistered tomatoes.

Caesar Whole Cauliflower

Prep time: 20 minutes | Cook time: 30 minutes |

Serves 2 to 4

3 tablespoons olive oil	Kosher salt and freshly ground
2 tablespoons red wine vinegar	black pepper, to taste
2 tablespoons Worcestershire	1 small head cauliflower (about
sauce	1 pound / 454 g), green leaves
2 tablespoons grated Parmesan	trimmed and stem trimmed
cheese	flush with the bottom of the
1 tablespoon Dijon mustard	head
4 garlic cloves, minced	1 tablespoon roughly chopped
4 oil-packed anchovy fillets,	fresh flat-leaf parsley (optional)
drained and finely minced	

1. In a liquid measuring cup, whisk together the olive oil, vinegar, Worcestershire, Parmesan, mustard, garlic, anchovies, and salt and pepper to taste. Place the cauliflower head upside down on a cutting board and use a paring knife to make an "x" through the full length of the core. Transfer the cauliflower head to a large bowl and pour half the dressing over it. Turn the cauliflower head to coat it in the dressing, then let it rest, stem-side up, in the dressing for at least 10 minutes and up to 30 minutes to allow the dressing to seep into all its nooks and crannies. 2. Transfer the cauliflower head, stem-side down, to the air fryer and air fry at 340ºF (171ºC) for 25 minutes. Drizzle the remaining dressing over the cauliflower and air fry at 400ºF (204ºC) until the top of the cauliflower is golden brown and the core is tender, about 5 minutes more. 3. Remove the basket from the air fryer and transfer the cauliflower to a large plate. Sprinkle with the parsley, if you like, and serve hot.

Simple Zucchini Crisps

Prep time: 5 minutes | Cook time: 14 minutes |

Serves 4

2 zucchini, sliced into ¼ to	⅛ teaspoon sea salt
½-inch-thick rounds (about 2	Freshly ground black pepper, to
cups)	taste (optional)
¼ teaspoon garlic granules	Cooking spray

1. Preheat the air fryer to 392ºF (200ºC). Spritz the air fryer basket with cooking spray. 2. Put the zucchini rounds in the air fryer basket, spreading them out as much as possible. Top with a sprinkle of garlic granules, sea salt, and black pepper (if desired). Spritz the zucchini rounds with cooking spray. 3. Roast for 14 minutes, flipping the zucchini rounds halfway through, or until the zucchini rounds are crisp-tender. 4. Let them rest for 5 minutes and serve.

Hawaiian Brown Rice

Prep time: 10 minutes | Cook time: 12 to 16 minutes

| Serves 4 to 6

¼ pound (113 g) ground	¼ cup minced bell pepper
sausage	2 cups cooked brown rice
1 teaspoon butter	1 (8-ounce / 227-g) can crushed
¼ cup minced onion	pineapple, drained

1. Shape sausage into 3 or 4 thin patties. Air fry at 390ºF (199ºC) for 6 to 8 minutes or until well done. Remove from air fryer, drain, and crumble. Set aside. 2. Place butter, onion, and bell pepper in baking pan. Roast at 390ºF (199ºC) for 1 minute and stir. Cook 3 to 4 minutes longer or just until vegetables are tender. 3. Add sausage, rice, and pineapple to vegetables and stir together. 4. Roast for 2 to 3 minutes, until heated through.

Roasted Brussels Sprouts with Orange and Garlic

Prep time: 5 minutes | Cook time: 10 minutes |

Serves 4

1 pound (454 g) Brussels	2 tablespoons olive oil
sprouts, quartered	½ teaspoon salt
2 garlic cloves, minced	1 orange, cut into rings

1. Preheat the air fryer to 360ºF(182ºC). 2. In a large bowl, toss the quartered Brussels sprouts with the garlic, olive oil, and salt until well coated. 3. Pour the Brussels sprouts into the air fryer, lay the orange slices on top of them, and roast for 10 minutes. 4. Remove from the air fryer and set the orange slices aside. Toss the Brussels sprouts before serving.

Cheesy Loaded Broccoli

Prep time: 10 minutes | Cook time: 10 minutes |
Serves 2

3 cups fresh broccoli florets	¼ cup sour cream
1 tablespoon coconut oil	4 slices cooked sugar-free
¼ teaspoon salt	bacon, crumbled
½ cup shredded sharp Cheddar	1 medium scallion, trimmed
cheese	and sliced on the bias

1. Place broccoli into ungreased air fryer basket, drizzle with coconut oil, and sprinkle with salt. Adjust the temperature to 350ºF (177ºC) and roast for 8 minutes. Shake basket three times during cooking to avoid burned spots. 2. Sprinkle broccoli with Cheddar and cook for 2 additional minutes. When done, cheese will be melted and broccoli will be tender. 3. Serve warm in a large serving dish, topped with sour cream, crumbled bacon, and scallion slices.

Roasted Radishes with Sea Salt

Prep time: 5 minutes | Cook time: 18 minutes |
Serves 4

1 pound (454 g) radishes, ends	2 tablespoons olive oil
trimmed if needed	½ teaspoon sea salt

1. Preheat the air fryer to 360°F(182ºC). 2. In a large bowl, combine the radishes with olive oil and sea salt. 3. Pour the radishes into the air fryer and roast for 10 minutes. Stir or turn the radishes over and roast for 8 minutes more, then serve.

Mole-Braised Cauliflower

Prep time: 10 minutes | Cook time: 15 minutes |
Serves 2

8 ounces (227 g) medium	peanuts
cauliflower florets	1 tablespoon toasted sesame
1 tablespoon vegetable oil	seeds, plus more for garnish
Kosher salt and freshly ground	1 tablespoon finely chopped
black pepper, to taste	golden raisins
1½ cups vegetable broth	1 teaspoon kosher salt
2 tablespoons New Mexico	1 teaspoon dark brown sugar
chile powder (or regular chili	½ teaspoon dried oregano
powder)	¼ teaspoon cayenne pepper
2 tablespoons salted roasted	⅛ teaspoon ground cinnamon

1. In a large bowl, toss the cauliflower with the oil and season with salt and black pepper. Transfer to a cake pan. Place the pan in the air fryer and roast at 375ºF (191ºC) until the cauliflower is tender and lightly browned at the edges, about 10 minutes, stirring halfway through. 2. Meanwhile, in a small blender, combine the broth, chile powder, peanuts, sesame seeds, raisins, salt, brown sugar, oregano, cayenne, and cinnamon and purée until smooth. Pour into a small saucepan or skillet and bring to a simmer over medium heat, then cook until reduced by half, 3 to 5 minutes. 3. Pour the hot mole sauce over the cauliflower in the pan, stir to coat, then cook until the sauce is thickened and lightly charred on the cauliflower, about 5 minutes more. Sprinkle with more sesame seeds and serve warm.

Chili Fingerling Potatoes

Prep time: 10 minutes | Cook time: 16 minutes |
Serves 4

1 pound (454 g) fingerling	1 teaspoon black pepper
potatoes, rinsed and cut into	1 teaspoon cayenne pepper
wedges	1 teaspoon nutritional yeast
1 teaspoon olive oil	½ teaspoon garlic powder
1 teaspoon salt	

1. Preheat the air fryer to 400ºF (204ºC). 2. Coat the potatoes with the rest of the ingredients. 3. Transfer to the air fryer basket and air fry for 16 minutes, shaking the basket at the halfway point. 4. Serve immediately.

Green Tomato Salad

Prep time: 10 minutes | Cook time: 8 to 10 minutes |
Serves 4

4 green tomatoes	2 teaspoons fresh lemon juice
½ teaspoon salt	2 tablespoons finely chopped
1 large egg, lightly beaten	fresh parsley
½ cup peanut flour	1 teaspoon dried dill
1 tablespoon Creole seasoning	1 teaspoon dried chives
1 (5-ounce / 142-g) bag arugula	½ teaspoon salt
Buttermilk Dressing:	½ teaspoon garlic powder
1 cup mayonnaise	½ teaspoon onion powder
½ cup sour cream	

1. Preheat the air fryer to 400ºF (204ºC). 2. Slice the tomatoes into ½-inch slices and sprinkle with the salt. Let sit for 5 to 10 minutes. 3. Place the egg in a small shallow bowl. In another small shallow bowl, combine the peanut flour and Creole seasoning. Dip each tomato slice into the egg wash, then dip into the peanut flour mixture, turning to coat evenly. 4. Working in batches if necessary, arrange the tomato slices in a single layer in the air fryer basket and spray both sides lightly with olive oil. Air fry until browned and crisp, 8 to 10 minutes. 5. To make the buttermilk dressing: In a small bowl, whisk together the mayonnaise, sour cream, lemon juice, parsley, dill, chives, salt, garlic powder, and onion powder. 6. Serve the tomato slices on top of a bed of the arugula with the dressing on the side.

Bacon-Wrapped Asparagus

Prep time: 10 minutes | Cook time: 10 minutes |

Serves 4

8 slices reduced-sodium bacon, cut in half
16 thick (about 1 pound / 454 g) asparagus spears, trimmed of woody ends

1. Preheat the air fryer to 350ºF (177ºC). 2. Wrap a half piece of bacon around the center of each stalk of asparagus. 3. Working in batches, if necessary, arrange seam-side down in a single layer in the air fryer basket. Air fry for 10 minutes until the bacon is crisp and the stalks are tender.

Sweet and Crispy Roasted Pearl Onions

Prep time: 5 minutes | Cook time: 18 minutes |

Serves 3

1 (14½ ounces / 411 g) package frozen pearl onions (do not thaw)
2 tablespoons extra-virgin olive oil
2 tablespoons balsamic vinegar
2 teaspoons finely chopped fresh rosemary
½ teaspoon kosher salt
¼ teaspoon black pepper

1. In a medium bowl, combine the onions, olive oil, vinegar, rosemary, salt, and pepper until well coated. 2. Transfer the onions to the air fryer basket. Set the air fryer to 400ºF (204ºC) for 18 minutes, or until the onions are tender and lightly charred, stirring once or twice during the cooking time.

Mashed Sweet Potato Tots

Prep time: 10 minutes | Cook time: 12 to 13 minutes

per batch | Makes 18 to 24 tots

1 cup cooked mashed sweet potatoes
1 egg white, beaten
⅛ teaspoon ground cinnamon
1 dash nutmeg
2 tablespoons chopped pecans
1½ teaspoons honey
Salt, to taste
½ cup panko bread crumbs
Oil for misting or cooking spray

1. Preheat the air fryer to 390ºF (199ºC). 2. In a large bowl, mix together the potatoes, egg white, cinnamon, nutmeg, pecans, honey, and salt to taste. 3. Place panko crumbs on a sheet of wax paper. 4. For each tot, use about 2 teaspoons of sweet potato mixture. To shape, drop the measure of potato mixture onto panko crumbs and push crumbs up and around potatoes to coat edges. Then turn tot over to coat other side with crumbs. 5. Mist tots with oil or cooking spray and place in air fryer basket in single layer. 6. Air fry at 390ºF (199ºC) for 12 to 13 minutes, until browned and crispy. 7. Repeat steps 5 and 6 to cook remaining tots.

Butter and Garlic Fried Cabbage

Prep time: 5 minutes | Cook time: 9 minutes | Serves 2

Oil, for spraying
½ head cabbage, cut into bite-size pieces
2 tablespoons unsalted butter, melted
1 teaspoon granulated garlic
½ teaspoon coarse sea salt
¼ teaspoon freshly ground black pepper

1. Line the air fryer basket with parchment and spray lightly with oil. 2. In a large bowl, mix together the cabbage, butter, garlic, salt, and black pepper until evenly coated. 3. Transfer the cabbage to the prepared basket and spray lightly with oil. 4. Air fry at 375ºF (191ºC) for 5 minutes, toss, and cook for another 3 to 4 minutes, or until lightly crispy.

Five-Spice Roasted Sweet Potatoes

Prep time: 10 minutes | Cook time: 12 minutes |

Serves 4

½ teaspoon ground cinnamon
¼ teaspoon ground cumin
¼ teaspoon paprika
1 teaspoon chile powder
⅛ teaspoon turmeric
½ teaspoon salt (optional)
Freshly ground black pepper, to taste
2 large sweet potatoes, peeled and cut into ¾-inch cubes (about 3 cups)
1 tablespoon olive oil

1. In a large bowl, mix together cinnamon, cumin, paprika, chile powder, turmeric, salt, and pepper to taste. 2. Add potatoes and stir well. 3. Drizzle the seasoned potatoes with the olive oil and stir until evenly coated. 4. Place seasoned potatoes in a baking pan or an ovenproof dish that fits inside your air fryer basket. 5. Cook for 6 minutes at 390ºF (199ºC), stop, and stir well. 6. Cook for an additional 6 minutes.

Roasted Potatoes and Asparagus

Prep time: 5 minutes | Cook time: 23 minutes |

Serves 4

4 medium potatoes
1 bunch asparagus
⅓ cup cottage cheese
⅓ cup low-fat crème fraiche
1 tablespoon wholegrain mustard
Salt and pepper, to taste
Cooking spray

1. Preheat the air fryer to 390ºF (199ºC). Spritz the air fryer basket with cooking spray. 2. Place the potatoes in the basket. Air fry the potatoes for 20 minutes. 3. Boil the asparagus in salted water for 3 minutes. 4. Remove the potatoes and mash them with rest of ingredients. Sprinkle with salt and pepper. 5. Serve immediately.

Crispy Garlic Sliced Eggplant

Prep time: 5 minutes | Cook time: 25 minutes |

Serves 4

1 egg	½ teaspoon salt
1 tablespoon water	½ teaspoon paprika
½ cup whole wheat bread crumbs	1 medium eggplant, sliced into ¼-inch-thick rounds
1 teaspoon garlic powder	1 tablespoon olive oil
½ teaspoon dried oregano	

1. Preheat the air fryer to 360°F(182°C). 2. In a medium shallow bowl, beat together the egg and water until frothy. 3. In a separate medium shallow bowl, mix together bread crumbs, garlic powder, oregano, salt, and paprika. 4. Dip each eggplant slice into the egg mixture, then into the bread crumb mixture, coating the outside with crumbs. Place the slices in a single layer in the bottom of the air fryer basket. 5. Drizzle the tops of the eggplant slices with the olive oil, then fry for 15 minutes. Turn each slice and cook for an additional 10 minutes.

Potato with Creamy Cheese

Prep time: 5 minutes | Cook time: 15 minutes |

Serves 2

2 medium potatoes	1 teaspoon chives
1 teaspoon butter	1½ tablespoons grated
3 tablespoons sour cream	Parmesan cheese

1. Preheat the air fryer to 350°F (177°C). 2. Pierce the potatoes with a fork and boil them in water until they are cooked. 3. Transfer to the air fryer and air fry for 15 minutes. 4. In the meantime, combine the sour cream, cheese and chives in a bowl. Cut the potatoes halfway to open them up and fill with the butter and sour cream mixture. 5. Serve immediately.

Easy Greek Briami (Ratatouille)

Prep time: 15 minutes | Cook time: 40 minutes |

Serves 6

2 russet potatoes, cubed	1 teaspoon dried oregano
½ cup Roma tomatoes, cubed	½ teaspoon salt
1 eggplant, cubed	½ teaspoon black pepper
1 zucchini, cubed	¼ teaspoon red pepper flakes
1 red onion, chopped	⅓ cup olive oil
1 red bell pepper, chopped	1 (8-ounce / 227-g) can tomato
2 garlic cloves, minced	paste
1 teaspoon dried mint	¼ cup vegetable broth
1 teaspoon dried parsley	¼ cup water

1. Preheat the air fryer to 320°F(160°C). 2. In a large bowl, combine the potatoes, tomatoes, eggplant, zucchini, onion, bell pepper, garlic, mint, parsley, oregano, salt, black pepper, and red pepper flakes. 3. In a small bowl, mix together the olive oil, tomato paste, broth, and water. 4. Pour the oil-and-tomato-paste mixture over the vegetables and toss until everything is coated. 5. Pour the coated vegetables into the air fryer basket in an even layer and roast for 20 minutes. After 20 minutes, stir well and spread out again. Roast for an additional 10 minutes, then repeat the process and cook for another 10 minutes.

Shishito Pepper Roast

Prep time: 4 minutes | Cook time: 9 minutes | Serves 4

Cooking oil spray (sunflower, safflower, or refined coconut)	1 tablespoon soy sauce
1 pound (454 g) shishito, Anaheim, or bell peppers, rinsed	2 teaspoons freshly squeezed lime juice
	2 large garlic cloves, pressed

1. Insert the crisper plate into the basket and the basket into the unit. Preheat the unit by selecting AIR ROAST, setting the temperature to 390°F (199°C), and setting the time to 3 minutes. Select START/ STOP to begin. 2. Once the unit is preheated, spray the crisper plate and the basket with cooking oil. Place the peppers into the basket and spray them with oil. 3. Select AIR ROAST, set the temperature to 390°F (199°C), and set the time to 9 minutes. Select START/ STOP to begin. 4. After 3 minutes, remove the basket and shake the peppers. Spray the peppers with more oil. Reinsert the basket to resume cooking. Repeat this step again after 3 minutes. 5. While the peppers roast, in a medium bowl, whisk the soy sauce, lime juice, and garlic until combined. Set aside. 6. When the cooking is complete, several of the peppers should have lots of nice browned spots on them. If using Anaheim or bell peppers, cut a slit in the side of each pepper and remove the seeds, which can be bitter. 7. Place the roasted peppers in the bowl with the sauce. Toss to coat the peppers evenly and serve.

Sesame-Ginger Broccoli

Prep time: 10 minutes | Cook time: 15 minutes |

Serves 4

3 tablespoons toasted sesame oil	½ teaspoon kosher salt
	½ teaspoon black pepper
2 teaspoons sesame seeds	1 (16 ounces / 454 g) package
1 tablespoon chili-garlic sauce	frozen broccoli florets (do not
2 teaspoons minced fresh ginger	thaw)

1. In a large bowl, combine the sesame oil, sesame seeds, chili-garlic sauce, ginger, salt, and pepper. Stir until well combined. Add the broccoli and toss until well coated. 2. Arrange the broccoli in the air fryer basket. Set the air fryer to 325°F (163°C) for 15 minutes, or until the broccoli is crisp, tender, and the edges are lightly browned, gently tossing halfway through the cooking time.

Glazed Sweet Potato Bites

Prep time: 10 minutes | Cook time: 25 minutes | Serves 4

Oil, for spraying

3 medium sweet potatoes, peeled and cut into 1-inch pieces

2 tablespoons honey

1 tablespoon olive oil

2 teaspoons ground cinnamon

1. Line the air fryer basket with parchment and spray lightly with oil. 2. In a large bowl, toss together the sweet potatoes, honey, olive oil, and cinnamon until evenly coated. 3. Place the potatoes in the prepared basket. 4. Air fry at 400ºF (204ºC) for 20 to 25 minutes, or until crispy and easily pierced with a fork.

Roasted Grape Tomatoes and Asparagus

Prep time: 5 minutes | Cook time: 12 minutes | Serves 6

2 cups grape tomatoes

1 bunch asparagus, trimmed

2 tablespoons olive oil

3 garlic cloves, minced

½ teaspoon kosher salt

1. Preheat the air fryer to 380ºF(193ºC). 2. In a large bowl, combine all of the ingredients, tossing until the vegetables are well coated with oil. 3. Pour the vegetable mixture into the air fryer basket and spread into a single layer, then roast for 12 minutes.

Breaded Green Tomatoes

Prep time: 15 minutes | Cook time: 30 minutes | Serves 4

½ cup all-purpose flour

2 eggs

½ cup yellow cornmeal

½ cup panko bread crumbs

1 teaspoon garlic powder

Salt and freshly ground black pepper, to taste

2 green tomatoes, cut into ½-inch-thick rounds

Cooking oil spray

1. Place the flour in a small bowl. 2. In another small bowl, beat the eggs. 3. In a third small bowl, stir together the cornmeal, panko, and garlic powder. Season with salt and pepper. 4. Dip each tomato slice into the flour, the egg, and finally the cornmeal mixture to coat. 5. Insert the crisper plate into the basket and the basket into the unit. Preheat the unit by selecting AIR FRY, setting the temperature to 400ºF (204ºC), and setting the time to 3 minutes. Select START/STOP to begin. 6. Once the unit is preheated, spray the crisper plate and the basket with cooking oil. Working in batches, place the tomato slices in the air fryer in a single layer. Do not stack them. Spray the tomato slices with the cooking oil. 7. Select AIR FRY, set

the temperature to 400ºF (204ºC), and set the time to 10 minutes. Select START/STOP to begin. 8. After 5 minutes, use tongs to flip the tomatoes. Resume cooking for 4 to 5 minutes, or until crisp. 9. When the cooking is complete, transfer the fried green tomatoes to a plate. Repeat steps 6, 7, and 8 for the remaining tomatoes.

Garlic Parmesan-Roasted Cauliflower

Prep time: 5 minutes | Cook time: 15 minutes | Serves 6

1 medium head cauliflower, leaves and core removed, cut into florets

2 tablespoons salted butter, melted

½ tablespoon salt

2 cloves garlic, peeled and finely minced

½ cup grated Parmesan cheese, divided

1. Toss cauliflower in a large bowl with butter. Sprinkle with salt, garlic, and ¼ cup Parmesan. 2. Place florets into ungreased air fryer basket. Adjust the temperature to 350ºF (177ºC) and roast for 15 minutes, shaking basket halfway through cooking. Cauliflower will be browned at the edges and tender when done. 3. Transfer florets to a large serving dish and sprinkle with remaining Parmesan. Serve warm.

Parmesan Herb Focaccia Bread

Prep time: 10 minutes | Cook time: 10 minutes | Serves 6

1 cup shredded Mozzarella cheese

1 ounce (28 g) full-fat cream cheese

1 cup blanched finely ground almond flour

¼ cup ground golden flaxseed

¼ cup grated Parmesan cheese

½ teaspoon baking soda

2 large eggs

½ teaspoon garlic powder

¼ teaspoon dried basil

¼ teaspoon dried rosemary

2 tablespoons salted butter, melted and divided

1. Place Mozzarella, cream cheese, and almond flour into a large microwave-safe bowl and microwave for 1 minute. Add the flaxseed, Parmesan, and baking soda and stir until smooth ball forms. If the mixture cools too much, it will be hard to mix. Return to microwave for 10 to 15 seconds to rewarm if necessary. 2. Stir in eggs. You may need to use your hands to get them fully incorporated. Just keep stirring and they will absorb into the dough. 3. Sprinkle dough with garlic powder, basil, and rosemary and knead into dough. Grease a baking pan with 1 tablespoon melted butter. Press the dough evenly into the pan. Place pan into the air fryer basket. 4. Adjust the temperature to 400ºF (204ºC) and bake for 10 minutes. 5. At 7 minutes, cover with foil if bread begins to get too dark. 6. Remove and let cool at least 30 minutes. Drizzle with remaining butter and serve.

Tingly Chili-Roasted Broccoli

Prep time: 5 minutes | Cook time: 10 minutes | Serves 2

12 ounces (340 g) broccoli florets
2 tablespoons Asian hot chili oil
1 teaspoon ground Sichuan peppercorns (or black pepper)

2 garlic cloves, finely chopped
1 (2-inch) piece fresh ginger, peeled and finely chopped
Kosher salt and freshly ground black pepper, to taste

1. In a bowl, toss together the broccoli, chili oil, Sichuan peppercorns, garlic, ginger, and salt and black pepper to taste. 2. Transfer to the air fryer and roast at 375°F (191°C), shaking the basket halfway through, until lightly charred and tender, about 10 minutes. Remove from the air fryer and serve warm.

Air Fried Potatoes with Olives

Prep time: 15 minutes | Cook time: 40 minutes | Serves 1

1 medium russet potatoes, scrubbed and peeled
1 teaspoon olive oil
¼ teaspoon onion powder
⅛ teaspoon salt

Dollop of butter
Dollop of cream cheese
1 tablespoon Kalamata olives
1 tablespoon chopped chives

1. Preheat the air fryer to 400°F (204°C). 2. In a bowl, coat the potatoes with the onion powder, salt, olive oil, and butter. 3. Transfer to the air fryer and air fry for 40 minutes, turning the potatoes over at the halfway point. 4. Take care when removing the potatoes from the air fryer and serve with the cream cheese, Kalamata olives and chives on top.

Flatbread

Prep time: 5 minutes | Cook time: 7 minutes | Serves 2

1 cup shredded Mozzarella cheese
¼ cup blanched finely ground

almond flour
1 ounce (28 g) full-fat cream cheese, softened

1. In a large microwave-safe bowl, melt Mozzarella in the microwave for 30 seconds. Stir in almond flour until smooth and then add cream cheese. Continue mixing until dough forms, gently kneading it with wet hands if necessary. 2. Divide the dough into two pieces and roll out to ¼-inch thickness between two pieces of parchment. Cut another piece of parchment to fit your air fryer basket. 3. Place a piece of flatbread onto your parchment and into the air fryer, working in two batches if needed. 4. Adjust the temperature to 320°F (160°C) and air fry for 7 minutes. 5. Halfway through the cooking time flip the flatbread. Serve warm.

Sesame Taj Tofu

Prep time: 5 minutes | Cook time: 25 minutes | Serves 4

1 block firm tofu, pressed and cut into 1-inch thick cubes
2 tablespoons soy sauce
2 teaspoons toasted sesame

seeds
1 teaspoon rice vinegar
1 tablespoon cornstarch

1. Preheat the air fryer to 400°F (204°C). 2. Add the tofu, soy sauce, sesame seeds, and rice vinegar in a bowl together and mix well to coat the tofu cubes. Then cover the tofu in cornstarch and put it in the air fryer basket. 3. Air fry for 25 minutes, giving the basket a shake at five-minute intervals to ensure the tofu cooks evenly. 4. Serve immediately.

Parmesan-Rosemary Radishes

Prep time: 5 minutes | Cook time: 15 to 20 minutes | Serves 4

1 bunch radishes, stemmed, trimmed, and quartered
1 tablespoon avocado oil
2 tablespoons finely grated fresh Parmesan cheese

1 tablespoon chopped fresh rosemary
Sea salt and freshly ground black pepper, to taste

1. Place the radishes in a medium bowl and toss them with the avocado oil, Parmesan cheese, rosemary, salt, and pepper. 2. Set the air fryer to 375°F (191°C). Arrange the radishes in a single layer in the air fryer basket. Roast for 15 to 20 minutes, until golden brown and tender. Let cool for 5 minutes before serving.

Dijon Roast Cabbage

Prep time: 10 minutes | Cook time: 10 minutes | Serves 4

1 small head cabbage, cored and sliced into 1-inch-thick slices
2 tablespoons olive oil, divided

½ teaspoon salt
1 tablespoon Dijon mustard
1 teaspoon apple cider vinegar
1 teaspoon granular erythritol

1. Drizzle each cabbage slice with 1 tablespoon olive oil, then sprinkle with salt. Place slices into ungreased air fryer basket, working in batches if needed. Adjust the temperature to 350°F (177°C) and air fry for 10 minutes. Cabbage will be tender and edges will begin to brown when done. 2. In a small bowl, whisk remaining olive oil with mustard, vinegar, and erythritol. Drizzle over cabbage in a large serving dish. Serve warm.

Stuffed Red Peppers with Herbed Ricotta and Tomatoes

Prep time: 10 minutes | Cook time: 20 minutes |

Serves 4

2 red bell peppers

1 cup cooked brown rice

2 Roma tomatoes, diced

1 garlic clove, minced

¼ teaspoon salt

¼ teaspoon black pepper

4 ounces (113 g) ricotta

3 tablespoons fresh basil, chopped

3 tablespoons fresh oregano, chopped

¼ cup shredded Parmesan, for topping

1. Preheat the air fryer to 360°F(182ºC). 2. Cut the bell peppers in half and remove the seeds and stem. 3. In a medium bowl, combine the brown rice, tomatoes, garlic, salt, and pepper. 4. Distribute the rice filling evenly among the four bell pepper halves. 5. In a small bowl, combine the ricotta, basil, and oregano. Put the herbed cheese over the top of the rice mixture in each bell pepper. 6. Place the bell peppers into the air fryer and roast for 20 minutes. 7. Remove and serve with shredded Parmesan on top.

Spiced Honey-Walnut Carrots

Prep time: 5 minutes | Cook time: 12 minutes |

Serves 6

1 pound (454 g) baby carrots

2 tablespoons olive oil

¼ cup raw honey

¼ teaspoon ground cinnamon

¼ cup black walnuts, chopped

1. Preheat the air fryer to 360°F(182ºC). 2. In a large bowl, toss the baby carrots with olive oil, honey, and cinnamon until well coated. 3. Pour into the air fryer and roast for 6 minutes. Shake the basket, sprinkle the walnuts on top, and roast for 6 minutes more. 4. Remove the carrots from the air fryer and serve.

Air-Fried Okra

Prep time: 10 minutes | Cook time: 10 minutes |

Serves 4

1 egg

½ cup almond milk

½ cup crushed pork rinds

¼ cup grated Parmesan cheese

¼ cup almond flour

1 teaspoon garlic powder

¼ teaspoon freshly ground black pepper

½ pound (227 g) fresh okra, stems removed and chopped into 1-inch slices

1. Preheat the air fryer to 400ºF (204ºC). 2. In a shallow bowl, whisk together the egg and milk. 3. In a second shallow bowl, combine the pork rinds, Parmesan, almond flour, garlic powder, and black pepper. 4. Working with a few slices at a time, dip the okra into the egg mixture followed by the crumb mixture. Press lightly to ensure an even coating. 5. Working in batches if necessary, arrange the okra in a single layer in the air fryer basket and spray lightly with olive oil. Pausing halfway through the cooking time to turn the okra, air fry for 10 minutes until tender and golden brown. Serve warm.

Roasted Salsa

Prep time: 15 minutes | Cook time: 30 minutes |

Makes 2 cups

2 large San Marzano tomatoes, cored and cut into large chunks

½ medium white onion, peeled and large-diced

½ medium jalapeño, seeded and large-diced

2 cloves garlic, peeled and diced

½ teaspoon salt

1 tablespoon coconut oil

¼ cup fresh lime juice

1. Place tomatoes, onion, and jalapeño into an ungreased round nonstick baking dish. Add garlic, then sprinkle with salt and drizzle with coconut oil. 2. Place dish into air fryer basket. Adjust the temperature to 300ºF (149ºC) and bake for 30 minutes. Vegetables will be dark brown around the edges and tender when done. 3. Pour mixture into a food processor or blender. Add lime juice. Process on low speed 30 seconds until only a few chunks remain. 4. Transfer salsa to a sealable container and refrigerate at least 1 hour. Serve chilled.

Broccoli with Sesame Dressing

Prep time: 5 minutes | Cook time: 10 minutes |

Serves 4

6 cups broccoli florets, cut into bite-size pieces

1 tablespoon olive oil

¼ teaspoon salt

2 tablespoons sesame seeds

2 tablespoons rice vinegar

2 tablespoons coconut aminos

2 tablespoons sesame oil

½ teaspoon Swerve

¼ teaspoon red pepper flakes (optional)

1. Preheat the air fryer to 400ºF (204ºC). 2. In a large bowl, toss the broccoli with the olive oil and salt until thoroughly coated. 3. Transfer the broccoli to the air fryer basket. Pausing halfway through the cooking time to shake the basket, air fry for 10 minutes until the stems are tender and the edges are beginning to crisp. 4. Meanwhile, in the same large bowl, whisk together the sesame seeds, vinegar, coconut aminos, sesame oil, Swerve, and red pepper flakes (if using). 5. Transfer the broccoli to the bowl and toss until thoroughly coated with the seasonings. Serve warm or at room temperature.

Creamed Spinach

Prep time: 10 minutes | Cook time: 15 minutes | Serves 4

Vegetable oil spray

1 (10-ounce / 283-g) package frozen spinach, thawed and squeezed dry

½ cup chopped onion

2 cloves garlic, minced

4 ounces (113 g) cream cheese, diced

½ teaspoon ground nutmeg

1 teaspoon kosher salt

1 teaspoon black pepper

½ cup grated Parmesan cheese

1. Spray a baking pan with vegetable oil spray. 2. In a medium bowl, combine the spinach, onion, garlic, cream cheese, nutmeg, salt, and pepper. Transfer to the prepared pan. 3. Place the pan in the air fryer basket. Set the air fryer to 350°F (177°C) for 10 minutes. Open and stir to thoroughly combine the cream cheese and spinach. 4. Sprinkle the Parmesan cheese on top. Set the air fryer to 400°F (204°C) for 5 minutes, or until the cheese has melted and browned.

Garlic and Thyme Tomatoes

Prep time: 10 minutes | Cook time: 15 minutes | Serves 2 to 4

4 Roma tomatoes

1 tablespoon olive oil

Salt and freshly ground black pepper, to taste

1 clove garlic, minced

½ teaspoon dried thyme

1. Preheat the air fryer to 390°F (199°C). 2. Cut the tomatoes in half and scoop out the seeds and any pithy parts with your fingers. Place the tomatoes in a bowl and toss with the olive oil, salt, pepper, garlic and thyme. 3. Transfer the tomatoes to the air fryer, cut side up. Air fry for 15 minutes. The edges should just start to brown. Let the tomatoes cool to an edible temperature for a few minutes and then use in pastas, on top of crostini, or as an accompaniment to any poultry, meat or fish.

Spinach and Sweet Pepper Poppers

Prep time: 10 minutes | Cook time: 8 minutes | Makes 16 poppers

4 ounces (113 g) cream cheese, softened

1 cup chopped fresh spinach leaves

½ teaspoon garlic powder

8 mini sweet bell peppers, tops removed, seeded, and halved lengthwise

1. In a medium bowl, mix cream cheese, spinach, and garlic powder. Place 1 tablespoon mixture into each sweet pepper half and press down to smooth. 2. Place poppers into ungreased air fryer basket. Adjust the temperature to 400°F (204°C) and air fry for 8 minutes. Poppers will be done when cheese is browned on top and peppers are tender-crisp. Serve warm.

Chapter 9 Vegetarian Mains

Spinach-Artichoke Stuffed Mushrooms

Prep time: 10 minutes | Cook time: 10 to 14 minutes | Serves 4

2 tablespoons olive oil	crumbled
4 large portobello mushrooms, stems removed and gills scraped out	½ cup chopped marinated artichoke hearts
½ teaspoon salt	1 cup frozen spinach, thawed and squeezed dry
¼ teaspoon freshly ground pepper	½ cup grated Parmesan cheese
4 ounces (113 g) goat cheese,	2 tablespoons chopped fresh parsley

1. Preheat the air fryer to 400ºF (204ºC). 2. Rub the olive oil over the portobello mushrooms until thoroughly coated. Sprinkle both sides with the salt and black pepper. Place top-side down on a clean work surface. 3. In a small bowl, combine the goat cheese, artichoke hearts, and spinach. Mash with the back of a fork until thoroughly combined. Divide the cheese mixture among the mushrooms and sprinkle with the Parmesan cheese. 4. Air fry for 10 to 14 minutes until the mushrooms are tender and the cheese has begun to brown. Top with the fresh parsley just before serving.

Garlic White Zucchini Rolls

Prep time: 20 minutes | Cook time: 20 minutes | Serves 4

2 medium zucchini	½ cup full-fat ricotta cheese
2 tablespoons unsalted butter	¼ teaspoon salt
¼ white onion, peeled and diced	½ teaspoon garlic powder
½ teaspoon finely minced roasted garlic	¼ teaspoon dried oregano
¼ cup heavy cream	2 cups spinach, chopped
2 tablespoons vegetable broth	½ cup sliced baby portobello mushrooms
⅛ teaspoon xanthan gum	¾ cup shredded Mozzarella cheese, divided

1. Using a mandoline or sharp knife, slice zucchini into long strips lengthwise. Place strips between paper towels to absorb moisture. Set aside. 2. In a medium saucepan over medium heat, melt butter. Add onion and sauté until fragrant. Add garlic and sauté 30 seconds. 3. Pour in heavy cream, broth, and xanthan gum. Turn off heat and whisk mixture until it begins to thicken, about 3 minutes. 4. In a medium bowl, add ricotta, salt, garlic powder, and oregano and mix well. Fold in spinach, mushrooms, and ½ cup Mozzarella. 5. Pour half of the sauce into a round baking pan. To assemble the rolls, place two strips of zucchini on a work surface. Spoon 2 tablespoons of ricotta mixture onto the slices and roll up. Place seam side down on top of sauce. Repeat with remaining ingredients. 6. Pour remaining sauce over the rolls and sprinkle with remaining Mozzarella. Cover with foil and place into the air fryer basket. 7. Adjust the temperature to 350ºF (177ºC) and bake for 20 minutes. 8. In the last 5 minutes, remove the foil to brown the cheese. Serve immediately.

Crispy Fried Okra with Chili

Prep time: 5 minutes | Cook time: 10 minutes | Serves 4

3 tablespoons sour cream	Salt and black pepper, to taste
2 tablespoons flour	1 pound (454 g) okra, halved
2 tablespoons semolina	Cooking spray
½ teaspoon red chili powder	

1. Preheat the air fryer to 400ºF (204ºC). Spray the air fryer basket with cooking spray. 2. In a shallow bowl, place the sour cream. In another shallow bowl, thoroughly combine the flour, semolina, red chili powder, salt, and pepper. 3. Dredge the okra in the sour cream, then roll in the flour mixture until evenly coated. 4. Arrange the okra in the air fryer basket and air fry for 10 minutes, flipping the okra halfway through, or until golden brown and crispy. 5. Cool for 5 minutes before serving.

Garlicky Sesame Carrots

Prep time: 5 minutes | Cook time: 16 minutes | Serves 4 to 6

1 pound (454 g) baby carrots	Freshly ground black pepper, to taste
1 tablespoon sesame oil	6 cloves garlic, peeled
½ teaspoon dried dill	3 tablespoons sesame seeds
Pinch salt	

1. Preheat the air fryer to 380ºF (193ºC). 2. In a medium bowl, drizzle the baby carrots with the sesame oil. Sprinkle with the dill, salt, and pepper and toss to coat well. 3. Place the baby carrots in the air fryer basket and roast for 8 minutes. 4. Remove the basket and stir in the garlic. Return the basket to the air fryer and roast for another 8 minutes, or until the carrots are lightly browned. 5. Serve sprinkled with the sesame seeds.

Mushroom and Pepper Pizza Squares

Prep time: 10 minutes | Cook time: 10 minutes |

Serves 10

1 pizza dough, cut into squares
1 cup chopped oyster
mushrooms
1 shallot, chopped

¼ red bell pepper, chopped
2 tablespoons parsley
Salt and ground black pepper,
to taste

1. Preheat the air fryer to 400ºF (204ºC). 2. In a bowl, combine the oyster mushrooms, shallot, bell pepper and parsley. Sprinkle some salt and pepper as desired. 3. Spread this mixture on top of the pizza squares. 4. Bake in the air fryer for 10 minutes. 5. Serve warm.

Loaded Cauliflower Steak

Prep time: 5 minutes | Cook time: 7 minutes | Serves 4

1 medium head cauliflower
¼ cup hot sauce
2 tablespoons salted butter,

melted
¼ cup blue cheese crumbles
¼ cup full-fat ranch dressing

1. Remove cauliflower leaves. Slice the head in ½-inch-thick slices. 2. In a small bowl, mix hot sauce and butter. Brush the mixture over the cauliflower. 3. Place each cauliflower steak into the air fryer, working in batches if necessary. 4. Adjust the temperature to 400ºF (204ºC) and air fry for 7 minutes. 5. When cooked, edges will begin turning dark and caramelized. 6. To serve, sprinkle steaks with crumbled blue cheese. Drizzle with ranch dressing.

Lush Summer Rolls

Prep time: 15 minutes | Cook time: 15 minutes |

Serves 4

1 cup shiitake mushroom, sliced
thinly
1 celery stalk, chopped
1 medium carrot, shredded
½ teaspoon finely chopped
ginger

1 teaspoon sugar
1 tablespoon soy sauce
1 teaspoon nutritional yeast
8 spring roll sheets
1 teaspoon corn starch
2 tablespoons water

1. In a bowl, combine the ginger, soy sauce, nutritional yeast, carrots, celery, mushroom, and sugar. 2. Mix the cornstarch and water to create an adhesive for the spring rolls. 3. Scoop a tablespoonful of the vegetable mixture into the middle of the spring roll sheets. Brush the edges of the sheets with the cornstarch adhesive and enclose around the filling to make spring rolls. 4. Preheat the air fryer to 400ºF (204ºC). When warm, place the rolls inside and air fry for 15 minutes or until crisp. 5. Serve hot.

Air Fryer Veggies with Halloumi

Prep time: 5 minutes | Cook time: 14 minutes |

Serves 2

2 zucchinis, cut into even
chunks
1 large eggplant, peeled, cut
into chunks
1 large carrot, cut into chunks

6 ounces (170 g) halloumi
cheese, cubed
2 teaspoons olive oil
Salt and black pepper, to taste
1 teaspoon dried mixed herbs

1. Preheat the air fryer to 340ºF (171ºC). 2. Combine the zucchinis, eggplant, carrot, cheese, olive oil, salt, and pepper in a large bowl and toss to coat well. 3. Spread the mixture evenly in the air fryer basket and air fry for 14 minutes until crispy and golden, shaking the basket once during cooking. Serve topped with mixed herbs.

Mediterranean Pan Pizza

Prep time: 5 minutes | Cook time: 8 minutes | Serves 2

1 cup shredded Mozzarella
cheese
¼ medium red bell pepper,
seeded and chopped
½ cup chopped fresh spinach

leaves
2 tablespoons chopped black
olives
2 tablespoons crumbled feta
cheese

1. Sprinkle Mozzarella into an ungreased round nonstick baking dish in an even layer. Add remaining ingredients on top. 2. Place dish into air fryer basket. Adjust the temperature to 350ºF (177ºC) and bake for 8 minutes, checking halfway through to avoid burning. Top of pizza will be golden brown and the cheese melted when done. 3. Remove dish from fryer and let cool 5 minutes before slicing and serving.

Air Fryer Winter Vegetables

Prep time: 5 minutes | Cook time: 16 minutes |

Serves 2

1 parsnip, sliced
1 cup sliced butternut squash
1 small red onion, cut into
wedges
½ chopped celery stalk

1 tablespoon chopped fresh
thyme
2 teaspoons olive oil
Salt and black pepper, to taste

1. Preheat the air fryer to 380ºF (193ºC). 2. Toss all the ingredients in a large bowl until the vegetables are well coated. 3. Transfer the vegetables to the air fryer basket and air fry for 16 minutes, shaking the basket halfway through, or until the vegetables are golden brown and tender. 4. Remove from the basket and serve warm.

Cayenne Tahini Kale

Prep time: 5 minutes | Cook time: 15 minutes |
Serves 2 to 4

Dressing:
¼ cup tahini
¼ cup fresh lemon juice
2 tablespoons olive oil
1 teaspoon sesame seeds
½ teaspoon garlic powder
¼ teaspoon cayenne pepper

Kale:
4 cups packed torn kale leaves
(stems and ribs removed and
leaves torn into palm-size
pieces)
Kosher salt and freshly ground
black pepper, to taste

1. Preheat the air fryer to 350°F (177°C). 2. Make the dressing: Whisk together the tahini, lemon juice, olive oil, sesame seeds, garlic powder, and cayenne pepper in a large bowl until well mixed. 3. Add the kale and massage the dressing thoroughly all over the leaves. Sprinkle the salt and pepper to season. 4. Place the kale in the air fryer basket in a single layer and air fry for about 15 minutes, or until the leaves are slightly wilted and crispy. 5. Remove from the basket and serve on a plate.

Parmesan Artichokes

Prep time: 10 minutes | Cook time: 10 minutes |
Serves 4

2 medium artichokes, trimmed
and quartered, center removed
2 tablespoons coconut oil
1 large egg, beaten
½ cup grated vegetarian

Parmesan cheese
¼ cup blanched finely ground
almond flour
½ teaspoon crushed red pepper
flakes

1. In a large bowl, toss artichokes in coconut oil and then dip each piece into the egg. 2. Mix the Parmesan and almond flour in a large bowl. Add artichoke pieces and toss to cover as completely as possible, sprinkle with pepper flakes. Place into the air fryer basket. 3. Adjust the temperature to 400°F (204°C) and air fry for 10 minutes. 4. Toss the basket two times during cooking. Serve warm.

Rice and Eggplant Bowl

Prep time: 15 minutes | Cook time: 10 minutes |
Serves 4

¼ cup sliced cucumber
1 teaspoon salt
1 tablespoon sugar
7 tablespoons Japanese rice
vinegar
3 medium eggplants, sliced
3 tablespoons sweet white miso

paste
1 tablespoon mirin rice wine
4 cups cooked sushi rice
4 spring onions
1 tablespoon toasted sesame
seeds

1. Coat the cucumber slices with the rice wine vinegar, salt, and sugar. 2. Put a dish on top of the bowl to weight it down completely. 3. In a bowl, mix the eggplants, mirin rice wine, and miso paste. Allow to marinate for half an hour. 4. Preheat the air fryer to 400°F (204°C). 5. Put the eggplant slices in the air fryer and air fry for 10 minutes. 6. Fill the bottom of a serving bowl with rice and top with the eggplants and pickled cucumbers. 7. Add the spring onions and sesame seeds for garnish. Serve immediately.

Fried Root Vegetable Medley with Thyme

Prep time: 10 minutes | Cook time: 22 minutes |
Serves 4

2 carrots, sliced
2 potatoes, cut into chunks
1 rutabaga, cut into chunks
1 turnip, cut into chunks
1 beet, cut into chunks
8 shallots, halved

2 tablespoons olive oil
Salt and black pepper, to taste
2 tablespoons tomato pesto
2 tablespoons water
2 tablespoons chopped fresh
thyme

1. Preheat the air fryer to 400°F (204°C). 2. Toss the carrots, potatoes, rutabaga, turnip, beet, shallots, olive oil, salt, and pepper in a large mixing bowl until the root vegetables are evenly coated. 3. Place the root vegetables in the air fryer basket and air fry for 12 minutes. Shake the basket and air fry for another 10 minutes until they are cooked to your preferred doneness. 4. Meanwhile, in a small bowl, whisk together the tomato pesto and water until smooth. 5. When ready, remove the root vegetables from the basket to a platter. Drizzle with the tomato pesto mixture and sprinkle with the thyme. Serve immediately.

Greek Stuffed Eggplant

Prep time: 15 minutes | Cook time: 20 minutes |
Serves 2

1 large eggplant
2 tablespoons unsalted butter
¼ medium yellow onion, diced
¼ cup chopped artichoke hearts

1 cup fresh spinach
2 tablespoons diced red bell
pepper
½ cup crumbled feta

1. Slice eggplant in half lengthwise and scoop out flesh, leaving enough inside for shell to remain intact. Take eggplant that was scooped out, chop it, and set aside. 2. In a medium skillet over medium heat, add butter and onion. Sauté until onions begin to soften, about 3 to 5 minutes. Add chopped eggplant, artichokes, spinach, and bell pepper. Continue cooking 5 minutes until peppers soften and spinach wilts. Remove from the heat and gently fold in the feta. 3. Place filling into each eggplant shell and place into the air fryer basket. 4. Adjust the temperature to 320°F (160°C) and air fry for 20 minutes. 5. Eggplant will be tender when done. Serve warm.

Baked Turnip and Zucchini

Prep time: 5 minutes | Cook time: 15 to 20 minutes |

Serves 4

3 turnips, sliced

1 large zucchini, sliced

1 large red onion, cut into rings

2 cloves garlic, crushed

1 tablespoon olive oil

Salt and black pepper, to taste

1. Preheat the air fryer to 330ºF (166ºC). 2. Put the turnips, zucchini, red onion, and garlic in a baking pan. Drizzle the olive oil over the top and sprinkle with the salt and pepper. 3. Place the baking pan in the preheated air fryer and bake for 15 to 20 minutes, or until the vegetables are tender. 4. Remove from the basket and serve on a plate.

Zucchini and Spinach Croquettes

Prep time: 9 minutes | Cook time: 7 minutes | Serves 6

4 eggs, slightly beaten

½ cup almond flour

½ cup goat cheese, crumbled

1 teaspoon fine sea salt

4 garlic cloves, minced

1 cup baby spinach

½ cup Parmesan cheese, grated

⅓ teaspoon red pepper flakes

1 pound (454 g) zucchini, peeled and grated

⅓ teaspoon dried dill weed

1. Thoroughly combine all ingredients in a bowl. Now, roll the mixture to form small croquettes. 2. Air fry at 340ºF (171ºC) for 7 minutes or until golden. Tate, adjust for seasonings and serve warm.

Crispy Tofu

Prep time: 30 minutes | Cook time: 15 to 20 minutes | Serves 4

1 (16 ounces / 454 g) block extra-firm tofu

2 tablespoons coconut aminos

1 tablespoon toasted sesame oil

1 tablespoon olive oil

1 tablespoon chili-garlic sauce

1½ teaspoons black sesame seeds

1 scallion, thinly sliced

1. Press the tofu for at least 15 minutes by wrapping it in paper towels and setting a heavy pan on top so that the moisture drains. 2. Slice the tofu into bite-size cubes and transfer to a bowl.

Drizzle with the coconut aminos, sesame oil, olive oil, and chili-garlic sauce. Cover and refrigerate for 1 hour or up to overnight. 3. Preheat the air fryer to 400ºF (204ºC). 4. Arrange the tofu in a single layer in the air fryer basket. Pausing to shake the pan halfway through the cooking time, air fry for 15 to 20 minutes until crisp. Serve with any juices that accumulate in the bottom of the air fryer, sprinkled with the sesame seeds and sliced scallion.

Vegetable Burgers

Prep time: 10 minutes | Cook time: 12 minutes |

Serves 4

8 ounces (227 g) cremini mushrooms

2 large egg yolks

½ medium zucchini, trimmed and chopped

¼ cup peeled and chopped

yellow onion

1 clove garlic, peeled and finely minced

½ teaspoon salt

¼ teaspoon ground black pepper

1. Place all ingredients into a food processor and pulse twenty times until finely chopped and combined. 2. Separate mixture into four equal sections and press each into a burger shape. Place burgers into ungreased air fryer basket. Adjust the temperature to 375ºF (191ºC) and air fry for 12 minutes, turning burgers halfway through cooking. Burgers will be browned and firm when done. 3. Place burgers on a large plate and let cool 5 minutes before serving.

Caprese Eggplant Stacks

Prep time: 5 minutes | Cook time: 12 minutes |

Serves 4

1 medium eggplant, cut into ¼-inch slices

2 large tomatoes, cut into ¼-inch slices

4 ounces (113 g) fresh

Mozzarella, cut into ½-ounce / 14-g slices

2 tablespoons olive oil

¼ cup fresh basil, sliced

1. In a baking dish, place four slices of eggplant on the bottom. Place a slice of tomato on top of each eggplant round, then Mozzarella, then eggplant. Repeat as necessary. 2. Drizzle with olive oil. Cover dish with foil and place dish into the air fryer basket. 3. Adjust the temperature to 350ºF (177ºC) and bake for 12 minutes. 4. When done, eggplant will be tender. Garnish with fresh basil to serve.

Chapter 10 Desserts

Baked Cheesecake

Prep time: 30 minutes | Cook time: 35 minutes | Serves 6

½ cup almond flour

1½ tablespoons unsalted butter, melted

2 tablespoons erythritol

1 (8 ounce / 227-g) package cream cheese, softened

¼ cup powdered erythritol

½ teaspoon vanilla paste

1 egg, at room temperature

Topping:

1½ cups sour cream

3 tablespoons powdered erythritol

1 teaspoon vanilla extract

1. Thoroughly combine the almond flour, butter, and 2 tablespoons of erythritol in a mixing bowl. Press the mixture into the bottom of lightly greased custard cups. 2. Then, mix the cream cheese, ¼ cup of powdered erythritol, vanilla, and egg using an electric mixer on low speed. Pour the batter into the pan, covering the crust. 3. Bake in the preheated air fryer at 330ºF (166ºC) for 35 minutes until edges are puffed and the surface is firm. 4. Mix the sour cream, 3 tablespoons of powdered erythritol, and vanilla for the topping; spread over the crust and allow it to cool to room temperature. 5. Transfer to your refrigerator for 6 to 8 hours. Serve well chilled.

Cream Cheese Danish

Prep time: 20 minutes | Cook time: 15 minutes | Serves 6

¾ cup blanched finely ground almond flour

1 cup shredded Mozzarella cheese

5 ounces (142 g) full-fat cream cheese, divided

2 large egg yolks

¾ cup powdered erythritol, divided

2 teaspoons vanilla extract, divided

1. In a large microwave-safe bowl, add almond flour, Mozzarella, and 1 ounce (28 g) cream cheese. Mix and then microwave for 1 minute. 2. Stir and add egg yolks to the bowl. Continue stirring until soft dough forms. Add ½ cup erythritol to dough and 1 teaspoon vanilla. 3. Cut a piece of parchment to fit your air fryer basket. Wet your hands with warm water and press out the dough into a ¼-inch-thick rectangle. 4. In a medium bowl, mix remaining cream cheese, erythritol, and vanilla. Place this cream cheese mixture on the right half of the dough rectangle. Fold over the left side of the dough and press to seal. Place into the air fryer basket. 5.

Adjust the temperature to 330ºF (166ºC) and bake for 15 minutes. 6. After 7 minutes, flip over the Danish. 7. When done, remove the Danish from parchment and allow to completely cool before cutting.

Shortcut Spiced Apple Butter

Prep time: 5 minutes | Cook time: 1 hour | Makes 1¼ cups

Cooking spray

2 cups store-bought unsweetened applesauce

⅔ cup packed light brown sugar

3 tablespoons fresh lemon juice

½ teaspoon kosher salt

¼ teaspoon ground cinnamon

⅛ teaspoon ground allspice

1. Spray a cake pan with cooking spray. Whisk together all the ingredients in a bowl until smooth, then pour into the greased pan. Set the pan in the air fryer and bake at 340ºF (171ºC) until the apple mixture is caramelized, reduced to a thick purée, and fragrant, about 1 hour. 2. Remove the pan from the air fryer, stir to combine the caramelized bits at the edge with the rest, then let cool completely to thicken. Scrape the apple butter into a jar and store in the refrigerator for up to 2 weeks.

Strawberry Pecan Pie

Prep time: 15 minutes | Cook time: 10 minutes | Serves 6

1½ cups whole shelled pecans

1 tablespoon unsalted butter, softened

1 cup heavy whipping cream

12 medium fresh strawberries, hulled

2 tablespoons sour cream

1. Place pecans and butter into a food processor and pulse ten times until a dough forms. Press dough into the bottom of an ungreased round nonstick baking dish. 2. Place dish into air fryer basket. Adjust the temperature to 320ºF (160ºC) and set the timer for 10 minutes. Crust will be firm and golden when done. Let cool 20 minutes. 3. In a large bowl, whisk cream until fluffy and doubled in size, about 2 minutes. 4. In a separate large bowl, mash strawberries until mostly liquid. Fold strawberries and sour cream into whipped cream. 5. Spoon mixture into cooled crust, cover, and place in refrigerator for at least 30 minutes to set. Serve chilled.

Indian Toast and Milk

Prep time: 10 minutes | Cook time: 20 minutes |

Serves 4

1 cup sweetened condensed milk	4 slices white bread
1 cup evaporated milk	2 to 3 tablespoons ghee or butter, softened
1 cup half-and-half	2 tablespoons crushed pistachios, for garnish (optional)
1 teaspoon ground cardamom, plus additional for garnish	
1 pinch saffron threads	

1. In a baking pan, combine the condensed milk, evaporated milk, half-and-half, cardamom, and saffron. Stir until well combined. 2. Place the pan in the air fryer basket. Set the air fryer to 350ºF (177ºC) for 15 minutes, stirring halfway through the cooking time. Remove the sweetened milk from the air fryer and set aside. 3. Cut each slice of bread into two triangles. Brush each side with ghee. Place the bread in the air fryer basket. Set the air fryer to 350ºF (177ºC) for 5 minutes or until golden brown and toasty. 4. Remove the bread from the air fryer. Arrange two triangles in each of four wide, shallow bowls. Pour the hot milk mixture on top of the bread and let soak for 30 minutes. 5. Garnish with pistachios if using, and sprinkle with additional cardamom.

Molten Chocolate Almond Cakes

Prep time: 5 minutes | Cook time: 13 minutes |

Serves 3

Butter and flour for the ramekins	or almond extract
4 ounces (113 g) bittersweet chocolate, chopped	1 tablespoon all-purpose flour
	3 tablespoons ground almonds
½ cup (1 stick) unsalted butter	8 to 12 semisweet chocolate discs (or 4 chunks of chocolate)
2 eggs	Cocoa powder or powdered sugar, for dusting
2 egg yolks	
¼ cup sugar	Toasted almonds, coarsely chopped
½ teaspoon pure vanilla extract,	

1. Butter and flour three (6 ounces / 170-g) ramekins. (Butter the ramekins and then coat the butter with flour by shaking it around in the ramekin and dumping out any excess.) 2. Melt the chocolate and butter together, either in the microwave or in a double boiler. In a separate bowl, beat the eggs, egg yolks and sugar together until light and smooth. Add the vanilla extract. Whisk the chocolate mixture into the egg mixture. Stir in the flour and ground almonds. 3. Preheat the air fryer to 330ºF (166ºC). 4. Transfer the batter carefully to the buttered ramekins, filling halfway. Place two or three chocolate discs in the center of the batter and then fill the ramekins to ½-inch below the top with the remaining batter. Place the ramekins into the air fryer basket and air fry at 330ºF (166ºC) for 13 minutes. The sides of the cake should be set, but the centers should be slightly soft. Remove the ramekins from the air fryer and let the cakes sit for 5 minutes. (If you'd like the cake a little less molten, air fry for 14 minutes and let the cakes sit for 4 minutes.) 5. Run a butter knife around the edge of the ramekins and invert the cakes onto a plate. Lift the ramekin off the plate slowly and carefully so that the cake doesn't break. Dust with cocoa powder or powdered sugar and serve with a scoop of ice cream and some coarsely chopped toasted almonds.

Halle Berries-and-Cream Cobbler

Prep time: 10 minutes | Cook time: 25 minutes |

Serves 4

12 ounces (340 g) cream cheese (1½ cups), softened	unsalted butter, cut into pieces
1 large egg	¼ teaspoon fine sea salt
¾ cup Swerve confectioners'-style sweetener or equivalent amount of powdered sweetener	Frosting:
	2 ounces (57 g) cream cheese (¼ cup), softened
½ teaspoon vanilla extract	1 tablespoon Swerve confectioners'-style sweetener or equivalent amount of powdered or liquid sweetener
¼ teaspoon fine sea salt	
1 cup sliced fresh raspberries or strawberries	
Biscuits:	1 tablespoon unsweetened, unflavored almond milk or heavy cream
3 large egg whites	
¾ cup blanched almond flour	Fresh raspberries or strawberries, for garnish
1 teaspoon baking powder	
2½ tablespoons very cold	

1. Preheat the air fryer to 400ºF (204ºC). Grease a pie pan. 2. In a large mixing bowl, use a hand mixer to combine the cream cheese, egg, and sweetener until smooth. Stir in the vanilla and salt. Gently fold in the raspberries with a rubber spatula. Pour the mixture into the prepared pan and set aside. 3. Make the biscuits: Place the egg whites in a medium-sized mixing bowl or the bowl of a stand mixer. Using a hand mixer or stand mixer, whip the egg whites until very fluffy and stiff. 4. In a separate medium-sized bowl, combine the almond flour and baking powder. Cut in the butter and add the salt, stirring gently to keep the butter pieces intact. 5. Gently fold the almond flour mixture into the egg whites. Use a large spoon or ice cream scooper to scoop out the dough and form it into a 2-inch-wide biscuit, making sure the butter stays in separate clumps. Place the biscuit on top of the raspberry mixture in the pan. Repeat with remaining dough to make 4 biscuits. 6. Place the pan in the air fryer and bake for 5 minutes, then lower the temperature to 325ºF (163ºC) and bake for another 17 to 20 minutes, until the biscuits are golden brown. 7. While the cobbler cooks, make the frosting: Place the cream cheese in a small bowl and stir to break it up. Add the sweetener and stir. Add the almond milk and stir until well combined. If you prefer a thinner frosting, add more almond milk. 8. Remove the cobbler from the air fryer and allow to cool slightly, then drizzle with the frosting. Garnish with fresh raspberries. 9. Store leftovers in an airtight container in the refrigerator for up to 3 days. Reheat the cobbler in a preheated 350ºF (177ºC) air fryer for 3 minutes, or until warmed through.

Oatmeal Raisin Bars

Prep time: 15 minutes | Cook time: 15 minutes |

Serves 8

⅓ cup all-purpose flour

¼ teaspoon kosher salt

¼ teaspoon baking powder

¼ teaspoon ground cinnamon

¼ cup light brown sugar, lightly packed

¼ cup granulated sugar

½ cup canola oil

1 large egg

1 teaspoon vanilla extract

1⅓ cups quick-cooking oats

⅓ cup raisins

1. Preheat the air fryer to 360ºF (182ºC). 2. In a large bowl, combine the all-purpose flour, kosher salt, baking powder, ground cinnamon, light brown sugar, granulated sugar, canola oil, egg, vanilla extract, quick-cooking oats, and raisins. 3. Spray a baking pan with nonstick cooking spray, then pour the oat mixture into the pan and press down to evenly distribute. Place the pan in the air fryer and bake for 15 minutes or until golden brown. 4. Remove from the air fryer and allow to cool in the pan on a wire rack for 20 minutes before slicing and serving.

Chocolate Lava Cakes

Prep time: 5 minutes | Cook time: 15 minutes |

Serves 2

2 large eggs, whisked

¼ cup blanched finely ground almond flour

½ teaspoon vanilla extract

2 ounces (57 g) low-carb chocolate chips, melted

1. In a medium bowl, mix eggs with flour and vanilla. Fold in chocolate until fully combined. 2. Pour batter into two ramekins greased with cooking spray. Place ramekins into air fryer basket. Adjust the temperature to 320ºF (160ºC) and bake for 15 minutes. Cakes will be set at the edges and firm in the center when done. Let cool 5 minutes before serving.

Coconut Flour Cake

Prep time: 10 minutes | Cook time: 25 minutes |

Serves 6

2 tablespoons salted butter, melted

⅓ cup coconut flour

2 large eggs, whisked

½ cup granular erythritol

1 teaspoon baking powder

1 teaspoon vanilla extract

½ cup sour cream

1. Mix all ingredients in a large bowl. Pour batter into an ungreased round nonstick baking dish. 2. Place baking dish into air fryer basket. Adjust the temperature to 300ºF (149ºC) and bake for 25 minutes. The cake will be dark golden on top, and a toothpick inserted in the center should come out clean when done. 3. Let cool in dish 15 minutes before slicing and serving.

Cardamom Custard

Prep time: 10 minutes | Cook time: 25 minutes |

Serves 2

1 cup whole milk

1 large egg

2 tablespoons plus 1 teaspoon sugar

¼ teaspoon vanilla bean paste or pure vanilla extract

¼ teaspoon ground cardamom, plus more for sprinkling

1. In a medium bowl, beat together the milk, egg, sugar, vanilla, and cardamom. 2. Place two 8 ounces (227 g) ramekins in the air fryer basket. Divide the mixture between the ramekins. Sprinkle lightly with cardamom. Cover each ramekin tightly with aluminum foil. Set the air fryer to 350ºF (177ºC) for 25 minutes, or until a toothpick inserted in the center comes out clean. 3. Let the custards cool on a wire rack for 5 to 10 minutes. 4. Serve warm, or refrigerate until cold and serve chilled.

Brownies for Two

Prep time: 5 minutes | Cook time: 15 minutes |

Serves 2

½ cup blanched finely ground almond flour

3 tablespoons granular erythritol

3 tablespoons unsweetened cocoa powder

½ teaspoon baking powder

1 teaspoon vanilla extract

2 large eggs, whisked

2 tablespoons salted butter, melted

1. In a medium bowl, combine flour, erythritol, cocoa powder, and baking powder. 2. Add in vanilla, eggs, and butter, and stir until a thick batter forms. 3. Pour batter into two ramekins greased with cooking spray and place ramekins into air fryer basket. Adjust the temperature to 325ºF (163ºC) and bake for 15 minutes. Centers will be firm when done. Let ramekins cool 5 minutes before serving.

Apple Wedges with Apricots

Prep time: 5 minutes | Cook time: 15 to 18 minutes |

Serves 4

4 large apples, peeled and sliced into 8 wedges

2 tablespoons olive oil

½ cup dried apricots, chopped

1 to 2 tablespoons sugar

½ teaspoon ground cinnamon

1. Preheat the air fryer to 350ºF (180ºC). 2. Toss the apple wedges with the olive oil in a mixing bowl until well coated. 3. Place the apple wedges in the air fryer basket and air fry for 12 to 15 minutes. 4. Sprinkle with the dried apricots and air fry for another 3 minutes. 5. Meanwhile, thoroughly combine the sugar and cinnamon in a small bowl. 6. Remove the apple wedges from the basket to a plate. Serve sprinkled with the sugar mixture.

Dark Chocolate Lava Cake

Prep time: 5 minutes | Cook time: 10 minutes |

Serves 4

Olive oil cooking spray	½ teaspoon baking powder
¼ cup whole wheat flour	¼ cup raw honey
1 tablespoon unsweetened dark chocolate cocoa powder	1 egg
⅛ teaspoon salt	2 tablespoons olive oil

1. Preheat the air fryer to 380ºF(193ºC). Lightly coat the insides of four ramekins with olive oil cooking spray. 2. In a medium bowl, combine the flour, cocoa powder, salt, baking powder, honey, egg, and olive oil. 3. Divide the batter evenly among the ramekins. 4. Place the filled ramekins inside the air fryer and bake for 10 minutes. 5. Remove the lava cakes from the air fryer and slide a knife around the outside edge of each cake. Turn each ramekin upside down on a saucer and serve.

Vanilla and Cardamon Walnuts Tart

Prep time: 5 minutes | Cook time: 13 minutes |

Serves 6

1 cup coconut milk	2 eggs
½ cup walnuts, ground	1 teaspoon vanilla essence
½ cup Swerve	¼ teaspoon ground cardamom
½ cup almond flour	¼ teaspoon ground cloves
½ stick butter, at room temperature	Cooking spray

1. Preheat the air fryer to 360ºF (182ºC). Coat a baking pan with cooking spray. 2. Combine all the ingredients except the oil in a large bowl and stir until well blended. Spoon the batter mixture into the baking pan. 3. Bake in the preheated air fryer for approximately 13 minutes. Check the tart for doneness: If a toothpick inserted into the center of the tart comes out clean, it's done. 4. Remove from the air fryer and place on a wire rack to cool. Serve immediately.

Lemon Raspberry Muffins

Prep time: 5 minutes | Cook time: 15 minutes |

Serves 6

2 cups almond flour	¼ teaspoon salt
¾ cup Swerve	2 eggs
1¼ teaspoons baking powder	1 cup sour cream
⅓ teaspoon ground allspice	½ cup coconut oil
⅓ teaspoon ground anise star	½ cup raspberries
½ teaspoon grated lemon zest	

1. Preheat the air fryer to 345ºF (174ºC). Line a muffin pan with 6 paper liners. 2. In a mixing bowl, mix the almond flour, Swerve, baking powder, allspice, anise, lemon zest, and salt. 3. In another mixing bowl, beat the eggs, sour cream, and coconut oil until well mixed. Add the egg mixture to the flour mixture and stir to combine. Mix in the raspberries. 4. Scrape the batter into the prepared muffin cups, filling each about three-quarters full. 5. Bake for 15 minutes, or until the tops are golden and a toothpick inserted in the middle comes out clean. 6. Allow the muffins to cool for 10 minutes in the muffin pan before removing and serving.

Crustless Peanut Butter Cheesecake

Prep time: 10 minutes | Cook time: 10 minutes |

Serves 2

4 ounces (113 g) cream cheese, softened	1 tablespoon all-natural, no-sugar-added peanut butter
2 tablespoons confectioners' erythritol	½ teaspoon vanilla extract
	1 large egg, whisked

1. In a medium bowl, mix cream cheese and erythritol until smooth. Add peanut butter and vanilla, mixing until smooth. Add egg and stir just until combined. 2. Spoon mixture into an ungreased springform pan and place into air fryer basket. Adjust the temperature to 300ºF (149ºC) and bake for 10 minutes. Edges will be firm, but center will be mostly set with only a small amount of jiggle when done. 3. Let pan cool at room temperature 30 minutes, cover with plastic wrap, then place into refrigerator at least 2 hours. Serve chilled.

Pretzels

Prep time: 10 minutes | Cook time: 10 minutes |

Serves 6

1½ cups shredded Mozzarella cheese	melted, divided
1 cup blanched finely ground almond flour	¼ cup granular erythritol, divided
2 tablespoons salted butter,	1 teaspoon ground cinnamon

1. Place Mozzarella, flour, 1 tablespoon butter, and 2 tablespoons erythritol in a large microwave-safe bowl. Microwave on high 45 seconds, then stir with a fork until a smooth dough ball forms. 2. Separate dough into six equal sections. Gently roll each section into a 12-inch rope, then fold into a pretzel shape. 3. Place pretzels into ungreased air fryer basket. Adjust the temperature to 370ºF (188ºC) and set the timer for 8 minutes, turning pretzels halfway through cooking. 4. In a small bowl, combine remaining butter, remaining erythritol, and cinnamon. Brush ½ mixture on both sides of pretzels. 5. Place pretzels back into air fryer and cook an additional 2 minutes at 370ºF (188ºC). 6. Transfer pretzels to a large plate. Brush on both sides with remaining butter mixture, then let cool 5 minutes before serving.

Bourbon Bread Pudding

Prep time: 10 minutes | Cook time: 20 minutes | Serves 4

3 slices whole grain bread, cubed

1 large egg

1 cup whole milk

2 tablespoons bourbon

½ teaspoons vanilla extract

¼ cup maple syrup, divided

½ teaspoons ground cinnamon

2 teaspoons sparkling sugar

1. Preheat the air fryer to 270ºF (132ºC). 2. Spray a baking pan with nonstick cooking spray, then place the bread cubes in the pan. 3. In a medium bowl, whisk together the egg, milk, bourbon, vanilla extract, 3 tablespoons of maple syrup, and cinnamon. Pour the egg mixture over the bread and press down with a spatula to coat all the bread, then sprinkle the sparkling sugar on top and bake for 20 minutes. 4. Remove the pudding from the air fryer and allow to cool in the pan on a wire rack for 10 minutes. Drizzle the remaining 1 tablespoon of maple syrup on top. Slice and serve warm.

Coconut Muffins

Prep time: 5 minutes | Cook time: 25 minutes | Serves 5

½ cup coconut flour

2 tablespoons cocoa powder

3 tablespoons erythritol

1 teaspoon baking powder

2 tablespoons coconut oil

2 eggs, beaten

½ cup coconut shred

1. In the mixing bowl, mix all ingredients. 2. Then pour the mixture into the molds of the muffin and transfer in the air fryer basket. 3. Cook the muffins at 350ºF (177ºC) for 25 minutes.

Orange-Anise-Ginger Skillet Cookie

Prep time: 20 minutes | Cook time: 15 minutes | Serves 2 to 4

Cookie:

Vegetable oil

1 cup plus 2 tablespoons all-purpose flour

1 tablespoon grated orange zest

1 teaspoon ground ginger

1 teaspoon aniseeds, crushed

¼ teaspoon kosher salt

4 tablespoons (½ stick) unsalted

butter, at room temperature

½ cup granulated sugar, plus more for sprinkling

3 tablespoons dark molasses

1 large egg

Icing:

½ cup confectioners' sugar

2 to 3 teaspoons milk

1. For the cookie: Generously grease a baking pan with vegetable oil. 2. In a medium bowl, whisk together the flour, orange zest, ginger, aniseeds, and salt. 3. In a medium bowl using a hand

mixer, beat the butter and sugar on medium-high speed until well combined, about 2 minutes. Add the molasses and egg and beat until light in color, about 2 minutes. Add the flour mixture and mix on low until just combined. Use a rubber spatula to scrape the dough into the prepared pan, spreading it to the edges and smoothing the top. Sprinkle with sugar. 4. Place the pan in the basket. Set the air fryer to 325ºF (163ºC) for 15 minutes, or until sides are browned but the center is still quite soft. 5. Let cool in the pan on a wire rack for 15 minutes. Turn the cookie out of the pan onto the rack. 6. For the icing: Whisk together the sugar and 2 teaspoons of milk. Add 1 teaspoon milk if needed for the desired consistency. Spread, or drizzle onto the cookie.

Fried Cheesecake Bites

Prep time: 30 minutes | Cook time: 2 minutes | Makes 16 bites

8 ounces (227 g) cream cheese, softened

½ cup plus 2 tablespoons Swerve, divided

4 tablespoons heavy cream, divided

½ teaspoon vanilla extract

½ cup almond flour

1. In a stand mixer fitted with a paddle attachment, beat the cream cheese, ½ cup of the Swerve, 2 tablespoons of the heavy cream, and the vanilla until smooth. Using a small ice-cream scoop, divide the mixture into 16 balls and arrange them on a rimmed baking sheet lined with parchment paper. Freeze for 45 minutes until firm. 2. Line the air fryer basket with parchment paper and preheat the air fryer to 350ºF (177ºC). 3. In a small shallow bowl, combine the almond flour with the remaining 2 tablespoons Swerve. 4. In another small shallow bowl, place the remaining 2 tablespoons cream. 5. One at a time, dip the frozen cheesecake balls into the cream and then roll in the almond flour mixture, pressing lightly to form an even coating. Arrange the balls in a single layer in the air fryer basket, leaving room between them. Air fry for 2 minutes until the coating is lightly browned.

Almond Butter Cookie Balls

Prep time: 5 minutes | Cook time: 10 minutes | Makes 10 balls

1 cup almond butter

1 large egg

1 teaspoon vanilla extract

¼ cup low-carb protein powder

¼ cup powdered erythritol

¼ cup shredded unsweetened coconut

¼ cup low-carb, sugar-free chocolate chips

½ teaspoon ground cinnamon

1. In a large bowl, mix almond butter and egg. Add in vanilla, protein powder, and erythritol. 2. Fold in coconut, chocolate chips, and cinnamon. Roll into 1-inch balls. Place balls into a round baking pan and put into the air fryer basket. 3. Adjust the temperature to 320ºF (160ºC) and bake for 10 minutes. 4. Allow to cool completely. Store in an airtight container in the refrigerator up to 4 days.

Easy Chocolate Donuts

Prep time: 5 minutes | Cook time: 8 minutes | Serves 8

1 (8-ounce / 227-g) can jumbo biscuits

Cooking oil

Chocolate sauce, for drizzling

1. Preheat the air fryer to 375ºF (191ºC) 2. Separate the biscuit dough into 8 biscuits and place them on a flat work surface. Use a small circle cookie cutter or a biscuit cutter to cut a hole in the center of each biscuit. You can also cut the holes using a knife. 3. Spray the air fryer basket with cooking oil. 4. Put 4 donuts in the air fryer. Do not stack. Spray with cooking oil. Air fry for 4 minutes. 5. Open the air fryer and flip the donuts. Air fry for an additional 4 minutes. 6. Remove the cooked donuts from the air fryer, then repeat steps 3 and 4 for the remaining 4 donuts. 7. Drizzle chocolate sauce over the donuts and enjoy while warm.

Vanilla Scones

Prep time: 20 minutes | Cook time: 10 minutes | Serves 6

4 ounces (113 g) coconut flour

½ teaspoon baking powder

1 teaspoon apple cider vinegar

2 teaspoons mascarpone

¼ cup heavy cream

1 teaspoon vanilla extract

1 tablespoon erythritol

Cooking spray

1. In the mixing bowl, mix coconut flour with baking powder, apple cider vinegar, mascarpone, heavy cream, vanilla extract, and erythritol. 2. Knead the dough and cut into scones. 3. Then put them in the air fryer basket and sprinkle with cooking spray. 4. Cook the vanilla scones at 365ºF (185ºC) for 10 minutes.

Applesauce and Chocolate Brownies

Prep time: 10 minutes | Cook time: 15 minutes | Serves 8

¼ cup unsweetened cocoa powder

¼ cup all-purpose flour

¼ teaspoon kosher salt

½ teaspoons baking powder

3 tablespoons unsalted butter, melted

½ cup granulated sugar

1 large egg

3 tablespoons unsweetened applesauce

¼ cup miniature semisweet chocolate chips

Coarse sea salt, to taste

1. Preheat the air fryer to 300ºF (149ºC). 2. In a large bowl, whisk together the cocoa powder, all-purpose flour, kosher salt, and baking powder. 3. In a separate large bowl, combine the butter, granulated sugar, egg, and applesauce, then use a spatula to fold in the cocoa powder mixture and the chocolate chips until well combined. 4. Spray a baking pan with nonstick cooking spray, then pour the mixture into the pan. Place the pan in the air fryer and bake for 15 minutes or until a toothpick comes out clean when inserted in the middle. 5. Remove the brownies from the air fryer, sprinkle some coarse sea salt on top, and allow to cool in the pan on a wire rack for 20 minutes before cutting and serving.

Funnel Cake

Prep time: 10 minutes | Cook time: 5 minutes | Serves 4

Oil, for spraying

1 cup self-rising flour, plus more for dusting

1 cup fat-free vanilla Greek

yogurt

½ teaspoon ground cinnamon

¼ cup confectioners' sugar

1. Preheat the air fryer to 375ºF (191ºC). Line the air fryer basket with parchment and spray lightly with oil. 2. In a large bowl, mix together the flour, yogurt, and cinnamon until the mixture forms a ball. 3. Place the dough on a lightly floured work surface and knead for about 2 minutes. 4. Cut the dough into 4 equal pieces, then cut each of those into 6 pieces. You should have 24 total pieces. 5. Roll the pieces into 8- to 10-inch-long ropes. Loosely mound the ropes into 4 piles of 6 ropes. 6. Place the dough piles in the prepared basket and spray liberally with oil. You may need to work in batches, depending on the size of your air fryer. 7. Cook for 5 minutes, or until lightly browned. 8. Dust with the confectioners' sugar before serving.

Zucchini Nut Muffins

Prep time: 15 minutes | Cook time: 15 minutes | Serves 4

¼ cup vegetable oil, plus more for greasing

¾ cup all-purpose flour

¾ teaspoon ground cinnamon

¼ teaspoon kosher salt

¼ teaspoon baking soda

¼ teaspoon baking powder

2 large eggs

½ cup sugar

½ cup grated zucchini

¼ cup chopped walnuts

1. Generously grease four 4 ounces (113-g) ramekins or a baking pan with vegetable oil. 2. In a medium bowl, sift together the flour, cinnamon, salt, baking soda, and baking powder. 3. In a separate medium bowl, beat together the eggs, sugar, and vegetable oil. Add the dry ingredients to the wet ingredients. Add the zucchini and nuts and stir gently until well combined. Transfer the batter to the prepared ramekins or baking pan. 4. Place the ramekins or pan in the air fryer basket. Set the air fryer to 325ºF (163ºC) for 15 minutes, or until a cake tester or toothpick inserted into the center comes out clean. If it doesn't, cook for 3 to 5 minutes more and test again. 5. Let cool in the ramekins or pan on a wire rack for 10 minutes. Carefully remove from the ramekins or pan and let cool completely on the rack before serving.

Bourbon and Spice Monkey Bread

Prep time: 5 minutes | Cook time: 25 minutes | Serves 6 to 8

1 (16.3-ounce / 462-g) can store-bought refrigerated biscuit dough

¼ cup packed light brown sugar

1 teaspoon ground cinnamon

½ teaspoon freshly grated nutmeg

½ teaspoon ground ginger

½ teaspoon kosher salt

¼ teaspoon ground allspice

⅛ teaspoon ground cloves

4 tablespoons (½ stick) unsalted butter, melted

½ cup powdered sugar

2 teaspoons bourbon

2 tablespoons chopped candied cherries

2 tablespoons chopped pecans

1. Open the can and separate the biscuits, then cut each into quarters. Toss the biscuit quarters in a large bowl with the brown sugar, cinnamon, nutmeg, ginger, salt, allspice, and cloves until evenly coated. Transfer the dough pieces and any sugar left in the bowl to a cake pan and drizzle evenly with the melted butter. Place the pan in the air fryer and bake at 310°F (154°C) until the monkey bread is golden brown and cooked through in the middle, about 25 minutes. Transfer the pan to a wire rack and let cool completely. Unmold from the pan.
2. In a small bowl, whisk the powdered sugar and the bourbon into a smooth glaze. Drizzle the glaze over the cooled monkey bread and, while the glaze is still wet, sprinkle with the cherries and pecans to serve.

Dark Brownies

Prep time: 10 minutes | Cook time: 11 to 13 minutes | Serves 4

1 egg

½ cup granulated sugar

¼ teaspoon salt

½ teaspoon vanilla

¼ cup butter, melted

¼ cup flour, plus 2 tablespoons

¼ cup cocoa

Cooking spray

Optional:

Vanilla ice cream

Caramel sauce

Whipped cream

1. Beat together egg, sugar, salt, and vanilla until light. 2. Add melted butter and mix well. 3. Stir in flour and cocoa. 4. Spray a baking pan lightly with cooking spray. 5. Spread batter in pan and bake at 330°F (166°C) for 11 to 13 minutes. Cool and cut into 4 large squares or 16 small brownie bites.

Air Fryer Cooking Chart

Beef

Item	Temp (°F)	Time (mins)	Item	Temp (°F)	Time (mins)
Beef Eye Round Roast (4 lbs.)	400 °F	45 to 55	Meatballs (1-inch)	370 °F	7
Burger Patty (4 oz.)	370 °F	16 to 20	Meatballs (3-inch)	380 °F	10
Filet Mignon (8 oz.)	400 °F	18	Ribeye, bone-in (1-inch, 8 oz)	400 °F	10 to 15
Flank Steak (1.5 lbs.)	400 °F	12	Sirloin steaks (1-inch, 12 oz)	400 °F	9 to 14
Flank Steak (2 lbs.)	400 °F	20 to 28			

Chicken

Item	Temp (°F)	Time (mins)	Item	Temp (°F)	Time (mins)
Breasts, bone in (1 ¼ lb.)	370 °F	25	Legs, bone-in (1 ¾ lb.)	380 °F	30
Breasts, boneless (4 oz)	380 °F	12	Thighs, boneless (1 ½ lb.)	380 °F	18 to 20
Drumsticks (2 ½ lb.)	370 °F	20	Wings (2 lb.)	400 °F	12
Game Hen (halved 2 lb.)	390 °F	20	Whole Chicken	360 °F	75
Thighs, bone-in (2 lb.)	380 °F	22	Tenders	360 °F	8 to 10

Pork & Lamb

Item	Temp (°F)	Time (mins)	Item	Temp (°F)	Time (mins)
Bacon (regular)	400 °F	5 to 7	Pork Tenderloin	370 °F	15
Bacon (thick cut)	400 °F	6 to 10	Sausages	380 °F	15
Pork Loin (2 lb.)	360 °F	55	Lamb Loin Chops (1-inch thick)	400 °F	8 to 12
Pork Chops, bone in (1-inch, 6.5 oz)	400 °F	12	Rack of Lamb (1.5 – 2 lb.)	380 °F	22

Fish & Seafood

Item	Temp (°F)	Time (mins)	Item	Temp (°F)	Time (mins)
Calamari (8 oz)	400 °F	4	Tuna Steak	400 °F	7 to 10
Fish Fillet (1-inch, 8 oz)	400 °F	10	Scallops	400 °F	5 to 7
Salmon, fillet (6 oz)	380 °F	12	Shrimp	400 °F	5
Swordfish steak	400 °F	10			

Air Fryer Cooking Chart

Vegetables					
INGREDIENT	AMOUNT	PREPARATION	OIL	TEMP	COOK TIME
Asparagus	2 bunches	Cut in half, trim stems	2 Tbsp	420°F	12-15 mins
Beets	1½ lbs	Peel, cut in ½-inch cubes	1Tbsp	390°F	28-30 mins
Bell peppers (for roasting)	4 peppers	Cut in quarters, remove seeds	1Tbsp	400°F	15-20 mins
Broccoli	1 large head	Cut in 1-2-inch florets	1Tbsp	400°F	15-20 mins
Brussels sprouts	1lb	Cut in half, remove stems	1Tbsp	425°F	15-20 mins
Carrots	1lb	Peel, cut in ¼-inch rounds	1 Tbsp	425°F	10-15 mins
Cauliflower	1 head	Cut in 1-2-inch florets	2 Tbsp	400°F	20-22 mins
Corn on the cob	7 ears	Whole ears, remove husks	1 Tbps	400°F	14-17 mins
Green beans	1 bag (12 oz)	Trim	1 Tbps	420°F	18-20 mins
Kale (for chips)	4 oz	Tear into pieces,remove stems	None	325°F	5-8 mins
Mushrooms	16 oz	Rinse, slice thinly	1 Tbps	390°F	25-30 mins
Potatoes, russet	1½ lbs	Cut in 1-inch wedges	1 Tbps	390°F	25-30 mins
Potatoes, russet	1lb	Hand-cut fries, soak 30 mins in cold water, then pat dry	½ -3 Tbps	400°F	25-28 mins
Potatoes, sweet	1lb	Hand-cut fries, soak 30 mins in cold water, then pat dry	1 Tbps	400°F	25-28 mins
Zucchini	1lb	Cut in eighths lengthwise, then cut in half	1 Tbps	400°F	15-20 mins

Appendix Recipes Index

C

D

Made in the USA
Las Vegas, NV
29 October 2023

79866122R00059